Jacques Lacan and Feminist Epistemology

How does feminism change the way we can know ourselves and others?

Jacques Lacan and Feminist Epistemology outlines a compelling new agenda for feminist theories of identity and social relations. Using Lacanian psycho-analysis with feminist epistemology, this book sets out a groundbreaking psychoanalytic social theory. Campbell's work offers answers to the important contemporary question of how feminism can change the formation of gendered subjectivities and social relations. Drawing on the work of the third wave, the book shows how feminism can provide new political models of knowing and disrupt foundational ideas of sexual identity.

Kirsten Campbell engages the reader with an original interpretation of Lacanian psychoanalysis and offers a compelling argument for a fresh com-mitment to the politics of feminism. *Jacques Lacan and Feminist Epistemology* will be essential reading for anyone with interests in gender studies, cultural studies, psychoanalytic studies or social and political theory.

Kirsten Campbell is a lecturer in the sociology department at Goldsmiths College, University of London.

Transformations: Thinking Through Feminism

Edited by
Maureen McNeil, *Institute of Women's Studies, Lancaster University*
Lynne Pearce, *Department of English, Lancaster University*
Beverley Skeggs, *Department of Sociology, Manchester University*

Books in the series include:

Jacques Lacan and Feminist Epistemology

Kirsten Campbell

Routledge
Taylor & Francis Group

LONDON AND NEW YORK

First published 2004
by Routledge
11 New Fetter Lane, London EC4P 4EE

Simultaneously published in the USA and Canada
by Routledge
29 West 35th Street, New York, NY 10001

Routledge is an imprint of the Taylor & Francis Group

Typeset in Times by
Keystroke, Jacaranda Lodge, Wolverhampton
Printed and bound in Great Britain
by The Cromwell Press, Trowbridge, Wiltshire

British Library Cataloguing in Publication Data
A catalogue record for this book is available from the British Library

Library of Congress Cataloging in Publication Data
Campbell, Kirsten
  Jacques Lacan and feminist epistemology / Kirsten Campbell.
      p.   cm. – (Transformations)
Includes bibliographical references and index.
  1. Psychoanalysis and feminism. 2. Lacan, Jacques, 1901– I. Title.
II. Series.
  BF175.4.F45 .C37 2004
  305.42–dc22

                                          2003021154

ISBN 0–415–30087–8 (hbk)
ISBN 0–415–30088–6 (pbk)

For David Bausor

Contents

Acknowledgements

In this book I argue that feminist knowledges are affective and collective. This book is no exception. Many people have helped with this book, which began its first draft as my doctoral dissertation. My thanks to John Lechte and Robyn Ferrell for their supervision of its early stages. I would particularly like to thank my doctoral supervisor, Malcolm Bowie, for his exemplary and inspiring intellectual generosity and guidance. I was also fortunate to have Mari Shullaw of Routledge and Maureen McNeil of the Transformations series as editors. I would also like to thank Parveen Adams, Suki Ali, Steve Cross, and Kate Nash for their encouragement and engagement with earlier drafts of the text. I am very grateful for the love and support of my friends and family, without whom this book would not have been written. This book is dedicated to David Bausor, and it marks my immeasurable debt and love.

I would like to thank the Davies Group, Publishers for their permission to print a revised version of K. Campbell (2002) 'New Feminist Communities For The Third Wave', in Michael Strysick (ed.) *The Politics of Community*, Aurora, CO: Davies, pp. 221–241, © Michael Strysick. All rights reserved.

Abbreviations

The following abbreviations have been used to refer to Jacques Lacan's works:

FC *Les complexes familiaux dans la formation de l'individu: Essai d'analyse d'une fonction en psychologie*, Paris: Navarin, 1984.

É *Écrits*, trans. A. Sheridan, London: Routledge, 2001.

Éc *Écrits*, Paris: Seuil, 1966.

S1 *The Seminar of Jacques Lacan. Book I. Freud's Papers on Technique, 1953–1954*, trans. John Forrestor, ed. Jacques-Alain Miller, New York and London: Norton, 1991.

S2 *The Seminar of Jacques Lacan. Book II. The Ego in Freud's Theory and in the Technique of Psychoanalysis, 1954–1955*, trans. Sylvana Tomaselli, ed. Jacques-Alain Miller, New York and London: Norton, 1991.

S3 *The Seminar of Jacques Lacan. Book III. The Psychoses, 1955–1956*, trans. Russell Grigg, ed. Jacques-Alain Miller, London: Routledge, 1993.

S4 *Le Séminaire. Livre IV. La relation d'objet, 1956–1957*, ed. Jacques-Alain Miller, Paris: Seuil, 1994.

S5 *Le Séminaire. Livre V. Les Formations de l'inconscient, 1957–1958*, ed. Jacques-Alain Miller, Paris: Seuil, 1998.

S7 *The Seminar of Jacques Lacan. Book VII. The Ethics of Psychoanalysis, 1959–1960*, trans. Dennis Porter, ed. Jacques-Alain Miller, London: Routledge, 1992.

S8 *Le Séminaire. Livre VIII. Le Transfert, 1960–1961*, ed. Jacques-Alain Miller, Paris: Seuil, 2000.

S11 *The Four Fundamental Concepts of Psycho-Analysis*, trans. Alan Sheridan, ed. Jacques-Alain Miller, London: Peregrine, 1986.

S17 *Le Séminaire. Livre XVII. L'envers de la psychanalyse, 1969–1970*, ed. Jacques-Alain Miller, Paris: Seuil, 1991.

S20 *The Seminar of Jacques Lacan. Book XX. Encore: On Feminine Sexuality, the Limits of Love and Knowledge, 1972–1973*, trans. Bruce Fink, ed. Jacques-Alain Miller, New York and London: Norton, 1998.

Introduction

Third-wave politics

> Because our lives have been shaped by struggles between various feminisms as well as by cultural backlash against feminism and activism, we argue that contradiction . . . marks the desires and strategies of third wave feminists.
>
> (Drake and Heywood 1997a: 2)

In 1990, Judith Butler claimed that '[c]ontemporary feminist debates over the meanings of gender lead time and time again to a certain sense of trouble' (vii). A decade later, it is meanings of politics that trouble contemporary feminism. In current debates the category 'feminist politics' itself becomes a site of contestation. This problem of the political is attributable to a broader social conservatism that characterizes radicalism as obsolete and feminism as irrelevant. However, it is also an effect of internal debates that question foundational second-wave narratives of a women's liberation movement. The emergence of third-wave feminisms can be seen as symptomatic of this contemporary problem. This new generation claims to continue the second-wave work of collective action for and by women.[1] However, it also insists that this work requires new models of identity, collectivity and practice. For this reason, third-wave feminism engages in a continual questioning of its very foundation: 'feminist politics'.

In this book, I take up this contemporary engagement with feminist politics. However, rather than ask what that politics is or should be, I examine how feminism changes the way in which we understand ourselves and our others. I use feminist theories of knowledge to explore this question because of their central concern with how feminism enables us to know the world differently. This diverse and interdisciplinary field of research contends that knowledge is a practice that attributes certain meanings to reality. For this reason, I use feminist epistemologies to explore how politics can change the meanings that we give to our selves and our relations to others.

In Chapter 1, I explore the field of feminist epistemology, setting out the key ideas and contemporary debates that constitute this area of research. I argue that these debates do not offer a satisfactory answer to the question of the politics of feminist knowledge, as they too often reiterate circular arguments for and against identity politics or for and against modern or postmodern politics as foundations of models of knowing. These debates have become circular because they idealize and fix their foundational concepts of identity and of political truth. Their models of identity generally presume either a given sexual identity (the female knower) or a given political identity (the feminist knower). Rather than presuming the prior existence of an identity with given qualities and attributes, we need to explain its *constitution*. For this reason, in Chapter 3 I consider the formation of that identity. Is there a relationship between female and feminist subjects? How do we become feminist subjects? Similarly, these debates present a model of feminism that too often presumes that it is an evident and given political truth. Instead of assuming the prior existence of feminist knowledge, I argue in Chapter 4 and Chapter 5 that we need to understand its *production*. How is feminism a practice that changes the meanings that we give to our selves and others? To understand feminist politics requires an understanding of the production of political identities and meanings.

Feminist discourses

To understand the production of political subjects and signification, I use feminist and psychoanalytic theory. For both feminism and psychoanalysis, sexual difference makes a difference to how we become subjects and to how we understand the world. I argue that it is necessary to engage with both the psychoanalytic insight that sexual identity is substantial and impossible, *and* the feminist insight that sexual identity is contingently tied to empirical social subjects and relations. Utilizing both these insights, this book offers an account of feminism as a practice that can shift the meaning of subjectivity and sociality.

In Chapter 2, I begin my exploration of feminist politics by considering the terms of the encounter between feminism and psychoanalysis. This chapter sets out Lacan's psychoanalytic model of knowledge, both his classical account of *Écrits* and his later account of discourse. I argue that Lacan's model of knowing offers feminist epistemology a theory of the relationship between signification, subject and social relation. In particular, I focus upon Lacan's theory of discourse. In the Lacanian sense, discourse is an ordering or structure of signifiers or symbolic elements that represent subjects and their social relations. In this theory, Lacan identifies four different and foundational types of subjects and social bonds. Each discourse represents four different positions of the subject – the master, the hysteric, the academic and the psychoanalyst – and four different forms of intersubjective relations – mastering, hysterical, academic and psychoanalytic. For Lacan, these formulae represent possible subjects, social bonds and structures of signification.

In Chapter 3, I address the production of feminist identities. Drawing upon the work of feminist epistemologists such as Naomi Scheman (1993a) and Susan Bordo (1986), I develop Lacan's Discourses of the Master and the University as an account of masculine models of knowledge. The Discourse of the Master produces a masculine subject that seeks to master itself and others in knowledge. It misrecognizes its objects as the same as its 'self', imagining the world as a reflection of its own desires. Such an account does not claim that all men are masters, or that women cannot take up a position of mastery. Rather, it contends that this discourse produces a contingent relation between masculine identity and mastering knowledge.

How then to resist the Discourse of the Master? Is it, as some commentators suggest, that feminism is a Discourse of the Hysteric? In certain moments of both Lacanian and feminist theory, the hysteric appears as a romantic and rebellious figure that refuses to be mastered. However, I argue that her position is one of symptomatic repetition that fails to disrupt or change the Master's representation of the world. She does not take up a political position that permits her to change the social discourse that produces her psychic and physical pain.

How then to explain the formation of feminist subjects and their social bonds? To provide an account of the constitution of feminist identities, I draw on Freudian and Lacanian accounts of maternal and paternal identification, which I reread through the work of Julia Kristeva (1987, 1993) and Luce Irigaray (1974, 1977) on the formation of feminine identity. If paternal identification forms masculine identity, identification with another woman forms a 'feminine' identity. According to this account, all subjects 'fail' to be complete and whole. However, masculinity and femininity fail differently, for the feminine subject lacks a stable subjective structure. Jacqueline Rose (1986) rightly points out that this conventional psychoanalytic account characterizes femininity as a 'problem'. However, I argue that this so-called 'problem' also provides the possibility of a non-phallic identification with a political signifier, 'feminism'. This is a symbolic identification that reconstitutes identity by reshaping its ego-ideal. This political identification with the signifier 'feminism' produces feminist identities. These imaginary identifications with other women and symbolic identifications with a political ideal form communities of knowers, or feminist epistemic communities. Drawing on the work of Lorraine Code (1991, 1995) and Helen Longino (1990), I argue that these epistemic communities in turn produce feminist discourses that articulate new identities and social bonds.

In Chapter 4, I theorize feminism as a discursive practice. This chapter explores the structure of feminist discourse and how it operates as a transformative practice. For Lacan, psychoanalysis is a revolutionary discourse because it enables the analysand to traverse her phantasies of identity and hence to rearticulate the discursive structures which determine them. For this reason, I use Lacan's model of psychoanalytic discourse as a template to analyse the structure of feminist discourse. Drawing on the work of Kaja Silverman (1992b) and Judith Butler (1993b, 1997b), I argue that social discourses produce dominant representations of what is to be a subject. These social discourses produce particular phantasmic identities of femininity.

Feminist discourse works through and resists these phantasmic identities. This traversing of phantasies of femininity permits feminism to articulate the social discourses that support them. In turn, that articulation reveals the foundational and excluded term of social discourses, the lived experience of women. Feminist discourse produces a new signifier, which represents that lived experience of women. By reinscribing that signifier into social discourses, it shifts the existing structures of social discourses, thus producing new discourses and new signification. This discourse provides a new signification of 'reality', which ascribes a different meaning to it.

In this model, feminist discourse is not a 'truth' in the philosophical sense of an adequate correspondence between idea and thing. Nor is it the 'truth' of psychoanalytic discourse, which represents inescapable division between the subject and its knowledge, the truth of the unconscious. However, it shares with the Lacanian conception of psychoanalytic knowledge an emphasis upon the signification of the excluded elements of discourse, and the production of new signifying chains that produce new forms of signification. In this sense, feminist discourse is a practice that produces new meaning.

This use of Lacan's model as a template to theorize feminist discourse does not propose or rely upon an identity between feminist and psychoanalytic 'knowledges'. It does not claim that feminism is psychoanalysis in another mode, nor that feminist politics relies on the clinical operations of resistance, transference and so on. It is evident that feminist knowing is not produced in the transferential relation of analyst and analysand. My use of the Lacanian model does not rely on such an analogy between feminist and psychoanalytic practices because it reconfigures that model in the feminist field. Rereading the Lacanian theory of discourse through feminism shifts it from psychoanalytic to political discourse.

In Chapter 5, I argue that political discourse changes the structure of existing social discourses, producing new representations of subjects and the relations between them. This discourse posits women as social subjects and so rearticulates the masculine social contract. This new social contract does not refuse women as the Other of lack, but posits them as speaking subjects who are members of the sociality. In this way, feminist discourses produce another social contract and symbolic order. Drawing on the work of Teresa Brennan (1993), Judith Butler (1990, 1993b), Juliet Flower MacCannell (1991) and Luce Irigaray (1974, 1977), I argue that this new socio-symbolic order permits a different representation of subjects and their relation to other subjects, producing new discourses of subjectivity and intersubjectivity that do not reproduce the fraternal discourses of modernity. Those new social discourses represent the female subject as a social subject and the social relation as a relation between feminine subjects, and feminine and masculine subjects. In this way, feminist politics operates as a discursive practice that can change how we understand our others and ourselves.

The book begins its exploration of feminist politics by setting out feminist and Lacanian epistemologies and considering their relationship in Chapters 1 and 2. The second section of the book develops a theory of feminist discourse. Each chapter of this section explores a different thematic element of this theory. Chapter 3 addresses the formation of feminist identities while Chapter 4 develops a model of feminism as a discursive practice. Chapter 5 considers how feminism is a modern discourse that changes fraternal discourses of subjectivity and social relations. This model of feminist politics conceives it as a symbolic and imaginary practice that produces new social discourses. In this way, it hopes to suggest a new and radical project for third-wave feminisms.

1   Feminist epistemologies

The emergence of 'feminist epistemology'

> Yesterday, 'feminist epistemology' was an oxymoron; today, it has name
> recognition, but its referent is not yet clear.
>
> (Alcoff and Potter 1993a: 1)

What *is* 'feminist epistemology'? When the second-wave theorists first began
to use the term 'feminist epistemology', it did not refer to a recognizable body
of work. Rather the term referred to a set of theoretical and political problems
concerning accounts of knowledge. These problems focused upon whether
there are 'distinctive feminist perspectives on epistemology, metaphysics,
methodology and philosophy of science' (Harding and Hintikka 1983a: ix).
In the 1980s, a number of works appeared which began explicitly to take up
these issues, such as Rose (1983), Jagger (1983) and the anthology *Discovering
Reality* (Harding and Hintikka 1983b). Contributors to this anthology included
Sandra Harding, Kathryn Pyne Addelson, Evelyn Fox Keller, Naomi Scheman,
Nancy Hartsock and Jane Flax, all of whom have since become significant
theorists in the area. The mid-1980s saw the publication of influential key texts
which were to shape the contemporary field, including Haraway's 'A Manifesto
for Cyborgs' (1985), Harding's *The Science Question in Feminism* ([1986]
(1991)) and Dorothy Smith's *The Everyday World as Problematic* (1987).

In the early 1990s, 'feminist epistemology' became a recognizable term
that named a distinctive area of research and an emerging body of work, which
included theorists such as Lorraine Code (1991), Patricia Hill Collins (1991),
Jane Duran (1991), Harding (1991), Susan Hekman (1990), Helen Longino
(1990) and Liz Stanley (1990). During this period, several influential anthologies on the theme of feminism and knowledge were also published, such
as *Gender/Body/Knowledge* (Bordo and Jagger 1989), *Feminist Knowledge*
(Gunew 1990), *Feminist Epistemologies* (Alcoff and Potter 1993b), and
Knowing the Difference: Feminist Perspectives in Epistemology (Lennon and
Whitford 1994b). By the mid-1990s, the sociological and philosophical

mainstream came to recognize feminist epistemology as a field of research, even if only to decide 'Feminist Epistemology: For and Against' (Haack 1994). By 1999, Alessandra Tanesini's *Introduction to Feminist Epistemologies* could assume that feminist epistemology constitutes an established and substantive body of work that has gained 'name recognition'. Less than twenty years after Harding and Hintikka asked whether feminism provides a distinctive perspective on epistemology, Jane Duran (2001) could legitimately conceive 'global feminist epistemologies' as an affirmative answer to that question.

The theoretical field of feminist epistemology

While the term 'feminist epistemology' may have 'name recognition', it remains true that its referent is still unclear. For example, like other commentators Tanesini stresses the plurality of this area, emphasizing its interdisciplinary formations and the different political and epistemological models that its theorists deploy (1999: 4). 'Feminist epistemology' represents a complex and heterogeneous area of research. How then can we define 'feminist epistemology'?

Most commentators, such as Tanesini or Duran (1998), classify feminist epistemologies according to their philosophical traditions, such as 'naturalized feminist epistemology', their disciplinary object of study, such as 'science', or their disciplinary themes, such as 'objectivity'. However, it is not helpful to define feminist epistemology according to these categories. For example, it is not possible to confine feminist epistemologies to a single academic discipline such as philosophy, as do Linda Alcoff and Elizabeth Potter (1993b: 1). Feminist epistemology may appear to be a philosophical enterprise because it often deploys the language and concepts of philosophy, and because epistemology has traditionally been regarded as a strictly philosophical concern. Moreover, influential theorists such as Addelson (1993) and Code (1991) engage with epistemology as philosophy traditionally defines it. However, while this research often utilizes philosophical terms and uses them as analytic categories, it also reshapes and recasts those terms and uses them as conceptual markers rather than as disciplinary claims. Code points out that her work:

> sits uneasily with epistemologists . . . because [its] questions are thought not to be properly epistemological at all, but to belong to ethics, or to the softer fringes of everyday talk about knowledge, rather than to the hard center of serious epistemological analysis.
>
> (1994: 3)

For theorists such as Code, feminist epistemology is necessarily political and interdisciplinary because it asks questions of epistemology which philosophy traditionally excludes from a theory of knowledge, or which conventional philosophy does not wish to answer. Philosophical feminist epistemologists thus present a critical engagement with the 'philosophical' enterprise rather than a simple continuation of its project.

This area of research is *multidisciplinary* and *interdisciplinary*, because it draws upon philosophy, social theory, sociology, literary theory and political theory that together form feminist theory. This can be seen in the diversity of the disciplines of its leading theorists: historians and philosophers of science, such as Donna Haraway (1991); philosophers such as Lynne Hankinson Nelson (1995); political theorists such as Jane Flax (1993); sociologists such as Patricia Hill Collins (1991); and cultural theorists such as Teresa de Lauretis (1988). For this reason too, it is not possible to identify this body of research with a dominant theoretical movement or 'master' thinker. It is not reducible to a theoretical movement such as 'poststructuralism' or 'deconstruction' or to 'Foucauldian' or 'Derridean' models. So, for example, Haraway draws on standpoint theorists such as Hartsock (1983) as well as philosophers of science such as Bruno Latour (1993).

If feminist epistemology emerges from a confluence of thinkers, theories and texts, how then is it possible to describe what appear to be widely disparate theories and thinkers? We require another means of describing a body of research besides the inadequate categories of academic discipline, theoretical model, or master thinker. None of these categories satisfactorily explains why we should classify these theories, as opposed to any other, as 'feminist epistemology'. We need to be able to describe the distinctive nature of research that fits within the 'category' of feminist epistemology, while also acknowledging its heterogeneity. Tanesini argues that 'there are many partly overlapping accounts of knowledge which rightly could be called "feminist" [because] of the characteristics and aims that feminist epistemologists appear to share' (1999: 4). What, then, are those characteristics and aims that mark feminist epistemology as distinct from other areas of research?

A less reductionist and more productive approach to the definition and analysis of areas of related research is to be found in the work of the intellectual historian Fritz Ringer. Ringer provides an account of intellectual fields, those related areas of concepts and theorists that emerge in the history of ideas. Drawing upon Pierre Bourdieu's notion of a field as 'a network, or a con-figuration, of objective relations between positions', Ringer's approach focuses upon the '*positional* or *relational* attributes of ideas' (1992: 5–7).[1] For Ringer, 'the field is not an aggregate of isolated elements; it is a configuration or a network of relationships' formed in related theoretical positions (1992: 5). An intellectual field describes a group of thinkers and ideas, which are united by a shared set of political and intellectual engagements and a set of common theoretical positions. The usefulness of Ringer's concept of the intellectual field is that it provides a means of analysing how heterogeneous work can constitute a unified body of research.

While Ringer's work provides a useful conceptual frame, he develops his concept of the 'intellectual field' and empirical methodology in the context of the discipline of intellectual history. However, the purpose of my analysis of feminist epistemology is not to provide an intellectual history of this area, but rather to understand a body of related research. For this reason, I use my concept of a 'theoretical field' rather than Ringer's 'intellectual field'. I define a 'theoretical field' as a diverse group of theorists and research projects that coalesce around shared political and theoretical engagements.

The concept of a theoretical field permits us to understand how feminist epistemology is a body of related ideas and theorists that forms a distinct area of research. It focuses upon how the relationship between these thinkers, ideas and problems forms a theoretical field. Conceiving feminist epistemology as a theoretical field reveals how its diversity of political and epistemological models forms a network of theoretical positions. This network of theories shares both an epistemic object and a project. The conflicts and negotiations of conceptual and political positions around that object and project constitute feminist epistemology as a theoretical field. The field of feminist epistemology therefore can be delineated by (1) its object of study, (2) its project or collective aims and (3) its set of common political and theoretical positions.

The object of the field of feminist epistemology

In their early formulation of feminist epistemology's object of study, Harding and Hintikka ask: '[a]re there – can there be – distinctive feminist perspectives on epistemology, metaphysics, methodology and philosophy of science?' (1983a: ix). This question does not take epistemology *qua* epistemology as its object, that is, it does not study epistemology as such. Instead, it examines the epistemological implications of feminist politics. For example, Harding argues that the focus of feminist epistemological theory is not 'to justify the truth of feminist claims to more accurate accounts of reality. Rather it is the relations between power and knowledge that concern these thinkers' (2000: 50). Feminist epistemology, then, explores the difference that feminism makes to our models of knowledge. In this sense, its object of study is feminism, and in particular, the difference that feminist politics makes to how we understand the world.

For this reason, it is not possible to simply 'name' the object of the field of feminist epistemology, for it is as large and diverse as feminism itself. It studies that heterogeneous body of research and activism which feminist politics inform, encompassing the interdisciplinary body of work named 'feminist theory' as well as the many knowledges that feminist activism generates. Against the claim of analytic philosophy that there is only one way to give an account of what and how we know, the productivity of feminist epistemology (like the theory and politics from which it derives) lies in the diversity and hybridity of the knowledges which form its object, and in the plurality of the accounts of that object.

For this reason too, it is not possible to simply fix the object of the field. Feminism is not singular but plural, as it emerges from debates concerning what its politics is or should be. It is therefore also a temporal object, which changes and shifts in relationship to those changing and shifting debates. For example, Tanesini argues that '[w]hat characterises feminist epistemology in its broadest sense is the belief that gender is a category which is relevant to the study of knowledge' (1999: 38). However, in the last twenty years our understanding of 'gender' has itself changed, with shifts in notions of feminist politics. An example of this shift can be seen in the influential work of Sandra Harding, her focus changing from the woman-centred analysis of *The Science Question in Feminism* (1991) to the intersectional analysis of *Is Science Multicultural?* (1998). Feminism may be the object of the field of feminist epistemology, but it is a heterogeneous and changing object.

By taking 'feminism' as its object of study, this field may appear to collapse the numerous and otherwise disparate epistemologies which inform feminist work into a single model of knowledge. However, the field of feminist episte-mologies includes many different models of knowing. Moreover, the alternative approach of only analysing narrow and discrete areas of research does not address the pluralism of feminism for two reasons. First, if it is possible to posit our models of feminist knowing only in relation to the particular area of research or practice that generates them, then those working in other areas cannot utilize them. For a model of feminist knowledge to be useful, it must be sustainable in relation to different areas of feminist work. For this reason, an epistemological theory necessarily implies a sufficient level of generality to enable feminists working in many diverse areas to use it in relation to their own practices. Second, concepts of the 'nature' of politics and knowledge inform all our truth-claims. A coherent account of feminist epistemologies permits the explicit, reflexive and sustained examination of those otherwise implicit models.

Despite the complexity of its object, feminist epistemology proposes that it is necessary and possible to provide a coherent account of feminism as epistemic practice. For example, Helen Longino identifies what she calls 'theoretical virtues', which are epistemic practices that she argues feminism privileges (1997: 21). Longino proposes a theory of feminist knowledge *qua* knowledge and so develops a model that it is possible to apply across a broad range of feminist research and practice. Longino shares with other feminist episte-mologists a commitment to feminist politics, and from that commitment arises the central project of the field of feminist epistemology: how do we understand our epistemic practices as political practices?

The project of the field of feminist epistemology

The project of the field of feminist epistemology is to produce feminist models of knowing. This project is not primarily epistemological, that is, its aim is not to provide a new and better model of feminist knowledge or of knowledge itself. For example, Alcoff and Potter argue that 'a general account of knowledge, one that uncovers justificatory standards a priori . . . is precisely the premise that feminist epistemologists have called into question' (1993a: 1). These theorists do not aim to provide an account of the conditions of universal truth but instead to provide an account of epistemic practice as feminist practice. This project is political, in the sense that it focuses upon feminism as a potentially trans-formative knowledge that can change not only how we understand objects, but also subjects and their relationships.

That potential lies in the disruption of dominant knowledges that give particular meanings to the world. Lennon and Whitford rightly argue that feminism's most powerful epistemological 'insight' is 'the recognition that legitimation of knowledge-claims is intimately tied to networks of domination and exclusion' (1994a: 1). Because networks of power form knowledge-claims, feminist epistemology aims to construct new models of knowing the social world in order to understand that world differently. For this reason, it aims to reconstruct epistemic practice as political practice. It links the production of knowledge to the transformative values of feminism and hence to the production of new models of epistemic practice.

This central project falls into two subsidiary projects that, while overlapping, have different aims. The first (earlier) project focuses upon deconstructive critiques of masculinist knowledges. Alcoff and Potter describe how early epistemological research of the late 1970s and early 1980s began with a critical engagement with masculinist forms of knowledge and knowing (1993a: 2). These deconstructive theories focus upon 'masculine' forms of knowledge. They argue that these knowledges presuppose a masculine subject whose dominating, instrumental and objectifying relation to what is known derives from cultural models of masculinity. This engagement continues in the influential work of Naomi Scheman (1987) on masculinity and Cartesian epistemology, and Genevieve Lloyd (1984, 1993) on the masculine tropes of reason.

The second area of research, which emerges in the late 1980s and early 1990s, engages with the reconstructive project of theorizing feminist knowledges. A narrow interpretation of that project perceives its aim as the reconstruction of traditional philosophical models of epistemology in terms of feminist values. For example, Alcoff and Potter characterize the phrase 'feminist epistemologies' as marking 'the uneasy alliance between feminism and philosophy' (1993a: 1). In contrast, a broader conception of its aim is the construction of new epistemological models from epistemic and political practices of the feminist movement. Those models have characterized these practices as women's styles of knowing and knowledges, or, more recently, as feminist activities and knowledges.[2]

This broader project addresses two key issues: first, how to describe feminist knowledges, and second, how to understand them as epistemic practices. Theories that address the first issue focus upon describing feminism as a social and political knowledge. The standpoint theories of Hartsock (1983) and Harding (1991), and Haraway's (1991) work on situated knowledges, have been particularly influential examples. This research focuses upon theorizing feminist knowledge as 'a critical vision consequent upon a critical positioning in inhomogeneous gendered social space' (Haraway 1991: 195). These theorists ask how can we understand the distinctive nature of feminist knowledge in terms of social and political relations.

The most recent area of reconstructive theoretical work analyses the epistemic practices that produce feminist knowledges. It is possible to divide these accounts according to distinct 'foundational' categories. The first set of theories contends that the foundational epistemic practice of feminist knowledge is reason, focusing upon models of rationality and objectivity. A good example of this work is the anthology, *A Mind of One's Own*, edited by Antony and Witt (1993). The second group of theories takes as their 'foundational' category the knowing subject, whether conceiving it as an individual female, a feminist, a female feminist, or as the collective feminist community. Grosz (1993), Code (1991), de Lauretis (1988) and Longino (1997) are respective examples of these different approaches to the knowing subject.

Theoretical positions of the field of feminist epistemology

This field represents an emerging area of theoretical work that is still in the process of constituting itself. However, it is possible to trace a shared set of theoretical positions or assumptions that emerge from the key debates in this area. In particular, there are three key positions that the diverse works of this field share:

1 we need to understand the models of knowing which we use to construct truth-claims so that we can make their politics explicit;
2 feminist theory and practice has important implications for epistemological theory;
3 we should construct new feminist models of knowledge from that theory and practice.

*We need to understand the models of knowing which we use to
construct truth-claims so that we can make their politics explicit*

This first position contends that it is necessary to make explicit the models of
the subject, politics and knowing which inform our accounts of the world.[3] It
argues that we need to articulate these otherwise implicit and unexamined
foundational models in order to reveal their gender politics. Typical examples
of this argument can be seen in the deconstructive work of feminist epistemology. For example, Fox Keller and Longino argue that feminist analyses
of science begin with the question 'what kind of knowledge do the sciences
provide us and what is the basis of their cognitive authority?' (1996: 1). This
position argues that our models of knowledge shape how we understand the
world, and that for this reason we need to provide a feminist analysis of them.

*Feminist theory and practice has important implications
for epistemological theory*

This second position argues that feminist theory and practice provide new
models of foundational epistemological concepts. In particular, it argues that
feminist accounts of the subject (ontology), politics (axiology) and epistemic
practice (epistemology) permit us to rethink traditional concepts of persons,
values and truth. Three key arguments inform this position:

1   the knowing subject is not external to social relations but is constituted by
    them;
2   political values are not excluded from knowledge but are epistemologically
    significant;
3   knowledge is not an objective mirror of the external world, as social
    practices construct it.

THE KNOWING SUBJECT IS NOT EXTERNAL TO SOCIAL RELATIONS BUT
IS CONSTITUTED BY THEM

The first argument concerns feminism's ontological claims, that is, its theories
of the subject. That argument posits a relationship between the knowing subject
(however it is defined) and what is known. It contends that there is a relationship
between ontology and epistemology, or between subjectivity and knowledge.
Feminist epistemologists do not claim that this relation is an essential condition
of knowledge (such as the Cartesian subject who is able to reason and thereby posits her own existence). Instead, this argument emphasizes the social
construction of that relationship, arguing that knowing subjects produce knowledges. Influential examples of this argument can be found in the work of Donna
Haraway (1991) on situated knowledges or in Sandra Harding's standpoint

theory (1991). These theorists argue that in a differentiated social space, different social positions produce different knowledges. Because different knowers have different knowledges, certain social positions produce 'better', that is, more accurate, descriptions of the social world. This knower is a social subject, in that social relations form its epistemological position. Moreover, it is an embodied knower, whose gender, ethnic and class identity situate it in particular social positions. Feminist epistemology thus introduces the problem of the knowing subject to accounts of knowing. In particular, it raises two issues: first, how to theorize the knower as a subject, and second, how to understand the relation between the female subject and the feminist knower.[4]

POLITICAL VALUES ARE NOT EXCLUDED FROM KNOWLEDGE BUT ARE EPISTEMOLOGICALLY SIGNIFICANT

The second argument concerns feminism's axiological claims – its theories of value. It argues that political values are epistemologically significant because there is a relationship between politics and knowledge. This argument contends that political values inform and shape our knowledge of the world. Just as sexist values can inform how we understand the world, so too can feminist values. Miranda Fricker argues that the novelty of feminist epistemology 'is not so much to have such a [political] commitment, but rather to make this commitment explicit' (1994: 95). While neglecting other explicitly political epistemologies (such as critical theory), Fricker takes up a foundational position of feminist epistemology: that politics matter to how and what we know. Feminist epistemology thus introduces the theoretical problem of how to understand the relationship between knowledge and politics. In particular, it raises two issues: first, how do we define feminist politics, and second, what is the relationship between theoretical and political projects.

KNOWLEDGE IS NOT AN OBJECTIVE MIRROR OF THE EXTERNAL WORLD, AS SOCIAL PRACTICES CONSTRUCT IT

The third argument concerns feminism's epistemological claims, which are its theories of the nature of knowledge. This argument contends that feminism reveals the social and political construction of knowledge, including feminist knowledges.[5] According to this argument, knowing is a social practice. It is a social practice that *produces* the meanings and values that we attribute to the world, rather than being a mirror of that world. This argument shifts away from the traditional epistemological question of the ground of truth to questioning the modes of production of knowledge.[6] For this reason, feminist epistemologists often focus upon the production of knowledge rather than the abstracted conditions of propositional knowledge. This constructivist position also offers an important resource to feminists, for if we construct our knowledge of the world, it is then possible to produce new and different knowledges that can understand the world in new and different ways. Feminist knowledge 'implies the transformation of the very structures and images of thought, not just the propositional content of the thoughts' (Braidotti 1992: 184). Feminist epistemology examines how it describes not just different propositions, but also different forms of knowing. This conception of knowledge thus introduces the problem of how to provide an account of knowing. In particular, it raises two issues: first, how to provide a theory of the production of knowledge, and second, how to produce new and radical knowledges.

We should construct new feminist models of knowledge from that theory and practice

The third key position of the field takes up this problem, assembling these claims to construct theories of feminist knowledge. It argues that we need to construct new models of knowing from feminist theory and practice. It contends that feminism needs to provide models of knowing that theorize its subjects, politics and epistemic practices. The attempt to construct new feminist models of knowledge is the most recent and least developed of these theoretical positions. Currently, the most elaborated example of this construction of feminist models of knowing is standpoint theory. This conception of a new political epistemology introduces the theoretical problem of how to undertake this task, that is, of how to construct feminist models of knowing.

These three theoretical positions constitute the field of feminist epistemology. These positions delineate the conceptual premises which frame contemporary approaches to feminist epistemology and which structure those analyses. These concepts and arguments constitute a theoretical formation that shapes contemporary problems within the field. In particular, these positions formulate the central conceptual problems of feminist epistemology, namely:

1   how to make models of knowing and their politics explicit;
2   how to develop feminist theory and practice as epistemological theory;
3   how to construct new feminist models of knowledge.

At present these conceptual problems dominate research in this area. The field has not yet developed these theoretical positions as coherent accounts of what feminist knowledge is or could be, or as commonly agreed models of feminist knowledges. This field, like the feminist knowledges it takes as its object, is in a continuing process of formation.

The formation of the field of feminist epistemology

Reading the formation of the field of feminist epistemology

How do we understand the contemporary formation of these theoretical positions? Jane Gallop argues that '[i]f we take seriously the notion of feminist criticism as a collective movement, then critical anthologies, especially those which purport to represent the entirety of that movement, may be the best place to hear that collective subject' (1992: 8). For this reason, reading the important and influential anthology, *Knowing the Difference: Feminist Perspectives in Epistemology* (Lennon and Whitford 1994b), as a collective project permits us to understand the formation of the current positions within the field.

While the essays of *Knowing the Difference* present diverse theoretical concerns and frameworks, a collective question unites them: what is a feminist knowledge? Their answers to this question form a 'constructive project', in which each of the contributors engages with 'epistemological concerns arising out of feminist projects, which prompt reflection on the nature of knowledge and our methods for attaining it' (Lennon and Whitford 1994a: 13–14). The task of the anthology is to produce reconstructive models of feminist knowledge, rather than deconstructive critiques of masculinist knowledge. This task structures the epistemological accounts in *Knowing the Difference*.

Like other recent reconstructive research, the theories of *Knowing the Difference* address the question of the constitution of feminist knowledge and make distinct claims as to its epistemic practices. These theories argue that reason, embodiment and community produce feminist knowledges. In this way, they use the key 'categories' of contemporary reconstructive research and do so in ways typical of accounts that draw on these categories. A careful reading of these theories enables us to trace how current accounts of these concepts both enable and limit the contemporary formation of feminist epistemologies.

Normative foundations

If social practices constitute knowledge as feminist claims, then feminist epistemologists face a relativist problem in relation to their political truth-claims. For example, on what grounds do we accept feminist claims that women are more likely to be poor or suffer domestic violence, or that we should change these social realities? While 'postmodern' feminists such as Jane Flax (1990) and Susan Hekman (1990) reject traditional foundationalist epistemologies, nevertheless postfoundationalist feminist epistemologies still need to address the problem of why we would accept one truth-claim over another. The difficulty is that '[f]eminists have to insist on a better account of the world; it is not enough to show radical historical contingency and modes of construction for everything' (Haraway 1991: 187). That 'better account' requires normative or regulatory practices that determine what will count as an adequate truth-claim and what will not. For this reason, contemporary feminist epistemology has increasingly engaged with the issue of normative epistemic practices.

In *Knowing the Difference*, the essays of Marnia Lazreg (1994), Sabina Lovibond (1994) and Miranda Fricker (1994) are typical examples of this engagement. These theorists argue that feminist politics requires a commitment to a concept of truth, which in turn requires normative practices that can determine it (Lovibond 1994: 72). For example, Lazreg argues that 'the idea of truth cannot simply be jettisoned' because there must be grounds of judgement which can determine 'correctness or incorrectness in judging reality' (1994: 56, 73). For similar reasons, Fricker argues that feminism requires a 'realist account of empirical belief' (1994: 95). These theorists claim that rationality and objectivity need to be norms of feminist knowledge, as these norms determine the truth or falsity of knowledge-claims. For this reason, these essays either offer a model of reworked objectivity or 'some new form of rationalism to inform our epistemic practices' (Lennon and Whitford 1994a: 7).

These theorists explore in creative and complex ways a particularly difficult problem in this field, namely that feminist politics requires regulatory practices in relation to what it claims to be true. However, they do not adequately address new forms of regulatory epistemic practice. For example, as is typical of these accounts, Lazreg rejects the empiricism of standpoint theory, and aims to reconstruct reason through her concept of 'neo-rationalism'. However, ultimately this concept appears to differ little from more traditional notions of rationality (1994: 57). Unfortunately, these accounts rarely adequately address the challenge of recent feminist work on 'rationality', which provides a compelling critique of its claim to be foundational. This critique reveals 'a crisis of reason's *inability to know itself*; a crisis posed as reason's inability to come outside of itself, to enclose and know itself from the outside; the inadequation of the subject and its other' (Grosz 1993: 189). It is necessary to address this challenge to existing models of rationality and objectivity in order to provide a more adequate account of feminist reason.

Such an account needs to recognize that if social practices constitute knowledge, then they must also constitute feminist knowledge. Feminist epistemology cannot rely on existing forms of rationality to situate feminist knowledge 'outside' history and sociality, as these regulatory practices are themselves historically and socially constituted. Fricker argues that if 'political convictions are to be more than historical accident', then we must have a 'regulatory ideal of a unitary truth' (1994: 85, 106). This argument presumes that feminism is a single, evident and given political truth outside of history and politics. However, the third wave cannot rely on such a notion of Truth, given the internal struggles within feminism as to what counts as 'truth'. Instead of assuming the given existence of the truth of feminism, we need to understand the *production* of feminist knowledge and to develop new models of its regulatory practices.

The subject of feminism

Longino argues that '[i]n modern epistemology, whether rationalist or empiricist, the individual consciousness that is the subject of knowledge is transparent to itself [and] operates according to principles that are independent of embodied experience' (1996: 266). In contrast, the second strand of feminist epistemologies of *Knowing the Difference* founds knowledge upon an 'embodied subject'. Rosi Braidotti (1994a), Liz Stanley (1994), Kimberly Hutchings (1994) and Caroline Williams (1994) all assume that an embodied female subject produces feminist knowledges. For example, Braidotti's essay, 'The Pornography of Representation', counterposes the visual work of reproductive technology on the body with feminist accounts of embodiment. Typical of this strand of feminist thinking, Braidotti argues that the importance of those accounts lies in their model of a relational, embodied feminist knowing subject (1994a: 28–29).

In these characteristic formulations, the 'embodied subject' represents a series of connected terms: materiality, the body, woman, femininity, marginality, and positionality. 'Embodiment' signifies the intersection of three associated concepts. First, it represents the material body of the knowing subject. Second, it represents the sexual difference of woman and femininity. Third, it represents the social differences between women by marking marginality, location and position. Examples of this figurative construction of the 'embodied knower' can be seen in the reliance of Stanley's narrating and experiencing subject upon an embodied subject; the reliance of Hutching's situated knowledge upon the embodied (spatial and temporal) subject; and the reliance of Williams's 'corporeal knowledge' upon the material body. The notion of the 'embodied' subject functions as a metaphor, in which 'embodiment' represents a sexed subject, and the embodied feminist knower represents the female subject. In this way, the 'embodied subject' stands in for 'woman' and 'femininity'. In that metaphorical substitution, 'embodiment' implies a notion of sexual difference, which operates as an assumed and given term.

These theories are representative of a significant and radical model of the embodied feminist knower. However, as is typical of these models, their imaginary configuration of the trope of the 'embodied subject' elides certain crucial questions. For example, these accounts often do not consider the question of the *production* of sexual difference and the sexed subject. Because the sexed subject remains undertheorized, an account of the sexed body disappears. For example, with the exception of Williams these accounts characteristically do not address how we become 'embodied', the experience of embodiment, or what embodiment might mean. Without an account of the production of sexed subjectivity, these descriptions of the knowing subject render 'embodiment' as having or being a 'body'. This notion of embodiment appears to essentialize the body as a given fact without social signification. An effect of this notion of the body is that it elides the complex significations of the body, such as the racialized or queer body. Strangely but typically, a second effect is an elision of the material body. The materiality of the body, its affects, drives and physicality, does not appear in these accounts. Because they do not inscribe the body's materiality, the body fades from these accounts of the knowing subject. A consequence of that disappearance of materiality is that it reinstates the knower as mind and, in particular, as conscious mind.

Second, this appeal to an embodied knower as the foundation of feminist knowledge masks a conceptual slide from 'embodiment' to 'femininity' to 'feminist' subject. In these accounts, the concept of an 'embodied knower' links the female subject and feminist politics. While it is certainly possible to argue that such a relationship exists, these accounts collapse subjectivity and politics. Typically of such theories of feminist knowers, embodiment comes to represent femininity (sexual difference) and/or feminism (feminist politics). An important and problematic consequence of the operation of 'embodiment' in these theories is that they do not engage with the epistemological relationship between sexual difference and feminist politics upon which they rely. Ultimately, the feminist knower remains undertheorized in these accounts because she is assumed as a given epistemic subject.

Concomitantly and characteristically, these accounts assume that being a sexed subject explains doing feminist politics. For this reason, they do not address the relationship between the feminist (sexed) subject and the signifying practice of feminist knowledges. With the exception of Gemma Corradi Fiumara's important discussion of the role of metaphor in the production of theory (1994), these accounts of the embodied subject do not consider the question of how to understand feminist knowledge as a symbolic practice.[7] However, a theory of feminist knowledge cannot ignore the relationship between the knower and her signifying practice. Otherwise, that theory fails to address the crucial question of the operation of knowing as a signifying practice. Feminist epistemology should acknowledge feminist subjects as the makers and users of signs, rather than reducing them to their bodies. It needs to consider the complex question of the relationship between these subjects and feminist politics, so that it addresses the *formation* of the feminist knower and the *production* of her epistemic practices.

Feminist communities

The third foundational category of *Knowing the Difference* is the concept of an epistemic community. Typically of such accounts, these theorists replace the concept of the feminist knowing subject with the concept of a feminist community of knowers, arguing that feminist epistemology should not reproduce the individualist model of traditional epistemology. Drawing on second-wave critiques of the autonomous and non-relational subject, these theories argue that it is communities, not individuals, who produce knowledge. In the anthology, Ismay Barwell (1994), Diana Sartori (1994) and Janna Thompson (1994) all describe epistemic communities as founding feminist knowledges. For example, Ismay Barwell uses the work of Harding and Longino to formulate her own model of objectivity, arguing that it can be rethought as a collective feminist practice (1994: 82). Barwell argues that collective accountability constructs objectivity (1994: 90–91). As Lennon and Whitford point out, Barwell's conception of objectivity, like that of Fricker and Sartori, insists 'on the accountability of our knowledge production . . . to the community of feminists' (1994a: 7).

This work is representative of some of the most interesting and fertile research in the field of feminist epistemology. However, it is also typical of the figurative constitution of this concept of a 'community of knowers'. This concept of 'feminist community' signifies a series of associated ideas. It designates a 'political collectivity', which represents 'political engagement', which in turn represents 'feminist unity and solidarity'. For example, it is possible to identify that conceptual slippage in Barwell's notion of a feminist community of knowers; in Sartori's reconception of scientific authority in relation to a community of women scientists; or in Thompson's concept of the 'collective rationality' of a feminist community. A metonymic slide from 'the community of feminists' to a unified and singular feminism can be seen at work in these models of a feminist epistemic community.

A common effect of the metonymic operation of the appeal to 'feminist community' is that it displaces the political and theoretical difficulty of the differences among women. For example, these accounts of feminist community do not address the cultural differences between women. In *Knowing the Difference*, Meena Dhanda (1994), Susan Strickland (1994) and Anne Seller (1994) explicitly address how differences between women might effect, change, and be a resource for, epistemic practice. However, those issues are not raised within the work on communities of knowers. Unfortunately but typically, the operation of the trope of 'community' hides the complex question of the relationship between the production of feminist knowledges and communities, between these different political communities, or between different communities of women. The expression 'feminist community' in effect displaces the issue of what a feminist community *is*. In that displacement, feminist knowledge becomes an innocent statement of political position rather than an epistemic practice formed in social relations. A theory of feminist knowledge that addresses its collective nature needs to address the *production* of that collectivity, its relationship to feminist politics, and how that collectivity in turn produces feminist knowledges.

The formation of the field of feminist epistemology

In their introduction to *Knowing the Difference*, Lennon and Whitford argue that feminist epistemology emerges at the intersection of key debates in feminist theory, and that '[i]t is against the background of these debates that the essays in the present volume have been written' (1994a: 4). Like many other commentators, their discussion of these key debates coheres around two central issues: 'postmodernism' and 'difference'. For Lennon and Whitford, feminist epistemology emerges from the rearticulation of second-wave feminisms in terms of notions of 'postmodernism' and 'difference'.

In the first narrative of the 'postmodern turn', second-wave feminism confronts paradigm shifts occurring in social theory, philosophy and literary criticism in the 1980s (Nicholson 1990a: 5). The 'postmodern turn' is a catch-all phrase often used to describe the influence of postmodern philosophy and sociological postmodernity, as well as poststructuralist theory. Regardless of the rubric ascribed to the 'postmodern' field, the confrontation between feminist and postmodern theory reflected a broader questioning of the modern Enlightenment foundations of knowledge. That general 'crisis' of the foundations of theory was played out in debates concerning the (im)possibility of a postmodern feminist theory, exemplified by the collection edited by Linda Nicholson, *Feminism/Postmodernism* (1990b).

As the 'feminism/postmodernism' debates developed, a second narrative emerged within the second-wave movement. This second narrative emerges from the debates around the question of 'difference', which are exemplified by the anthology *The Future of Difference*, edited by Hester Eisenstein and Alice Jardine (1980). Those debates concerned the question of sexual difference (the differences between men and women) and also social difference (the differences between women). The question of sexual difference arose with the increasing influence of 'French feminists' such as Irigaray, Julia Kristeva and Hélène Cixous – for example, see the introduction to the Elaine Marks and Isabelle de Coutrivron collection, *New French Feminisms* (1981). Female, 'feminine' and 'Woman' became (and still are) sites of work around the question of what sexual difference *is*. The social differences between women also explicitly emerge as an issue at this time. For example, theorists such as bell hooks (1981), Trinh Minh-ha (1989) and Gayatri Spivak (1987) become increasingly influential in this period. How to build an anti-racist feminist movement became (and still is) a central concern. The difference debates called the subject of feminism into question – Woman/woman/women – and with it the apparent foundation of the second-wave politics.

The theoretical positions of *Knowing the Difference* respond to, and in different ways attempt to suture, these narratives of a crisis of second-wave feminism that emerged in the 1980s. The theoretical position that appeals to rationality as the regulatory feminist practice responds to the 'crisis' of modern foundations of knowledge. For these theorists, rationality protects feminist 'Truth' against the depredations of a notional 'postmodernism' (for example, these accounts often collapse poststructuralism, philosophical postmodernism and historical postmodernity). These arguments deploy 'postmodernism' as a signifier of the perceived nihilism and relativism of contemporary theory. Thus 'rationality' comes to represent a bulwark against the perceived dangers of relativistic theories of knowledge for feminist politics. This formulation of normative epistemic practices argues against a feminist postmodernism and appeals for a return to a reworked Enlightenment project. For this reason, it resolves the 'crisis' which the 'postmodern turn' precipitates by grounding knowing in Enlightenment concepts of truth, and, in particular, in existing practices of rationalism. However, this 'resolution' too often fails to satisfactorily engage with the social constitution of these practices, and hence to offer new models of regulatory epistemic norms.

By contrast, for those theoretical positions that appeal to an embodied knower or community, the influence of the poststructuralist and feminist critiques of universal and rational knowing dislodge the possibility that such Enlightenment models might unproblematically inform them. 'Feminist empiricist and standpoint theories', Code argues, 'attest to the influence of postmodern criticisms of the epistemological projects of the Enlightenment' (1993: 140). At the same time, theories of 'difference' also form these positions, which results in their acknowledging the sexualized and racialized social relations that are the ground of their theory and practice. Because of these complex philosophical and political concerns, this strand of feminist epistemological thinking cannot simply appropriate Enlightenment models of knowledge.

However, the appeals to 'embodiment' and 'community' do not escape the narratives of the 'crisis' of difference that emerges in second-wave theories. These appeals to the 'embodied knower' and a 'community of knowers' conceal the (sexual and cultural) differences inherent in feminist theory and practice, and so fail to adequately address those differences as conceptual and practical issues. Because of the figurative construction of these concepts of knowing subjects, these models of feminist knowledge fail to adequately engage with the production of sexual and cultural difference in their accounts of epistemic practice.

Knowing the Difference in this way illustrates the formation of a field of feminist epistemology, because it reveals how the 'crises' of the broader feminist field shape these accounts of 'rationality', 'embodiment' and 'community'. An effect of that formation is a theoretical closure, which uses the concepts of reason, the female knower and the feminist community to secure feminist theories of knowledge, and yet does not adequately theorize those foundational terms. For this reason, recent debates in the field often appear to devolve into circular and unproductive discussions concerning the epistemological significance of these concepts. Duran describes how:

feminist epistemologists have had their hands full trying to adjudicate such disputes as those between theorists who would employ some aspects of analytic theory and those who would not, or those who might favor a Marxist-oriented standpoint approach over some type of work deemed to be postmodern. An observer might well be tempted to say that it is simply too difficult a task.

(2001: xi)

Like Duran, I believe that this task is not impossible but is challenging. The challenge for feminist epistemologies lies in not endlessly reproducing those same debates but reconceiving the way in which they understand the production of the feminist knower and the epistemic practices of feminism.

This task requires undertaking 'constructive and reconstructive work' that aims to 'reframe the problematic of knowledge' (Alcoff and Potter 1993a: 2). In this project, feminist epistemology finds an important theoretical alliance with the psychoanalytic work of Jacques Lacan. Lacanian theory reframes 'the problematic of knowledge' because it shifts from traditional models of thinking that are founded in individual consciousness to a theory of the formation of knowledge in real, imaginary and symbolic intersubjective relations. The importance of Lacanian theory for feminist epistemology lies in that radical reformulation of epistemic practice. The next chapter begins the reformulation of the problematic of feminist knowledge by placing it in the context of the encounter between Lacanian and feminist theory.

2   Lacanian epistemologies

Should feminists know better than to read Lacan?

> Does psychoanalysis provide the theory for politics? And which
> psychoanalysis?
>
> (Butler 2000c: 6)

Feminism/psychoanalysis

In the 1970s, the feminists of the Anglo-American second wave began to warn
women of the dangers of psychoanalysis. Betty Friedan, Germaine Greer and
Kate Millett argued that psychoanalysis is a patriarchal institution because
of its phallocentric prescription of normative femininity. By contrast, second-
wave 'French' feminists such as Julia Kristeva and Luce Irigaray argued that
psychoanalysis is a potential feminist ally, because of its account of the psychic
register of sexual oppression and liberation.[1] In his contemporaneous seminar,
Lacan warns these women not to confuse his revolutionary psychoanalysis
with the political and sexual revolution that they hope for (S17: 63).

These mutual narratives of the difficulties of feminism/psychoanalysis continue to haunt contemporary feminist and Lacanian movements. Certain strands
of Lacanian psychoanalysis regard feminism as a dangerous, if not impossible,
attempt to rewrite foundational sexual differences. A typical example could
be seen at an international conference of Lacanian analysts on the theme of 'The
Clinical Limits of Gender' (London, 1997), which figured the clinical limits
of gender as the clinical limit of politics. It seems that a rejection of feminist
and queer politics has become a truism of Lacanian orthodoxy: from the criticism that feminism fails to recognize 'the rock of castration', to the refusal to
recognize the legitimacy of same-sex families. These analysts confront feminism
with a conservatism which asks 'Replace the phallus? Why do that?' (Hoffman
Baruch and Serrano 1996: 48).

Similarly, 'ideal-typical anglophone feminist readings', such as Nancy
Fraser's, also reject Lacanian psychoanalysis because of its dangers (Aoki

1995: 47). For Fraser, if feminists seek to 'use or adapt the theory of Jacques Lacan', they will not be able to escape its structuralist determinism that naturalizes women's oppression (1992: 182). Fraser fears that Lacan, 'the ladies' man', the seductive Master Analyst, the prescriptive phallocrat, will seduce them and fundamentally compromise their politics. In this contemporary repudiation of psychoanalysis, 'Lacan' is a metaphor for the dangers of psycho-analysis for feminism, as 'Freud' was for the earlier feminist movement of the 1970s.

However, the history of the encounter between psychoanalysis and feminism is more rich and complex than either of these defensive positions allows. Juliet Mitchell and Jacqueline Rose (1982) show in their careful examinations of the history of feminism and psychoanalysis that neither movement is unified or homogenous. Their different strands interact to address different theoretical and political issues. For example, Lacan develops his later theory of female sexuality at the time of his exposure to the women's liberation movement, both in terms of its increasing visibility as a political movement and in terms of the ideas of his feminist students.[2] There has been a long and complex engagement between particular forms of psychoanalysis and of feminism, such as the feminist appropriation of Lacanian theories of 'female' subjectivity that emerge in the 1980s, to Fraser's 'severe puzzlement'.

Commenting in 1989 on this burgeoning field of feminist psychoanalytic theory, Richard Feldstein and Judith Roof observe that '[i]n recent years, feminist critics have characterised the exchanges between feminism and psycho-analysis as a two-party, one-on-one affair' (1989: 1). However, as Feldstein and Roof point out, much of this writing constructs the relation between psycho-analysis and feminism within a familial paradigm, as a narrative of conjunction and union that seeks to marry them. During the same period, another different narrative of feminism and psychoanalysis emerges in the diverse work of Teresa Brennan (1986), Jane Gallop (1987), Elizabeth Grosz (1990), Jacqueline Rose (1986) and Kaja Silverman (1988). This engagement with psychoanalysis has been taken up in the 1990s in the postcolonial and queer theories of Homi Bhabha (1994) and Judith Butler (1997b), and more recently in the work of Tim Dean (2000) and Kalpana Seshadri-Crooks (2000).

These works characterize their relationship to Lacanian theory not as a marriage but as productive appropriation. They argue that Lacanian theory is central to their projects while also recognizing its specificity. For example, Seshadri-Crooks describes how she has 'tried to work with the richest aspects of theory, and in the process have found it necessary to wrestle with it, and to exert considerable force in inducing it to address race' (2000: 3). This narra-tive of productive appropriation involves both the use of Lacanian theory and its development. In that formulation, one field of theory and practice critically deploys another, acknowledging the differences and difficulties of each field in order to stage a productive encounter between them.

My engagement with Lacanian theory takes up this contemporary narrative of productive appropriation. It asks what this particular psychoanalytic account does, or fails to do, *for* a specific feminist problematic. My question does not concern a possible union of feminism/psychoanalysis, but a specific engagement of feminist and Lacanian epistemology. Despite the interdicts of the Master and the Sister, this encounter is very useful for my project of providing an account of feminist politics.

The other scene – feminist or analytic?

However, my engagement with Lacan shifts his work from the psychoanalytic field into another field with a different object, project, and set of theoretical positions. Placing Lacanian theory within the field of feminist epistemology reconfigures that theory. This reconfiguration takes place because feminist practice differs from psychoanalytic practice; because feminist knowledge differs from psychoanalytic knowledge; and, above all, because feminism implies a commitment to a politics of social change.

This shift to the feminist field entails that it is necessary to reconsider Lacanian epistemology (an account of the relationship between psychoanalyst and analysand), in terms of feminist epistemology (an account of social relationships). An ethical relation to an other may structure the psychoanalytic relation, but an ethical relation to others forms feminist relations. Shifting Lacanian epistemology to the feminist field situates it within the social, because an account of feminist knowledge as social practice requires a theory of the social relationships of subjects. It also situates Lacanian epistemology within the political, because feminism is ultimately a political project with a commitment to changing social relations. For these reasons, my engagement with Lacanian epistemology reconfigures it through a feminist social theory and politics. Without such a reconfiguration, Lacanian epistemology remains 'outside' feminist politics.

The question of 'politics'

Understanding Lacan's work as 'outside' feminist politics does not entail conceiving Lacanian theory as 'outside' history and politics – as if 'psychoanalysis' is timeless and apolitical while 'feminism' represents history and politics. Teresa Brennan stresses that 'any notion of opposition between psychoanalysis and politics has to be qualified: psychoanalysis is a thoroughly political entity' (1986: 1). The 'analytic truth' of Lacan is a 'truth' of its historical and political moment, particularly in relation to feminism.

If Lacanian epistemology is 'thoroughly political' in and of itself, when brought within the domain of feminist theory it becomes political for feminist epistemologists. In its engagement with Lacanian epistemology, feminism encounters the theoretical and political desires of Lacanian psychoanalysis. For example, the difficulty of the politics of Lacanian theory can be seen in the vociferous debates concerning the ramifications of Lacan's phallocentrism. Lacanian theory is not feminist theory. If feminism is to appropriate Lacan's work, it must confront the specificity of Lacanian theory. It must take Lacanian theory on its terms, which it can then reconfigure in relation to its own problematic.

Lacanian epistemology is political not only because of the relation of Lacanian theory to feminism, but also because of the relation of feminism to Lacanian theory. Rose makes the important point that '[p]sychoanalysis is already political for feminism – political in the more obvious sense that it came into the arena of discussion in response to the internal needs of feminist debate' (1986: 84). The questions that feminists ask of Lacanian psychoanalysis are not neutral – and nor should they be. Feminist epistemology has its *own* history and its *own* theoretical and political projects that form its relation to Lacanian epistemology. Lacan's work is already political *for* feminist epistemology because it invokes that work to address a series of theoretical issues that remain unresolved within that field. The complex debates within feminist epistemology, which themselves emerge in the debates circulating within feminism, constitute these issues.

What are the internal needs of these feminist debates? Feminist epistemology needs to unravel the imaginary configurations of its debates and to unsettle the theoretical closure that characterizes them. It needs to resist reproducing the theoretical knot of existing accounts of the subject and its knowledges. Lacan's work provides a strategy for unravelling, unsettling and unknotting the existing configurations of current debates. It can be used to rework their constituent terms of the feminist knower, politics and knowledges, and hence to rework the problematic of the field, because it offers an account of the formation of the subject and of knowledge as a practice that changes how we understand ourselves and others.

Lacanian epistemology

> Freud's discovery puts truth into question, and there is no one who is not personally concerned by the truth.
>
> (*É*: 130)

Why does psychoanalysis put truth into question? For Lacan, its questioning of the truth emerges not from its knowledge of the unconscious, but from the implications of the unconscious for our models of knowing. The Freudian discovery of the unconscious radically challenges classical epistemological models that presume the conscious mind (*É*: 126). If these models understand knowledge as a truthful set of statements or as the accurate description of reality, Lacanian psychoanalysis proposes another model of truth. This model emerges from the psychoanalytic field – from Lacan's sustained and complex consideration of the status of truth in psychoanalysis. However, Lacan does not explicitly set out a psychoanalytic epistemology. Rather, his epistemological theory derives from his psychoanalytic theory. To delineate this epistemological theory requires a productive reading that sets out Lacan's model of truth and constructs 'Lacanian epistemology' from Lacanian psychoanalysis.

Reading Lacanian epistemology

> *Your style, etcetera.*
>
> (Lacan 1974: 45)

Écrits begins with the question of style with its opening claim that '[l]e style est l'homme même' (*style is the man himself*) (*Éc*: 9). Lacan situates his style not within the field of the academy but within the literary. Lacan's associative writing deploys a rhetoric that is aesthetically pleasurable and conceptually difficult. The evocation of the 'movement of discourse' within his writing performs both the representation, and the resistance to representation, of the unconscious (*É*: 147).

This infamous textual, aesthetic and theoretical complexity characterizes Lacan's *œuvre*, which commences with the publication of his specialist psychiatric papers in the late 1920s and concludes with the publication of his letter dissolving his psychoanalytic school in *Le Monde* in 1981. The texts that comprise Lacan's body of work are not in the form of traditional monographs. For the most part, that body of work consists of orally delivered papers and year-long seminars subsequently revised for publication, with a significant proportion of Lacan's major seminars of the 1970s still largely unpublished. Of those seminars that have been posthumously published, the status of the Lacanian text has been a matter of considerable debate.[3]

The textual slipperiness of Lacan's work exacerbates the difficulty of a style that is deliberately associative, elusive and opaque. Throughout his *œuvre* Lacan continually shifts and reformulates his theories, appearing to engage in a constant process of theorizing with only provisional concepts in place. This unstable and seemingly unfinished quality of Lacan's work is part of the Lacanian model itself, as it enacts the desire, incompleteness, and lack, of the unconscious. However, the difficulty of Lacan's work does not mean that it is incomprehensible or incoherent. In Lacan's work, there are a number of stable propositions that can be extracted from their psychoanalytic field (Milner 1995: 8). Despite its complexity, Lacan's work presents stable concepts and theories. It is possible to extract these stable concepts and ideas and to use them to build a model of what can be called 'Lacanian epistemology'.

Such a project requires a productive reading that constructs a Lacanian epistemology from his sustained and complex theories of psychoanalytic knowledge. Lacan does not directly present a theory of knowledge in his work. Rather, that theory emerges from his consideration of psychoanalytic knowledge and subjectivity. Lacanian epistemology thus emerges from his engagement with the specific question of knowledge in the psychoanalytic field – knowledge as it emerges from the practice and theory of the clinic. To construct a model of Lacanian epistemology therefore requires a productive reading of Lacan's work that is both synchronic and diachronic. This approach to Lacan's work avoids what Dylan Evans characterizes as the two most common errors made by readers of Lacan – namely, the presentation of his work as either being subject to radical epistemological breaks, such as a 'radically new "linguistic turn" in 1953, or alternatively as being a "single unfolding narrative"' (1996: x). Instead, a productive reading recognizes that Lacanian theory changes and shifts over the fifty years of its development, while also identifying those constant and stable theses upon which he bases his account of knowledge and which subsist throughout his work.

My productive reading does not aim to provide an exhaustive exegesis of Lacanian theory. Rather, it is a strategic reading of that theory which aims to extract relatively stable and transferable concepts for feminist epistemology. This reading constructs a Lacanian epistemology by first tracing its foundational theses in Lacan's seminal text, *Écrits* (1966). It then examines Lacan's later development of his account of knowledge in his theory of the discourse in later texts, such as the seminars of 1969–1970, *L'envers de la psychanalyse* (*The Other Side of Psychoanalysis*), and of 1972–1973, *Encore*.

The foundations of Lacanian epistemology

Before 1966, Lacan's reputation in intellectual and psychoanalytic circles derives mainly from his articles and seminars. However, 'the explosion of his influence in French society' begins with the publication of *Écrits* (Benevuto and Kennedy 1986: 22). In the light of the slow rate of publication, and slower translation, of Lacan's seminars, *Écrits* is likely to remain the seminal Lacanian text.[4] The French edition of *Écrits* includes those papers which Lacan selected as representative of his psychoanalytic work of thirty years, from the 1936 essay, 'Au-delà du "Principe de réalité"' (*Towards the 'Reality Principle'*) (*Éc*), to his paper of 1965, 'La science et la vérité' (*Science and Truth*). This collection of papers reveals Lacan in his most systematic mode, laying down the conceptual foundations of his theory. Zizek characterizes *Écrits* as the '"classical Lacan"', exploring central questions of the unconscious, subjectivity and language (1992: 130).

However, the papers collected in *Écrits* do not set out 'Lacanian theory', in the sense that Lacan does not present a series of elaborated, propositional arguments. He writes that '[m]y *Écrits* are unsuitable for a thesis, particularly an academic thesis: they are antithetical by nature: one either takes what they formulate or one leaves them' (1970a: vii). Lacan does not intend those writings to be read as an exposition of his theory but as an experience of the opacity and difficulty of the unconscious. His legendary 'baroque' style is marked by a poetic use of language that he intends to be a textual evocation of the unconscious.

In terms of both its style and its ideas, *Écrits* retains the difficulty and jaggedness of an unfolding work of theory. This stylistic and theoretical complexity is exacerbated by Lacan's refusal to 'systematise' his theories. For example, even John Muller and William Richardson, whose meticulous textual analysis examines *Écrits* line by line, at times are reduced to bewildered incomprehension.[5] However, *Écrits* also reveals moments of logic, structure and clarity, as well as moments of excess and resistance. Despite the difficulty of *Écrits*, nevertheless it is possible to trace within it those stable concepts that form a Lacanian theory of knowledge. In *Écrits*, three key concepts form Lacanian epistemology:

1   the relationship between *the subject and knowledge*;
2   *the knowing subject*:
    the knowing subject of the conscious mind;
    the knowing subject as analysand;
3   *the analyst's knowledge* as practice.

The subject and knowledge

The subject

Before Freud, Lacan argues, there was a radical disjuncture between the subject and object of knowledge. However, the Freudian discovery of the unconscious 'brought within the circle of science the boundary between the object and being that seemed to mark its outer limit' (*É*: 193). For Lacan, the Freudian experience reveals the epistemological relation of being to object, because it shows how the psychic reality of the subject forms that relation. The '"little reality"' of the psyche structures the relation of knowing subject to reality (*É*: 4). In Lacan's account, the structures of the subject form knowledge, linking subjectivity and knowing together. If epistemology is a theory of knowing and ontology is a theory of being, then Lacanian theory radically imbricates epistemology and ontology.

For Lacan, the question 'how do I know?' entails another question: 'who am I?' However, reflexive self-knowledge does not reveal the truth of who I am. As Lacan describes it, the self cannot be an object of its own knowledge because it is not possible to obey 'the empty adage "Know thyself"' (*É*: 191). Playing upon the Cartesian *cogito*, Lacan insists upon the 'excentricity' of the subject to itself: 'I think where I am not, therefore I am where I do not think' (*É*: 183). Accordingly, knowledge is not a question of knowing the self, but of knowing the subject. This distinction marks Lacan's divergence from Descartes, since for Lacan thought does not secure being. Rather, it is the 'being' of the subject that secures thought.

What is the nature of that subject? In his descriptions of the subject, Lacan fully exploits the resonant associations of the term. Lacan uses 'the subject' both in its philosophical sense of a thinking consciousness, and in its linguistic and logical sense of the 'subject' of a predicate. Lacan also deploys the term to refer to the subject of psychoanalysis, the analyst or the analysand, while at other times he uses it in the ordinary sense of an individual person. However, the Lacanian concept of the subject is not to be found in these different usages of the term.

From his earliest psychoanalytic papers, Lacan argues that the subject cannot be reduced to the first person '*I*' of consciousness. For example, in his paper of 1946 'Propos sur la causalité psychique' (*Remarks on Psychical Causality*), Lacan criticizes psychiatric theory for confusing the ego and the being of the subject (*Éc*: 178). These accounts of the subject mistakenly reduce it to its conscious ego, and so ignore or refuse the unconscious. The distinction between the conscious ego which forms the *I* of the self and the unconscious of the subject founds Lacan's theory of the mirror stage, and he clearly uses the ego, the *I*, and the subject as distinct terms in his early papers. By 1955, Lacan posits a 'fundamental distinction between the true subject of the unconscious and the ego' (*É*: 141), a distinction which he sustains in subsequent reformulations of his theory of subjectivity.

Lacan's papers of the 1950s, such as 'The Function and Field of Speech and Language in Psychoanalysis' (1953) (*É*), introduce what can be described as the classical Lacanian account of the subject. That account emphasizes the production of the subject in language. Lacan coins the neologism *parlêtre* – the 'speaking being' – to describe the speaking subject that comes into existence in the linguistic structures of the Symbolic order. In the later papers such as 'The Subversion of the Subject and the Dialectic of Desire in the Freudian Unconscious' (1960) (*É*), Lacan reformulates the question of the subject as 'who is speaking?' (331). This later elaboration of subjectivity makes clear that the subject is an effect of language. For Lacan, the subject comes into being in the Symbolic order of language (*É*: 337).[6]

The Lacanian subject is thus a speaking being that is produced in language. Such a conception of subjectivity should not be misunderstood as a final stage in a teleology of the development of a unified and unitary identity. In a typical polemic against developmental psychoanalysis, Lacan argues against '[t]his mythology of instinctual maturation' (*É*: 59). He argues that the subject in the present is a re-representation of the subject's past and future. Subjectivity marks a temporal structure which language produces.

The predication of the subject in language constitutes it as divided, radically split between the conscious and unconscious, and as 'excentric', radically other to its conscious self of identity (*É*: 189). The subject of the unconscious has no positive content as such – it marks the void or gap between the symbolic elements of language that produce it. As Bruce Fink describes it, '[t]here is nothing substantial about this subject; it has no *being*, no substratum or permanence in time' (1995: 42). In this sense, the Lacanian subject is not a substance or an essence (unlike the philosophical subject). Rather, it emerges from the relationship between the symbolic elements, or signifiers, which comprise language.

The knowing subject

A knowing subject therefore represents a position of signification rather than an ontological state or experience of knowing. The knower is a linguistic event, because language constitutes it as speaking subject. It is no more than a stable structure of signifiers, a subjective position in language. For this reason, the specific structures of signifiers that produce the subject also form its relationship to reality. The knowing subject therefore is not prior to, or separate from, its knowledge.

This account characterizes knowledge as a signifying relation to the known object and so as a practice by which the knowing subject gives meaning to that object. Knowing appears to be radically subjective, since it is an act of representation of the knower. However, for Lacan the sensuous experience or rational consciousness of the subject does not found knowledge, which instead derives from the signifying structures which produce the knowing subject. Lacan understands the subject as founding the epistemological relation of knower and known, but another scene produces that subject – the scene of the unconscious and of language.

Signification

In 'The Function and Field of Speech and Language in Psychoanalysis', Lacan situates psychoanalytic practice within the field of language. To theorize this field, Lacan deploys Ferdinand de Saussure's linguistic theory.[7] For Lacan, the importance of Saussure's work lies in his structural definition of language as a synchronic structure of signs. In Saussure's account, each sign is determined by its relation to other signs, that is, its place in a structure of the linguistic units that comprise language (1916: 112–113). He argues that the relation between the two elements of the sign is not necessary but is arbitrary, and hence the sign itself is arbitrary, bearing only a contingent relation to the object that it appears to represent (1916: 66–67). Each sign has two elements: the signifier and the signified. Saussure defines the signifier as the signifying element of a sign – the acoustic or sound image – while the signified is its conceptual element (1916: 66–67).

However, Lacan's transposition of Saussure's theory to the psychoanalytic field itself produces another and different model of linguistic process. For Lacan, language is not a structure of signs but a structure of signifiers, which have the property of 'combining according to a closed order' (*É*: 169). This closed order is the Symbolic order. 'In the end', Lacan argues, 'the notion of structure and that of the signifier appear inseparable' (S3: 184). Lacan reverses Saussure's diagram of the sign, privileging the signifier over the signified, and positing the signified itself as an effect of the signifier. In Lacan's account of the sign, the conceptual element of the sign is an effect of its signifying element.

For Lacan, the relationship between these two elements is radically barred. He comments that his diagram S/s, should be 'read as: the signifier over the signified, "over" corresponding to the bar separating the two stages' (*É*: 164). This bar 'mark[s] the irreducibility in which, in the relations between signifier and signified, the resistance of signification is constituted' (*É*: 181). This resistance of signification needs to be read with a psychoanalytic inflection. Lacan's algorithm emphasizes not the unity of the sign but the rupture between signifier and signified. This rupture has the effect that speech is not a neutral act of representation which allows us to say what we want to say (the conscious resistance to the expression of the unconscious wish), but is an overdetermined combination of signifying elements in which we always say more than we intend (the Freudian slip, the symptom).

For Lacan, the relation between the signifier and signified is not only arbitrary but is also unstable and shifting, such that the apparently fixed relation between signifying element and concept unravels, and the signified constantly slides under the signifier. While Saussure conceives the signifier and signified as tied in the sign, Lacan emphasizes the radically arbitrary nature of that relation, as signifieds incessantly slide beneath signifiers (*É*: 170). In Lacan's model, the signified is an effect of the relationship between signifiers. Signification is therefore a process in which the order of signifiers produces meaning.

In this model, knowledge consists of the matching of a signifier to its correlative signified, because it always involves the representation of an object in language. For Lacan, structures of signification fix signifier to signified, such that the meaning given to an object appears to be the correlate of reality. The meaning that a knowing subject gives to objects must then be a fixing of signifier to signified, or, the signifying element to the concept. 'Knowledge' is thus understood as a representation of the known object. That representation is not a transparent reflection of the object but is always overdetermined and bound up in the structures of the chain of signifiers.

In this way, Lacan rejects the classical model of truth as *adaequatio rei et intellectus*, that is, as a relationship of parity between the idea and object. In the Lacanian model of knowledge, there is no possibility of a neutral representation of reality, precisely because to describe an object involves representing it in language. For Lacan, 'there is no such thing as a metalanguage . . . no language able to say the truth about the truth, since truth is grounded in the fact that it speaks, and that it has no other means with which to do so' (1965: 16, *Éc*: 867–868). No language can represent the truth of the truth, because truth itself is expressed in language.

Knowing subjects

If Lacan posits a radical imbrication of ontology and epistemology, he counterposes the philosophical concept of the subject as consciousness to the psychoanalytic subject. Lacan often does not distinguish between the position of analyst and analysand in his more general discussions of psychoanalysis. However, he clearly differentiates between three different knowing subjects: the philosophical subject of the conscious mind, the analysand in relation to psychoanalytic practice, and the analyst in the relation to psychoanalytic theory.

The three different positions of the knowing subject which emerge in *Écrits* are:

1 the knowing subject of consciousness;
2 the knowing subject as analysand;
3 the knowing subject as analyst.

Being in error

Being and error

There is a state of knowing which Lacan characterizes as a state of error. The state of knowing as error is the position of the conscious knower. The conscious mind of the knower confines its knowledge to that which is admissible to consciousness and hence it can only know the conscious. In typically sweeping style, Lacan variously identifies this state in the ego-psychology of the International Psychoanalytic Association of his time; in the ego-driven American way of life; and in the philosophical concept of Cartesian *cogito* as rational consciousness. Jacques-Alain Miller describes how each of these 'states of error' represents for Lacan the '"modern ego", that is to say, the paranoiac subject of scientific civilisation, of which a warped psychology theorizes the imaginary, at the service of free enterprise' (*É*: 362).

The subject of consciousness

Lacan initially develops his theory of consciousness in his early papers on the theory of the mirror stage: 'Aggressivity in Psychoanalysis' (1948) (*É*) and 'The Mirror Stage as Formative of the Function of the I' (1949) (*É*). In these papers, Lacan argues that the ego is the nucleus of consciousness. In 'Aggressivity', Lacan distinguishes the agency of the ego from the perception-consciousness system of Freud's metapsychology and characterizes it instead by its phenomenological essence of *Verneinung* – negation (*É*: 17). The ego is a negation of the unconscious, which forms consciousness and the experience of self as *I*. For this reason, the ego appears as co-extensive with the *I* of consciousness.

Lacan argues that the *I* of consciousness is formed in the mirror stage. He draws on the work of the psychologist Henri Wallon to develop a theory of the formation of the *I* of the conscious in imaginary recognition. The mirror stage can be understood '*as an identification*', and in particular as a narcissistic identification. In the mirror stage, the infant identifies with the imago of its own body in a narcissistic 'jubilant assumption of his specular image'. With this operation of identification, 'the I is precipitated in a primordial form' (*É*: 2). That primordial form is the agency of the ego. This process constitutes the ego in the imaginary relations of the mirror stage, which is thus a narcissistic formation in the imaginary order.

The function of the imago of the infant's body is to establish 'a relation between the organism and its reality . . . between the *Innenwelt* and the *Umwelt*' (*É*: 4). The imago enables the infant to perceive its experience of a fragmented body as a totality, and so to establish a relation between the infant's inner and outer worlds. That experience of the body is 'orthopaedic', and forms 'an alienating identity' (*É*: 5). In a series of alienating identifications with its specular image, the infant perceives its imago as a rival other. The infant perceives the imago of its body as the form of the other and directs the aggression formerly directed at its own image to the ego's other. In this way, the infant uses the aggression formed in the distress of its original disorder to construct the relation of ego to other and object (*É*: 21). This process marks the ego with an aggressive and objectifying relation to its imagined other. For Lacan, this process of the construction of ego and other represents the transition from specular *I* to social *I* (*É*: 6).

The genesis of the ego in a series of alienating and objectifying identifications gives it a paranoiac structure (*É*: 23). The ego perceives its objects in relation to itself in a 'formal stagnation', which constitutes the ego and its objects 'with attributes of permanence, identity and of substantiality' (*É*: 19). The 'formal stagnation' that Lacan describes is the capture of the self and its objects in the imaginary order, such that the ego gives its objects and its self form, fixity and presence. The ego posits itself as having mastery and knowledge of its others and its objects, which it perceives as frozen reflections of its self. The ego 'is a function of mastery, a play of presence, of bearing (*prestance*), and of constituted rivalry' (*É*: 340). Accordingly, the ego is that which secures the *I* as a would-be masterful presence.

The knowing subject of consciousness

The first position of the knowing subject that emerges in Lacanian epistemology is that of conscious ego. That knower is a subject in the conventional philosophical sense of a conscious self. Lacanian epistemology clearly counterposes this self to the psychoanalytic subject of the unconscious. In this first position, the knower is a conscious self which appears to be transparent, certain and foundational. For this reason, I describe this knower as 'the knowing subject of consciousness'.

In Lacanian epistemology, the knowing subject of consciousness confuses *ego*, *I* and *subject*, so that the knower understands its 'self' as the *I* of consciousness. The knower's confusion of *I* and *ego* misrecognises the ego as self, and the self as the subject, in a defensive operation that repudiates the unconscious. That which is other to consciousness is inadmissible to it, not because there is something missing from its conscious knowledge, but rather because a repudiation of, and defence against, the unconscious orders its knowing.

This knowing subject is founded upon consciousness and secured by the conscious. This knower cannot recognize itself as other than *I* (*É*: 339). Because the knower takes up a defensive position against its unconscious other, it cannot know itself in its refusal of the unconscious. For this reason, Lacan is led to oppose any philosophy 'directly issuing from the *Cogito*' (*É*: 1).[8] For Lacan, both the Cartesian *cogito* and the Hegelian 'being conscious of self, the fully conscious self' are moments of the knowing subject of consciousness (*É*: 328).

This position of the knower can be characterized as an imaginary position. Because the imaginary order captures the knower, it perceives its self and its objects within the imaginary projections of the mirror of the ego (*É*: 19). It posits its self and its others in a relation of narcissistic and objectifying identification in which they appear as objects to be controlled. Accordingly, the knowing subject of consciousness claims mastery of the world and itself, and takes up an imaginary position of 'Absolute Master' (Lacan 1955: 47, *Éc*: 33). In that position, the knower projects consciousness, self and subject as a unified identity. That unity of identity enables the knowing subject to claim mastery and presence of self, and produces its relation to others as an aggressive relation of masterful ego to masterful ego.

Signification

For Lacan, the knower that founds itself in the conscious recognizes only that which is admissible to conscious thought. Its representation of the world is (and can only be) confined to conscious material. As such, that representation is characterized by the imaginary permanence, stability and rigidity of the ego (*É*: 19). It fixes the relation of signifier to signified, giving it an imaginary permanence and stability and producing the illusion of univocal meaning. This illusion of singular meaning is an effect of the knower's refusal of the unconscious. For Lacan, such a refusal of the unconscious entails that signification does not cross the bar of signification between signifier and signified (*É*: 181). The knowledge of the subject resists the movement of metaphor, and hence the possibility of new signification. The knower reproduces its symbolic economy, because it does not produce a new relation between signifiers, and so cannot produce new signifieds or meanings.

However, the signification of the knower is also marked by what it cannot represent, because its signification is always in (unconscious) excess of that which it (consciously) intends to represent. For Lacan, the unconscious is 'a chain of signifiers which . . . is repeated, and insists upon interfering in the breaks offered it by the effective discourse and the cogitation that it informs' (*É*: 329). The unconscious interferes in conscious discourse because it structures signification in a metonymic displacement of desire, a horizontal movement from signifier to signifier whereby 'the resistance of signification is maintained, the bar is not crossed, no new signified is produced' (Evans 1996: 114). Unconscious repetition structures the signification of the knower.

Connaissance – méconnaissance

For Lacan, the signifying economy of the knowing subject of consciousness produces a particular type of knowledge, for which he uses the term *méconnaissance*. *Méconnaissance* implies a flawed knowledge that involves ignorance, error and misrecognition. Exploiting these implications of *méconnaissance*, Lacan uses the term to designate an imaginary misrecognition. 'The *function of méconnaissance* that characterizes the ego in all its structures', is the capture of the knower and its objects in the specular reflection of the ego (*É*: 7). The knower mistakenly perceives itself as consciousness, and its consciousness as reality. The *méconnaissance* of the ego is 'the most general structure of human knowledge [*connaissance*]' (*É*: 19). *Méconnaissance* is a knowledge in the imaginary register. As such, it only reflects the subject's misrecognition of itself and its reality.

In this description of conscious knowledge, Lacan proposes a theory of a knower who suffers radical error, because it suffers the *méconnaissance* of the ego. The imaginary entrapments of the ego capture it, such that the knower can only know its self and its others through the imaginary misrecognitions of the ego's mirror. This misrecognition produces the relation of the knowing subject to its known object. That relation is an aggressive, objectifying and distorting mastery of its object, which refuses its difference. Because the knowing subject of consciousness does not produce new signifiers, and thus does not produce new meaning or knowledge, it continually reproduces its signifying economy of *méconnaissance*.

The Lacanian theory of the *méconnaissance* of the knowing subject of consciousness raises the question of how it is possible to think anything other than radical error. Lacan appears to suggest that, as an analyst, he is able to evade *méconnaissance*, since he claims to represent the truth of the unconscious both in his theoretical and textual practice. In that claim of psychoanalytic truth, Lacanian epistemology offers other models of knowledge that resist the *méconnaissance* of the ego. Those models are to be found in Lacan's theory of the analysand and analyst as knowing subjects, who he claims can escape the imaginary entrapments of the knowing subject of consciousness.

Knowing as becoming

The subject as analysand

The earlier papers of *Écrits*, such as 'The Mirror Stage' or 'Aggressivity in Psychoanalysis', develop a theory of the mirror stage, and the ego and consciousness, rather than directly addressing a theory of the unconscious. Lacan elaborates his theory of the unconscious and language in his papers of the 1950s: 'The Function and Field of Speech and Language in Psychoanalysis' (1953) (*É*); 'The Freudian Thing' (1955) (*É*); and 'The Agency of the Letter in the Unconscious or Reason since Freud' (1957) (*É*). In these papers, Lacan elaborates his theory of the relation of the subject and signifier, and his concept of psychoanalytic knowledge. From that set of engagements emerges a theory of the analysand as knowing subject. The analysand as knower is the second position of the knowing subject in the Lacanian epistemology of *Écrits*.

Lacan characterizes the analysand as a subject of the unconscious. That subject emerges in psychoanalytic practice because of the disintegration of the imaginary and defensive unity of the ego in transference: 'it is in the disintegration of the imaginary unity constituted by the ego that the subject finds the signifying material of his symptom' (*É*: 151). Analytic practice reveals the 'signifying material' of the analysand's desire, because the analysand brings into speech (that is, signifies) the Other of the unconscious: 'he has verbalised it . . . he has made it pass into the Word, or more precisely, into the *epos* by which he brings back into the present time the origins of his own person' (*É*: 51). The analysand therefore recognizes the truth of the subject. For Lacan, the truth of the subject is that of the unconscious, for it is the 'unconscious which speaks the truth about the truth' (1965: 16, *Éc*: 868).

For Lacan, psychoanalytic practice disrupts the imaginary order of the ego because it enables the analysand's recognition of the Other of the Symbolic order. With that recognition, the subject articulates the order of signifiers – the

Symbolic order – that structures it, and in doing so acknowledges its subjection to the signifier. In this way, the analysand yields mastery by understanding that it is other to its conscious self, and that its discourse is the discourse of the Other: 'I think where I am not, therefore I am where I do not think' (*É*: 183). 'I am where I do not think' is not a position of Hegelian self-consciousness in which the subject knows itself, but rather of an articulation of its formation by the Other of the Symbolic order. In that act of signification, the analysand comes to symbolic knowledge. For Lacan, symbolic knowledge, or '[s]peech, begins only with the passage from "pretence" to the order of the signifier' (*É*: 338).

In this account of psychoanalysis, the aim of analysis is therefore not to 'cure' the analysand but to enable the analysand to articulate the structure of signifiers which produce him or her as subject: '[i]n order to free the subject's speech, we introduce him into the language of his desire' (*É*: 89). As a result, the imaginary no longer traps the analysand, who enters the symbolic register. The analysand is then able to accept the 'symbolic debt' – the pound of flesh or limit to *jouissance* – which it pays for the entry into language as a necessary price of signification (*É*: 352–353). That acceptance of symbolic debt ideally marks the final moment of the analysis, in which the analysand is able to accept its division and lack and concomitantly to refuse the fantasy of the presence of self and illusion of its mastery.

The knowing subject as analysand

In Lacanian epistemology, the knowing subject as analysand is able to recognize its temporal and intersubjective nature. The analysand does not repudiate its unconscious and its desires, but instead speaks them in order to change them. The analysand brings into its symbolic system those signifiers of the Other which it was previously unable to articulate (*É*: 338–339). The analysand's knowledge is not a fixing of referentiality, but a discourse in the process of becoming (1951: 72, *Éc*: 226). It is a discourse in the process of change.

For this reason, the knowing subject as analysand comes to exist in the process of change. This process does not secure and fix its identity, but shifts it and makes it mobile. The analytic disintegration of the imaginary and defensive unity of the ego reveals to the knowing subject that it cannot found itself in the conscious self with its illusions of certainty and mastery. This process reveals that the knower's relation to its objects includes an imaginary yearning for their aggressive control. Instead, the analysand accepts that it is finite, divided and incomplete. The imaginary delusion that its objects and others are identical to it no longer traps the knower. This shift opens to movement and flux the relation to objects and others, because the knower no longer rigidly insists that they have an unchanging and identical relation to its self.

Meaning

For the knowing subject as analysand, the articulation of the Other restores the mobility of the signifying chain because it opens that structure to the richness of metaphoric substitution. The operation of metaphor founds the productivity of signification. In the metaphoric substitution of one signifier for another, the second signifier crosses the bar to signification, and so passes into the signifieds, producing a new signified or concept and shifting the previously fixed structure of the signifying chain. For Lacan, 'it is in the substitution of signifier for signifier that an effect of signification is produced that is creative or poetic, in other words, which is the advent of the signification' (*É*: 181). Knowing moves from being a rigid structure of the imaginary to being a process of significatory productivity and possibility.

In this account, the signifying chain is incomplete and shifting, and signification is an open and unstable process rather than a closed, immutable and frozen structure. This account offers the possibility of changing the structure of signifiers that produce the subject. In Lacan's formulation, the signifier is the material by which the subject gives meaning to the real. To change the subject's relation to the signifier is therefore also to change the subject's relation to the real. That change affects not only the relation of subject and real, but also the very 'being' of the subject. If the signifier enables the subject to give meaning to the world, it also produces the subject. Therefore, to change the structure of signifiers which produce the subject is also to change the subject itself: '[t]he slightest alteration in the relation between man and the signifier . . . changes the whole course of history by modifying the moorings that anchor his being' (*É*: 192).

In the Lacanian epistemology, therefore, the knowledge of the analysand is not understood as a correlation between concept and object, but rather as the production of meaning. That meaning is supple, mobile and mutable. For Lacan, the analysand's knowledge is not fixed, but can and does change. When it changes, it transforms how the analysand knows its 'self' and its others. This productivity of signification provides the possibility of shifting how the knowing subject understands itself and its objects.

Savoir

In his account of psychoanalytic knowledge, Lacan distinguishes between the 'domain of exactitude' and the 'register of truth' (1955: 35, *Éc*: 20). The field of exactitude is the measure of the real of the exact sciences, while the domain of truth is psychoanalytic. Exactitude and truth are thus different forms of knowledge and different registers of knowing. For Lacan, the analysand as knowing subject produces a particular form of knowledge: *savoir* or symbolic knowledge.

Savoir implies a movement from the order of the imaginary to that of the symbolic, from *méconnaissance* to *savoir*, as '*connaissance* (with its inevitable concomitant, "*méconnaissance*") belongs to the imaginary register, while *savoir* belongs to the symbolic register' (Sheridan 1977: xiii). For Lacan, *savoir* is knowledge in the symbolic register. *Savoir* implies knowledge of the subjection of the subject to the signifier, and hence a knowledge of the Other of the Symbolic order. This symbolic knowledge of the analysand is a practice of signification that represents the unconscious truth of subject.

As a truth of the subject, symbolic knowledge is a practice of becoming because ' "[t]here where it was . . . it is my duty that I should come into being" ' (*É*: 142). I, the analysand, acquire symbolic knowledge in my experience of psychoanalysis. It therefore has a temporal movement because it is a discursive moment in which the subject comes into being. Lacan links this form of knowledge to time because the object which it signifies – the unconscious – has a temporal structure (1964b: 267, *Éc*: 838). The signification of the unconscious, and therefore symbolic knowledge, has a temporal quality.[9]

Accordingly, symbolic knowledge is both finite and infinite. On the one hand, as a practice of signification of the unconscious, it is an infinite practice because it is not possible to signify the unconscious for once and for all. Echoing Freud, Lacan proposes that there is an unconscious kernel of the subject which can never be known and which can never be symbolized (*É*: 191). Symbolic knowledge is a process of knowing without end insofar as it is not possible to exhaust the signifying chain. On the other hand, it is also a practice of knowing that is radically limited, for the unconscious cannot be completely known. In neither sense is it a finite representation of the real that attempts a correspondence of signifier, signified and referent.

In his description of the knowledge of the analysand, Lacan proposes a model of knowing which is able to escape the entrapments of the *méconnaissance* of the conscious mind. Lacan argues that psychoanalytic practice dissolves the imaginary projections of the ego, and hence the analysand is able to articulate her or his desire. This model conceives knowledge as a practice of symbolization. This practice of symbolization enables the analysand to articulate *savoir* or symbolic knowledge, rather than reproduce *méconnaissance* or imaginary knowledge. That signifying act produces symbolic knowledge. It is not the product of a universal method that yields exactitude, but a signifying practice. The knower as analysand accepts the difference and otherness of its known object, and the radical finitude of its knowledge. With this acceptance, knowledge can represent a relation other than aggressive mastery to its objects and its others. This relation is produced in a practice of symbolization in which the subject comes to know its self and its others differently. In this model knowledge is radically intersubjective because it emerges from the psychoanalytic relationship of transference. It is not a reflection of reality but an act of representation which gives rise to a new understanding of reality. As an act of representation, it is a practice of signification. The knowledge of the analysand is a practice of signification.

However, the clinical practice of psychoanalysis founds the analysand's knowledge. If the knowing subject suffers *méconnaissance* outside analytic practice, then how is it possible to found knowledge outside the analytic experience? Is it possible to evade *méconnaissance* beyond the analytic couch? To account for Lacan's (and other analysts') theoretical knowledge, it must be possible to transpose the model of symbolic knowledge outside the analytic session. How does Lacan as analyst, rather than analysand, produce knowledge as *savoir* rather than *méconnaissance*?

This raises a second issue concerning how to construct a communicable, coherent and explanatory psychoanalytic theory. The knowledge of the analysand is a subjective practice, which raises the problem of its transmission to others. If the analysand produces symbolic knowledge, then is it the case that knowers who are not analysands produce different forms of knowledge? The analyst cannot rely on the empirical experience of the clinic nor on positivist verifications of that experience (although Lacan frequently does so) to found psychoanalytic theory because of the problem of *méconnaissance*. In particular, Lacan's own speaking position as analyst raises the question of how he knows in the symbolic register unless it is as an analysand.

Both these epistemological problems are internal to Lacan's theory of knowledge. Althusser argues that if Lacan is right to claim that psychoanalysis is a science, then it must possess 'a *theory* and a *technique* (method) that permit the knowledge and the transformation of its object in a specific *practice*' (1996: 18). Psychoanalytic theory determines its practices, not the converse. For this reason, these epistemological problems of the foundations of the analyst's knowledge vex Lacan throughout his work, since he must provide an account of the analyst's knowledge in order to legitimize his own practice. However, Lacan finds that epistemic legitimation in his theory of the analyst's knowledge as symbolic practice.

Knowledge as practice

The analyst's knowledge

Lacan develops his theory of analytic knowledge as a symbolic practice in his later papers of the 1960s: 'Position of the Unconscious' (1964b) (*Éc*) and 'Science and Truth' (1965) (*Éc*).[10] In that model, knowledge is a process or practice of symbolization. To know as an analyst is to know in the symbolic register because the analyst knows the laws of the Symbolic order. For Lacan, psychoanalysts are 'practitioners of the symbolic function' (*É*: 79). He suggests that the analyst's interpretation is based 'in the fact that the unconscious is structured in the most radical way like a language'. Because the unconscious is structured like a language, it operates according to the laws of the Symbolic order (*É*: 259). Insofar as structures of signifiers comprise the Symbolic order, it is possible to express those structures in terms of laws of signification.

Lacan uses '*law*' both in its sense of those codes that regulate human behaviour and its sense of a scientific law that expresses the regularity of natural phenomena. Lacanian epistemology deploys both these implications of 'law' to invoke two facets of the Symbolic order. The first is the paternal Law of the Father that founds the Symbolic order, the symbolic law that regulates social action in a community. The second emphasizes the regularity of the order of symbolic elements in language. The play on these senses of 'law' can be seen in Lacan's earlier paper, 'The Function and Field of Speech and Language in Psychoanalysis':

> No one is supposed to be ignorant of the law; this somewhat humorous formula taken direct from our Code of Justice nevertheless expresses the truth in which our experience is grounded, and which our experience confirms. No man is actually ignorant of it, since the law of man has been the law of language.
>
> (*É*: 67)

Knowledge in the symbolic register invokes 'law' in both senses. The structure of signifiers that comprise the Symbolic order is a regular phenomenon – it is an order of signifying elements – and therefore it is possible to express it as a law that describes that regularity. For this reason, Lacan argues that psychoanalysis studies the subject of the laws of the symbolic. For Lacan, psychoanalysis is a science because it does not study the individual but the subject formed in the signifying laws of the Symbolic order (1965: 10–12, *Éc*: 861–863).

At this moment, Lacanian epistemology engages with the issue of the relationship between psychoanalysis and science. Lacan does not propose that psychoanalysis replicates the methodology of the natural sciences. For Lacan, the measure of exactitude that forms the natural sciences cannot be a sufficient measure of truth for the conjectural sciences. Science fails not because of inexactitude but because it does not engage with the unconscious (1965: 22, *Éc*: 874). For Lacan, the question of psychoanalysis as a science does not concern whether psychoanalysis is within the field of science, but whether its praxis implies no other knowing subject than that of science (1965: 12, *Éc*: 863).

In these later papers, Lacan argues that the knowing subject of science is not the Cartesian *cogito* but the Cartesian subject of doubt. That subject is characterized by a radical and methodical doubt in its claim of 'a rejection of all knowledge' (1965: 5, *Éc*: 856) and its break 'with every assurance conditioned by intuition' (1964b: 261, *Éc*: 831). Lacan argues that its model of the knower – the subject of science – and the communicability of its knowledge define scientific praxis (1965: 24, *Éc*: 877).[11] Lacan believes that 'these ideals of scientism' are necessary for psychoanalysis (1965: 6, *Éc*: 857). For Lacan, the subject of doubt and the transmission of symbolic knowledge (*savoir*) are essential for the construction of a psychoanalytic knowledge (1965: 24, *Éc*: 877). In this way, Lacan perceives psychoanalysis and science as sharing a praxis of symbolic knowledge.

However, Lacan also argues that the classical foundations of scientific knowledge, empiricism (*É*: 325) and the methodology of positivism (S11: 8), cannot found psychoanalytic theory because of their participation in the imaginary order. This argument contradicts his contemporaneous claim that his own position of analytic theorist is authorized by his experience of psychoanalytic practice, and his earlier claim that psychoanalysis is a science because it is verifiable and replicable (*É*: 11). In the midst of these contradictory assertions, how then does Lacan found his own praxis of symbolic knowledges?

Lacan founds his position as knowing subject in the rationalist tradition. He uses examples from physics, mathematics, formal logic and topology to produce a model of knowing as the symbolization of signifying relations or laws. Examples of this practice can be seen throughout *Écrits* in the use of topological figures, as well as the algebraic graphs of the subject and signification. While the epistemological status of Lacan's formalized figures is a matter of controversy, these examples of formalization fulfil three functions in Lacan's work. First, Lacan's formalization follows a structuralist model which is implicit in his appropriation of the linguistic and anthropological theories of Saussure and Lévi-Strauss in the 1950s, and which becomes explicit in his work in the 1960s, such as 'Science and Truth'. Second, Lacan perceives these devices as enabling the transmission of psychoanalytic knowledge in symbolic form. Third, and most importantly, because they are in symbolic form, these devices serve as a means of evading the imaginary *méconnaissance* of conscious knowledge. They articulate the logical relations of signifiers and are an exemplary symbolic knowledge in that they distil the practice of symbolization of the laws of signification.

However, as a symbolic practice, this knowledge is not of itself immune to the laws of signification. If signification is imbricated in the unconscious laws of representation, then how is the analyst to communicate his or her *savoir*? While Lacan's formal representation of the unconscious attempts to represent the logic of that other scene by revealing the structural logic of unconscious thought, those formal devices also represent a radical limit of psychoanalytic (and other) knowledge. Lacan recognizes this difficulty in his seminar of 1966–1967, in which he describes his wish ' "to formulate decisive formulas about the unconscious, i.e. logical formulas" . . . to define "a logic that is not a logic, an entirely new logic that I have not named yet, for it needs to be instituted first." ' [12]

The Lacanian theoretical practice attempts to evade this difficulty through the institution of an 'entirely new' form of knowledge – the symbolization of the laws of the Symbolic order. In effect, the Lacanian drive to formalization is an attempt to evade the limits of language posed by the representation of the unconscious. The Lacanian account of the analyst's knowledge articulates and resists a limit of signification: the unconscious. For this reason, the Lacanian theory of symbolic knowledge does not only concern the content of that knowledge – what is known – but also its representation.[13]

For Lacan, knowledge as symbolic practice evades the problematic of the formal (representational) limits of knowledge and grounds the methodology and justification of the psychoanalyst's theoretical reflection on their practice. Lacan argues that analytic theory can justify and transmit its praxis with a model of symbolic knowledge constructed from rational and scientific praxis. Unsurprisingly, the final paper of *Écrits*, 'Science and Truth', considers how psychoanalysis is distinguishable from science and religion, and is an extended meditation on the problem of psychoanalytic knowledge. Lacan does not resolve this problem in 'Science and Truth', and it becomes central to the later Lacanian epistemology.

The later Lacanian epistemology: the four discourses

[T]here is no knowledge without discourse.

(Lacan 1970a: vii)

From the 1970s onwards, Lacan's work shifts its emphasis from the signifier to the 'matheme'.[14] Lacan invents his neologism of the matheme to describe the devices that he uses to formalize psychoanalytic knowledge. The matheme represents a further attempt to describe a model of symbolic knowledge that can escape *méconnaissance*. It designates a pure signifying relation that is a transmissible *savoir* (S20: 110). By 1973, Lacan characterizes his goal as mathematical formalization (S20: 119). Yet, Lacan's drive to mathematization is also 'accompanied by a tendency to emphasize the poetry and ambiguity of language' (Evans 1996: 97). In his later work, Lacan increasingly focuses upon what escapes the Symbolic order and engages in a reworking of his earlier concern with the limit of signification. For example, this focus can be seen in his creation of another neologism, 'la langue', to describe the poetic and associative dimensions of language, and, most importantly, in the development of the concept of the Real as that which is impossible to integrate in an order of representation.

The tension in the classical Lacanian epistemology of *Écrits* between the formalization and the excessive profusion of the unconscious heightens in the later Lacanian epistemology of the 1970s. In these final seminars, there is an evident contrast between Lacan's goal of mathematical formalization, with its increasingly elaborate algebraic equations and topologies, and his engagement with the ineffable and productive dimension of language, such as the writings of James Joyce, the Real and his own excessive, associative and elusive rhetoric. Lacan's later theory of knowledge is presented in perhaps his most difficult, obtuse and elliptical writing. The formal clarity of Lacan's mathematical formulae stands in contrast to his discussion of the ideas that they represent. He makes allusions to, and gestures towards, the concepts articulated by his mathemes throughout these texts, picking up his formulae for discussion and then discarding them shortly thereafter. Similarly to the earlier Lacanian epistemology of *Écrits*, Lacan's later theory of knowledge is neither a closed and finished explanatory structure nor a comprehensive theory.

The difficulty of explicating the later Lacanian epistemology is exacerbated by the questionable status of Lacan's seminars of the 1970s, which remain largely unpublished. The more or less correct reading of Lacan's later work is still much debated. My reading of the later Lacanian epistemology therefore is provisional as it necessarily derives from the published seminars from the 1970s. Nevertheless, as with Lacan's classical epistemology, it is possible to extract a cohesive and stable theoretical structure from these later texts through a productive and strategic reading. This reading is productive insofar as it describes the coherent epistemological account that is presented in Lacan's later theoretical work. It is also strategic because it does not aim to provide an exegesis of Lacanian theory of the 1970s but instead it focuses upon Lacan's theory of discourse. My analysis of the later Lacanian epistemology therefore focuses upon the published seminars – namely the seminar of 1969–1970, *L'envers de la psychanalyse* (S17), and the seminar of 1972–1973, *Encore* (S20) – which establish and develop the Lacanian theory of discourse.

Lacan's account of discourse encapsulates the theoretical shifts and ambiguities of his later work. For example, his understanding of language shifts from a structuralist conception of a closed order of signifiers to a discursive relation of signifiers that always produce a signifying remainder. This account of discourse forms the basis of the later Lacanian model of knowledge. This theory of the four foundational discourses of the master, the university, the hysteric, and the analyst, presents an account of knowledge as a symbolic and social network. It describes the fundamental structures of symbolic networks that form subjects and produce their understanding of their world. From my elaboration of that account, I develop a theory of the knowing subject as discursive subject and of knowledge as a product of discourse, which I describe as the 'later Lacanian epistemology'.

Discourse

As with many of his other central concepts, Lacan does not offer a definition of 'discourse'. Instead, he develops this concept in an increasingly complex way throughout his work. In the papers of *Écrits* of the 1950s and 1960s, Lacan draws upon both the general meaning of 'discourse' as speech, and its more technical linguistic meaning of an act of signification. For example, in 'The Agency of the Letter' (1957), Lacan distinguishes between the discourse of the subject and the universal structure of language: 'by "letter" I designate that material support that concrete discourse borrows from language' (*É*: 163). For Lacan, 'the letter' is the material support of discourse and is to be understood 'to the letter' of the signifier, or literally as 'the essentially localized structure of the signifier' (*É*: 169). In this sense, Lacan conceives discourse as a chain of signifiers that is structured by language.

However, the concept of discourse should not be understood simply as a formal structure of signifiers. In 'Function and Field of Speech' (1953), Lacan argues that the act of signification always involves an other in that 'the allocution of the subject entails an allocuter . . . the locuter is constituted in it as inter-subjectivity' (*É*: 54). For Lacan, discourse implies intersubjectivity because it always involves an address to, and of, the Other. The domain of psycho-analysis is that of 'concrete discourse, in so far as this is the field of the transindividual reality of the subject' (*É*: 54), a field of reality which is not reducible to the subject but lies 'across' and 'beyond' the subject. This field is the Other of the Symbolic order.

Lacan retains both senses of 'discourse' in *L'envers* and *Encore*. In these seminars, he uses 'discourse' to describe a necessary and stable structure of signification. Discourse is a signifying link, that is, a relationship of signifier to signifier. Those chains of signifiers represent fundamental structures, as language structures those signifiers in stable and subsisting relationships (S17: 11). As a structure of signifiers which language founds, the Symbolic order produces discourse.

In *L'envers* and *Encore*, Lacan further develops his conception of the trans-individuality of discourse, emphasizing its intersubjective nature. In *Encore*, he suggests that 'the notion of discourse should be taken as a social link (*lien social*), founded on language' (S20: 17). Once again, Lacan does not elucidate what is meant by that crucial phrase, 'the social tie'. However, in a later passage he argues that 'a discourse is what determines a form of social link' (S20: 82). Discourse thus produces the social link between subjects, because discursive chains of signifiers structure stable intersubjective relations. In the theory of the four discourses, the intersubjective relation is a discursive relation. This concept of discourse does not therefore imply a Hegelian intersubjectivity, which Lacan always associates with the imaginary order, but rather a symbolic relation between subjects.

The social bond of subjects is discursive because language anchors that relation (S20: 54). For Lacan, language produces a 'speaking being' – *l'être parlant* – and the relation between such subjects (S20: 54). In this way, the term 'discourse' implies a relation between speaking subjects. It represents the transindividual aspect of language that structures social bonds. The Lacanian concept of discourse links the structure of signification and the intersubjective relation because it describes signifying chains that form relations between subjects. In his theory of the four discourses, Lacan identifies four different and foundational types of social bonds of speaking subjects.

Lacan describes the subject of discourse as the 'subject of a signifier'. In a typically cryptic formulation, Lacan explains 'this minimal formula' further with a restatement of his earlier definition of the subject in *Écrits* whereby 'a signifier represents a subject to another signifier' (S20: 142). A signifier represents a subject for another signifier because a discursive relation between signifiers produces the subject. As in the Lacanian epistemology of *Écrits*, the subject describes a position in language. However, in the later Lacanian theory, specific discourses produce different subjects.

The four discourses

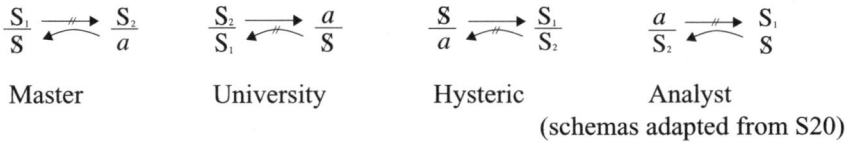

$$\frac{S_1}{S} \xrightarrow{\;/\!/\;} \frac{S_2}{a} \qquad \frac{S_2}{S_1} \xrightarrow{\;\;\;} \frac{a}{S} \qquad \frac{S}{a} \xrightarrow{\;\;\;} \frac{S_1}{S_2} \qquad \frac{a}{S_2} \xrightarrow{\;/\!/\;} \frac{S_1}{S}$$

Master   University   Hysteric   Analyst
                                               (schemas adapted from S20)

Lacan presents his formulae of the discourses of the master, the university, the hysteric and the psychoanalyst in his seminar of 1969–1970, *L'envers de la psychanalyse* (chapters I and II, S17). Each formula represents four different positions of the subject – the master, the academic, the hysteric and the psycho-analyst – and four different forms of the discursive social link – mastering, academic, hysterical and psychoanalytic. For Lacan, these formulae represent possible subject positions and social bonds within the psychoanalytic field.

Lacan elaborates this theory in two subsequent interviews, 'Radiophonie' (1970b) and *Télévision* (1974), and further develops it in his seminar of 1972–1973, *Encore* (S20). *L'envers* contains Lacan's most extended discussion of his theory of the four discourses. However, in *Encore* he provides more detailed schemas of the discourses and links his formulae to additional explanatory schemas. In *Encore*, Lacan provides an explanation of each of the elements of the schemas, further elaborates the relation between these elements, and sets out the complete formulae of the four discourses (S20: 16). For this reason, my discussion of the four discourses focuses upon the schemas of *Encore*, with additional reference to the explanatory material of *L'envers*.

As in *L'envers*, in *Encore* Lacan represents each of the discourses by a schema which sets out the relation of four terms: S_1, S_2, *a* and S. These terms designate respectively: the master signifier (*le signifiant maître*), knowledge (*le savoir*), surplus *jouissance* (*le plus-de-jouir*) and the subject (*le sujet*) (S20: 17). S_1 represents the master signifier, the symbolic element that represents the subject for another signifier. The master signifier marks the subject's position within the signifying chain and hence within the discursive social tie. S_2 designates the symbolic field, the chain or network of signifiers that form the subject. For this reason, S_2 represents the knowledge of the subject. It describes both the form of the subject's knowledge, for example, academic, psycho-analytic and so on, and the form of knowledge of the subject, such as the differing conceptions of the subject within the university and psychoanalysis.

The term *a* represents the 'left-over' or remainder of discourse. That remainder is the *jouissance* produced by, and surrendered to, language in the taking up of a speaking position by the subject. The *a* is an unassimilable excess to the discourse. There is no signifier of the *a*, as it is not possible to represent it in the signifying economy of the discourse. The subject attempts to structure its relationship to this unassimilable remainder by rendering it as an imaginary object – the *objet petit a*. The *a* thus both functions in the imaginary register, in which it appears as an imaginary object filled with phantasmic content, and in the symbolic register, in which it marks the excluded term of discourse, the gap in or void of its symbolic structure. For this reason, the *a* 'stands simul-taneously for the imaginary fantasmic lure/screen *and* for that which this lure is obfuscating, for the void behind the lure' (Zizek 1998a: 80). The fourth term, S, represents the *subject*. The *subject* does not represent the S of the conscious subject but the 'true' psychoanalytic subject of the unconscious. S designates the barred subject, in which the S of the conscious subject is struck through because of its division by the unconscious. The schemas of the discourses describe the relation of each of these terms, S_1, S_2, *a* and S.

A fifth schema explains the structure of that relation. It describes each of the places that the four terms occupy, as well as the distribution of those terms in the positions of agent (*l'agent*), other (*l'autre*), truth (*la vérité*) and production (*la production*) (S20: 17). This fifth schema can be understood as describ-ing the operation of the discourses. The agent represents the causation of the discourse. The *agent* is the speaking subject – the subject who speaks and thereby appears to inaugurate discourse. This position represents 'the point from which speech is enunciated' (Adams 1996: 72). Lacan argues that speech always involves an interlocutor, the other to whom the speech is addressed. For this reason, the position of the *other* designates the addressee of that dis-course. The third position, *production*, describes the result of the operation of the discourse (S20: 17). This position designates the product of the action of the agent upon its addressee, the other. Each discourse results in a product, for example, the Discourse of the Master produces the *a*, the left-over of meaning, while the Discourse of the Analyst produces the master signifier which represents the subject. The fourth position is that of *truth*, which does not represent knowledge but the 'truth' of the discourse. The term that occupies this position founds and subtends the discourse. For example, in the Discourse of the Master the unconscious speech of the subject (S) founds and subtends its conscious speech.

The Discourse of the Master

$$\frac{S_1}{S} \xrightarrow{\;\;/\!/\;\;} \frac{S_2}{a}$$

In the Discourse of the Master, S_1 stands in the place of the agent, S_2 in the place of the other, S in the place of truth, and a in the place of the product of the discourse (S20: 16). In the operation of the Master's Discourse, the master signifier is the cause of the subject. The subject addresses its speech to the Other of the Symbolic order, S_2, the network of signifiers which form the subject. The truth of the discourse is S, the unconscious of the divided subject. The product of its discourse is the a, that remnant of *jouissance* which is forbidden to the subject. Lacan nominates the Discourse of the Master as the fundamental relation because it represents the structure of signifiers that produce the speaking subject (S17: 13). The master signifier, which stands in the place of the agent or cause, dominates the Discourse. As this signifier represents the subject to another signifier, and hence produces it as a subject in the signifying chain, the cause of the discourse is also the 'cause' of the speaking subject (S17: 19–20). In this way, the S_1 of the Discourse of the Master represents the 'origin' of discourse as such, because it is the condition of the production of discourse as enunciation (S17: 11). For this reason, Lacan describes the foundational discourse as that of the Master.

The Discourse of the University

$$\frac{S_2}{S_1} \xrightarrow{\;\;/\!/\;\;} \frac{a}{S}$$

In the Discourse of the University, S_2 stands in the place of the agent, a in the place of the other, S_1 in the place of truth, and S in the place of the product (S20: 16). In the operation of the University's Discourse, knowledge is the cause of the subject because the Discourse represents an attempt to master the a, its excluded term. Its truth is the master signifier, which this discourse continually reproduces. For this reason, an anti-clockwise quarter-turn of the schema of the Discourse of the Master produces the schema of the Discourse of the University. The Discourse of the University installs the Discourse of the

Master, such that S_2 dominates and produces an illusory 'all-knowledge' (*tout-savoir*) (S17: 34). That knowledge of all is illusory because the *a* always escapes it. For this reason, the product of the Discourse of the University is the barred subject – the unconscious truth of the subject which that discourse refuses (S17: 70–71).

The Discourse of the Hysteric

$$\frac{S\!\!\!/}{a} \xrightarrow{\quad//\quad} \frac{S_1}{S_2}$$

In the Discourse of the Hysteric, $S\!\!\!/$ stands in the place of the agent, S_1 in the place of the other, *a* in the place of truth, and S_2 in the place of the product (S20: 16). The barred subject (representing the unconscious of the subject) acts as its cause, because the Hysteric begins her discourse from the question of castration (S17: 112). Her unconscious desire dominates her speech. Surplus *jouissance* is in the place of truth in her discourse, not only because of her pleasure in knowing but also because her subjectivity articulates the cost of entry into the Symbolic order (S17: 37). The Discourse of the Hysteric produces S_2 because she speaks of the loss inherent to subjectivity. For Lacan, the Discourse of the Hysteric articulates the 'truth' of the Master's Discourse: namely, that it is founded on the operation of castration and that its effect is the unconscious. For this reason, Lacan argues that the Discourse of the Hysteric opens the way for the Discourse of the Analyst (S20: 41).

The Discourse of the Analyst

$$\frac{a}{S_2} \xrightarrow{\quad//\quad} \frac{S_1}{S\!\!\!/}$$

In the Discourse of the Analyst, *a* stands in the place of the agent, the $S\!\!\!/$ in the place of the Other, S_2 in the place of truth, and S_1 in the place of the product (S20: 16). In this Discourse, the excluded *a* puts the subject to work and is the cause of its desire. The subject addresses its unconscious as other in its recognition that the Symbolic order produces the barred subject. In this discourse, 'the subject manifests himself in his gap, namely, in that which causes his desire' (S20: 11). Knowledge functions in the place of truth, that is, the truth of the subject. *Savoir* (S_2) functions as truth and thus symbolic knowledge is the register of the Analyst. In its articulation of the truth, the subject articulates the master signifier that represents it. For this reason, the master signifier is the product of the Discourse of the Analyst (S20: 16–17).

Lacan presents the four discourses in formal, algebraic notation. He does not intend these formulae to be figurative, but rather to formalize the structural workings of the unconscious (S20: 131). The epistemological status of Lacan's formulae is a matter of considerable debate. Lacan's critics, such as François Roustang (1990), argue that they are a sophistic misappropriation of mathematics, while others, such as Nathalie Charraud (1997), follow the Lacanian argument that they are important devices for escaping the imaginary order. However, it is not productive to reduce a discussion of Lacan's formulae of the discourses to the issue of whether or not they are able to perform mathematical operations. Their function is to transmit psychoanalytic knowledge; as such Lacan gives representational content to each of the algebraic elements of his schemas of the four discourses and these elements in turn find their meaning in a theory of psychoanalysis. In his discussion of the epistemological status of Lacan's matheme, Joël Dor argues that it should be understood as a 'metaphorical illustration' that allows a dynamic representation of psychoanalytic knowledge (1996: 117). I read the formulae of the four discourses as a dynamic representation of the discursive social link; as devices that formalize and elucidate fundamental forms of intersubjectivity. These models of the four discourses are a conceptual apparatus that can be used as skeleton keys to open the complexities of discourse.

Discourse and knowledge

In *Encore*, Lacan emphasizes the relation of the four discourses to the psychoanalytic field. He states that '[t]here are four of them only on the basis of the psychoanalytic discourse that I articulate . . . these categories, which are structured only on the basis of the existence of psychoanalytic discourse' (S20: 16). Three of the discourses evidently emerge from the clinic, namely, those of the master, the hysteric and the analyst. Why then does Lacan refer to the Discourse of the University? For Lacan, this Discourse above all concerns the production of knowledge. In particular, it aims to provide a guarantee of certain and complete knowledge, including of the unconscious. Accordingly, Lacan's theory concerns possible foundations of psychoanalytic knowledge, and presents an elaboration and critique of those discourses of psychoanalytic knowledge. For this reason, I describe Lacan's theory of the four foundational discourses as being a 'later Lacanian epistemology'.

In the theory of the four discourses, Lacan describes the different relations of the knower to other subjects and to its objects, and the different forms of those epistemological relations. Each discourse formalizes a position of a knowing subject, its relation to that which its discourse excludes, to its master signifier, and to its knowledge. The formulae represent the structural relation of these key elements, so that each represents a stable structure of discourse. Each schema describes a particular and specific form of knowledge. For example, the Discourse of the University attempts to know all, including that which it excludes. A desire for mastery and control of its objects dominates this discourse, which at the same time operates to reproduce the exclusions of its knowledge (S17: 70–71).

The foundational discourses thus articulate possible combinations of discursive elements, representing four possible positions of the knowing subject and four possible epistemological relations. However, the position of the knower and the form of its knowledge cannot be understood by simply examining the place of the barred subject (S) or of knowledge (S_2) in the formulae of the discourses. The knower does not take up the position of the S, just as S_2 does not represent its knowledge. Rather, Lacan suggests that a knowing subject takes up a particular speaking position (for example, that of the master, the hysteric or the analyst) and so produces a particular type of knowledge (mastering, hysterical, analytic). The discourses describe four possible forms of knowledge.

The four discourses present a theory of specific forms of knowledge. However, they also constitute an epistemological metatheory. Underlying these four models is a radical imbrication of knowledge and discourse because '[d]iscourse is a fundamental apparatus which is prior to and which determines the whole relation of subjects to subjects and subjects to objects' (Adams 1996: 72). For Lacan, discourse produces knowledge. It gives meaning to the world, and so how that world is known is contingent upon its symbolic network. Lacan's formulae do not represent a formal description of the conditions of true belief abstracted from reality. Rather, as speaking beings we are always already within the world of discourse. Reality is a function of discourse, for discourse produces both the world that is known, and the only world that can be known (S17: 13).

In this model, discourse has a necessary and stable structure which shapes the interplay of its elements and which produces signification. Lacan analyses discourses in terms of their constitutive elements, and the operation of those elements. The different combinations of a knowing subject, the barred subject, the signifying chain, the excluded from discourse (the a), and the master signifier, produce different forms of knowledge. Lacan reduces each discourse to its constituent components. In this way, Lacanian epistemology describes the structural logic or symbolic economy of knowledge.

In this model, knowledge is contingent upon the discursive position of the knower. However, that subjective structure is necessarily an effect of discursive structure. By taking up a speaking position, the knower thereby is enmeshed in the fundamental relations of discourse. In the Lacanian account, it is inscribed in every act of enunciation of a subject (S17: 11). In each of Lacan's schemas, the knower exists in a particular relation to S_2 – knowledge or *le savoir* (S20: 16). The knowledge of the Master differs from that of the Hysteric, and these subject positions articulate a different relation to that knowing. For example, Lacan contrasts the ignorance of the Master who does not want to know with the desire of the Hysteric to know. The discourse of the knowing subject produces its relation to the known object. This relation is inscribed in an order of signifiers such that 'knowledge' is a representation or signification of what is known. Accordingly, the different operations of discourse produce different forms of knowledge.

Lacanian epistemology therefore posits knowledge as a signification of a known object. The object is signified, rather than known in and of itself. Discourse produces the known object, since the object can only be represented through signifying structures. This model of knowledge conceives it as a signifying act. The act of knowing is an act of representation that the stable structures of signifying chains produce. Therefore, knowledge itself has a discursive structure and thereby is rethought as the product of signification. The later Lacanian epistemology does not describe the propositional content of knowledge, but instead describes how discursive networks produce a known object, and the relation between the knowing subject and its known object.

In the later Lacanian epistemology, what is known is inseparable from how it is known. Knowledge describes a relation to the real, and the structuring of that relation in discourse. Lacan argues that the world is known through the meaning given to it, and that meaning is always bound up in discourse (S17: 13), because every 'reality' is presented in discursive networks (S20: 32). Discourse describes the symbolic structure through which the knowing subject represents the world to itself and to other subjects. Knowledge is therefore a symbolic practice because it is an act of meaning of the knowing subject. This act of signification is the insertion of the known object into the signifying chain, placing it within a symbolic field that enwraps the object and gives it meaning.

Lacanian epistemology posits knowledge as a signification given to the object. What is known is therefore radically contingent upon the discourse of the knowing subject, and accordingly radically limited by it. If discourse produces knowledge, then discourse is a necessary condition of knowing. Forms of knowledge are therefore contingent upon discursive forms. In this way, Lacan's theory suggests that there exists a causal, if not determinative, relation between knowledge and discourse (S17: 13). Lacan does not argue that these concepts are identical or reducible to each other. However, his account does suggest that what can be known is conditional upon discursive networks. In this sense, discursive structures delimit what is thinkable and signifiable as knowledge, such that to change those structures is to change how we know the world (S20: 16).

In Lacan's theory, discourse produces signification. It structures signifiers by ordering their relation and so producing meaning. Discourse enables the otherwise arbitrary signifier to mean something not only to the knowing subject but also to other subjects. Discourse knots the signifier and signified together by functioning as the link that enables the circulation of the signifier between those who speak (S20: 30). The signifier is an arbitrary symbolic element that does not produce meaning until it is brought into relation with other signifiers.

In the signifying chains of discourse the signifier as word comes to signify or mean something, '[t]he word "reference", in this case, can only be situated on the basis of what discourse constitutes by way of a link (*lien*). The signifier as such refers to nothing if not to a discourse, in other words, a mode of functioning or a utilization of language qua link' (S20: 30). The discursive social link therefore also ties signifier and signified. Because subjects exist in a symbolic relation to one another, they are able to exchange meaning. In this model, different knowing subjects may use the same symbolic element to name a known object but each may attribute it with a different signified. For Lacan, what enables other knowing subjects to 'read' the signifier is the social link between knowing subjects.

For Lacan, the linguistic is the condition of the social, and hence also the condition of knowledge. In the classical Lacanian epistemology of *Écrits*, Lacan deploys an Aristotelian understanding of the social being as speaking being, arguing that speech enables the symbolization of relations between subjects (*Éc*: 469). Lacan echoes that concept of the speaking being over a decade later in *Encore*, where he declares that:

> [i]n the final analysis, there's nothing but that, the social link. I designate it with the term 'discourse' because there's no other way to designate it once we realize that the social link is instated only by anchoring itself in the way in which language is situated over and etched into what the place is crawling with, namely, speaking beings (*l'être parlant*).
>
> (S20: 54)

The social tie is language because its discursive chains form the link and the relationship between speaking subjects. For Lacan, discourse is not a transparent relation between subjects. It does not imply that its addressee receives the message sent by the sender, as Lacan starts out from the position that communication is necessarily a failure (Verhaeghe 1997: 100). Rather, discourse is a particular arrangement of signifiers that enables symbolic exchange between subjects.

In *L'envers*, Lacan argues that '[a] society is not something which can be defined just like that. What I am attempting to articulate, because analysis gives me the evidence, is what dominates it – to wit: the practice of language' (S17: 239, 1969b: 127). For Lacan, the practice of language 'dominates' the social because the social order is founded in the structures of language, the Symbolic order. The Symbolic order produces a number of stable discourses, which represent fundamental intersubjective relations. The four discourses therefore articulate four different and foundational social bonds (which in turn raises the possibility of the existence of other discourses).

In the later Lacanian epistemology, 'knowledge' is not only a relation of subject to object, but also of subject to subject. Lacan argues that the four discourses represent different forms of the social bond. The discourses that produce different forms of intersubjectivity also produce different forms of knowledge. In this way, the later Lacanian account of knowledge moves between subjective and intersubjective structures. Because Lacan's model describes not only the relation of subject to object, but also the relation of subjects, discourses of knowledge reveal the relation of the knower to its others. The Lacanian model thereby unfolds the epistemological relation of knowing subject, signifier and known object to include the relation of the knowing subject to other subjects.

The later Lacanian epistemology is a model of knowledge that posits it as a social practice in the sense that it is the product of the discursive social link. This model describes knowing as contingent upon social bonds which enable the subject to give meaning to, and make sense of, its world. It articulates discourses that structure how the knowing subject knows the world. To conceive knowledge in this way posits it as contingent upon our social bonds. For this reason, Lacan conceives knowledge or *savoir* as that which is inscribed in the social link (S20: 73). Lacanian epistemology thus provides an account of the intersubjective production of knowledge, and of knowing as a socially mediated act.

Lacan's theory of the four discourses is far from being an elaborated epistemology. For example, Lacan does not indicate whether the discourses are necessarily interlinked or whether they can operate as explanatory devices without reference to each other. Moreover, Lacan does not reveal why it is four (and only four) discourses that comprise the fundamental social bonds. Lacan argues that these four discourses represent fundamental social bonds within the psychoanalytic field and possible forms of psychoanalytic knowledge. However, he does not explain why these discourses of the master, the hysteric, the university and the psychoanalyst function as foundational social links, nor why he has chosen these four discourses out of all possible social discourses.

Despite these omissions, the later epistemological work provides a new and important means of understanding the production of knowledge. Lacanian epistemology analyses knowledge as a discursive practice that is the product of the operation of particular signifying structures. Knowledge is also a social practice, in that the discursive social link produces it. In Lacan's account, knowledge is understood as a discursive social practice. It does not reduce knowledge to the status of a proposition (as in many philosophical theories) nor to a social object (as in many sociological accounts). Rather, Lacanian epistemology offers feminist epistemology a theoretical apparatus to analyse the relation between knowledge, subjectivity and sociality.

However, for feminist epistemology the next question concerns the relationship between discourse and sexual difference. While Lacan provides a theory of the knower as speaking subject, he does not address it as a sexed subject.

Rather, he addresses sexed subjectivity separately in his theory of sexuation. In the next chapter, I explore the relationship between sexuation and discourse by bringing Lacan's theories of knowledge and sexuation together to develop an account of the sexed knower and its discourses.

3 Knowing subjects

Representation of the world, like the world itself, is the work of men; they describe it from their own point of view, which they confuse with absolute truth.

(de Beauvoir 1949: 175)

For feminist theories of knowledge, the gender of the knower is epistemologically significant. The deconstructive feminist epistemologies of the 1980s argue that the Western subject of reason is not sexually neutral but presupposes a masculine knower. The work of Evelyn Fox Keller (1985), Genevieve Lloyd (1984) and Susan Bordo (1986) exemplifies these arguments. For example, Lloyd's influential study of the tropes of masculinity and femininity in Western philosophy describes 'the maleness of the Man of Reason' (1984: ix). The reconstructive feminist epistemologies of the 1990s further displace the masculine knower. Theorists such as Sandra Harding (1990) and Patricia Hill Collins (1991) construct new models of knowledge 'that take women as the *subject* of knowledge [and] attempt to create new subject positions of knowing' (Grosz 1993: 206). For example, Harding argues that '[f]eminist standpoint theories direct us to start our research and scholarship from the perspectives of women's lives' (1990: 249). Rather than begin with a deconstructive inscription of the masculine knower, these theories of knowledge begin with a female and/or feminist knower.

Feminist epistemologists argue persuasively that we cannot ignore the sex of the knower. For this reason, these theories share the epistemic and political strategy of the reinscription of the sexed knower. However, that strategy requires an account of the sexed knower, which remains a central and strangely neglected problem in the field of feminist epistemology. In particular, the claim that there is a relation between the sexed knower and knowledge raises two questions which feminist epistemology has yet to fully answer:

1   How is the knower produced as a sexed subject?
2   What is the relationship between the process of becoming a sexed subject and becoming a feminist subject?

In this chapter, I unravel the overdetermined knot of the sexed knower in feminist epistemology, which slides from notions of embodied sexual difference to the sexual difference of the knower to the feminist knower. This chapter provides an account of the sexed knower and its relationship to feminism by developing Lacan's account of knowledge as a theory of the relationship between sexed knowers and their knowledges. Lacan's theory of knowledge provides a compelling description of the formation of the knower and its knowledge. However, it needs to be brought together with his theory of sexuation to understand the relation between formation of the sexed knower and the sexuation of knowledge. I begin by exploring the production of the masculine subject and its forms of knowing, before considering the relationship between feminine and feminist subjects.

The discourse of sex

The classical Lacanian epistemology of *Écrits* is silent on the sex of the knowing subject. Lacan presents his account of the knowing analyst and analysand as if his theory of sexed subjectivity is not relevant to his theory of knowledge, and the knowing subject is asexual. This presentation of the knower is in keeping with the concept of the psychoanalytic subject. The analyst and analysand may be either male or female, and so psychoanalysis needs to be a universal theory that applies to both men and women. However, psychoanalysis also presents a theory of sexed subjectivity that explains their sexual difference. The Lacanian resolution of this paradox is the argument that the phallic function that produces masculinity and femininity instantiates a desire that is indifferent to sexuation (É: 312–313). Lacan insists that psychoanalysis reveals the human condition of ontological lack, because it shows that all subjects suffer castration regardless of sex. All subjects suffer the *méconnaissance* of consciousness, and are riven by a desiring unconscious.

The later Lacanian epistemology also presents a subject that is sexually neutral, because the master, academic, hysteric and analyst are positions without gender. Since both men and women have to enter the intersubjective relations of discourse in order to become subjects, the subject as such does not have a sex. Bruce Fink argues that 'one could go so far as to say that the analyst qua analyst is sexless. The same holds true for the master' (1995: 194). The Master is sexless because all must enter the Discourse of the Master in order to become subjects. That discourse produces all speaking subjects, such that '[i]n the final analysis, the "person" always has to do with the master's discourse' (S20: 69).

Lacan makes his claim that the Discourse of the Master forms all subjects in *Encore*, (S20) the same seminar in which he also proposes that feminine sexuality and subjectivity are in excess of, rather than determined by, the phallic function. In his later work, Lacan repeatedly returns to the question of women's knowledge. In *Encore*, Lacan addresses a love letter to women in the form of a question: what do women know? Despite the fact that 'in all the time that people having been begging them, begging them on their hands and knees – I spoke last time of women psychoanalysts – to try to tell us, not a word!' (S20: 75). The figure of the knowing woman is both difficult and fascinating for the later Lacan. This difficulty reflects the paradox of the classical account of sexuation: the phallus is a sexually neutral signifier which produces all subjects, but men and women become sexed subjects because of their different relation to the phallus.

In Lacan's work, a different relationship to the phallic signifier defines the sexual difference of masculinity and femininity. In the description of the formation of the subject presented in *Écrits*, the child becomes an *I* and takes up a subject position in language after the intervention of the Law of the Father in the Oedipus complex. After the resolution of the Oedipus complex, subjectivity is assumed in the Symbolic order and the subject sexually differentiated by its relation to the phallus (*É*: 320–321). Similarly, Lacan's later account argues that the subject's relation to the phallic signifier produces it as sexed. As Lacan describes it in *Encore*, each speaking being must line up on one side or the other of the Graph of Sexuation (S20: 79). In this way, Lacan's account of the production of the subject turns on his concept of the phallus.

This pivotal role of the phallus in the formation of sexed subjectivity gives rise to the most strenuous feminist critiques of Lacan's work. Generally, the accusation of phallocentrism contains two objections: first, that Lacan ties his concept of the phallus to the biological organ of the penis, and second, by doing so Lacan privileges masculinity and the male body as his model of sexual difference and its formation. For example, Elizabeth Grosz contends that in the phallocentric model, '[s]exual difference becomes codified into the presence or absence of a single feature – the male sexual organ' (1990: 188).

In reply, Lacanians commonly accuse feminists of misreading this concept of the phallus. Typically, Bruce Fink argues that feminist authors such as Jane Gallop 'have thus provided the reading public with patently or partially false interpretations' (1995: 98). However, ironically it is Gallop who first identifies this trope of misreading in Lacanian and feminist exchanges. Gallop points out that 'this configuration suggests that "getting Lacan right", or simply reading accurately, particularly where the "phallic signifier" is concerned, may be harder than one would think' (1987: 22).

Following the 'Function and Field of Speech' (1953), Lacan's concept of the phallus becomes increasingly complex and central to his theory of sexed subjectivity. For Lacan, the phallus operates in the three registers of the imaginary, the symbolic and the real. In the Symbolic order, the phallus 'is the signifier for which there is no signified' (S20: 80); in the imaginary order it operates as a narcissistic object of the phallic image which fulfils that lack (*É*: 354); and in the real as the real phallus, the organ of the penis (*É*: 320).

While it is possible to differentiate between the concepts of the real, imaginary and symbolic phallus, these adjectival and conceptual distinctions are not necessarily clearly evident in the Lacanian text. Lacan frequently uses the concept inconsistently, and it is often unclear which phallus he is referring to. Reading the phallic signifier 'accurately' is difficult because Lacan's own use of the term 'phallus' often collapses these distinctions.

This ambiguity is most clearly evident in those passages where Lacan describes the signification of the symbolic phallus. In these passages, Lacan invokes the biological functions of the penis, which are then given symbolic significance in relation to the phallus. A representative example of the shifting meaning of the phallus can be found in Lacan's explanation of the relation between the symbolic phallus and the penis in 'The Signification of the Phallus':

> [i]t can be said that this signifier is chosen because it is the most tangible element in the real of sexual copulation, and also the most symbolic in the literal (typographical) sense of the term, since it is equivalent there to the (logical) copula. It might also be said that, by virtue of its turgidity, it is the image of the vital flow as it is transmitted in generation.
>
> (*É*: 318)

In this passage, the symbolic phallus operates as the privileged signifier because of its 'tangible' physical role in sexual intercourse, that is, because of its relation to the 'real' phallus. 'It can be said' that the phallus is a privileged signifier because the erect phallus (the biological organ of the penis) is the image of 'the vital flow' of reproduction. John Muller and William Richardson describe how 'the term "phallus" thus assumes a new ambiguity, oscillating as it does between its role as signifier and its role as real or imagined organ' (1994: 337). That ambiguity is an effect of the conceptual slide from the signifier of the phallus to the referent of the penis.

Lacan's later seminar, *L'envers*, in which he again returns to the question of sexed subjectivity, echoes this description of the relation between the phallus and the penis. In *L'envers*, Lacan repeats his concern with the relation between the privilege of the phallus and its biological function of erection. However, in this rendering of the signification of the phallus, Lacan shifts the privilege of the phallus from the possibility of its erection to the possibility of its failure. Lacan describes the phallus as the organ that is privileged in sexual relations because its enjoyment can be isolated, for tumescence and detumescence define it – 'une fois que c'est fini, c'est fini' (*once it is done, it is done*) (S17: 86). In this passage too, the phallus has a shifting and ambiguous relation to the penis. Failed or otherwise, the phallus rests on a copula, on a logical and symbolic link, to the biological organ of the penis.

The phallus does not therefore function as a sexually 'neutral' signifier. The relation of the subject to the phallic signifier is structured *with regard* to anatomical difference. For example, in Lacan's account of sexuation each subject assumes its ontological loss by a differentiated relation to the phallus, according to whether that subject is positioned as having or not having the phallus. The latter feminine position necessarily refers to a phallic 'lack'. The woman does not have the 'real' phallus: 'the man is "castrated" by not being total, just as the woman is "castrated" by not being a man' (Gallop 1984: 134). By implication, the 'lack' to which Lacan refers is the anatomical difference of woman, which he renders as the absence of a penis. Kaja Silverman argues that we should expect this confusion of phallus and penis because:

> in any [theoretical] passage centrally concerned with elaborating a lack specific to woman . . . that lack can only be elaborated through reference to the penis. The Lacanian phallus depends for its libidinal centrality upon the anatomical distinction between the sexes, and it cannot, consequently, be rigorously distinguished from the penis.
>
> (1992a: 96)

In this way, Lacan's account of ontological loss is predicated on the assumption of a body that suffers anatomical 'loss'.

For this reason, reference to a social signification of the body secures the Lacanian account of sexed subjectivity. Lacan emphasizes the contingency of the relation between biological and psychic sexual difference in his argument that the subject can have either masculine or feminine structures, regardless of biological sex (S20: 71). However, while sexuation may be contingent, the socio-symbolic field which assigns masculinity and femininity to male and female bodies also produces them as sexually different. Sexual subjectivity is not so contingent that it becomes possible to sever its production from the signification of the biological body. A concept of biological sexual difference thus secures which bodies come to be 'masculine' and 'feminine'. While biological sex does not determine sexed subjectivity, sexuation signifies what it is to have a 'male' or 'female' body.

Because 'masculine' and 'feminine' refer to a relation of the subject to the phallus, sexuation operates as the signification of biological sex in relation to the phallic signifier. For example, Lacan understands the Hysteric as a position of both men and women. Both sexes can be hysterics and, as analysands, become hysterical subjects. However, he repeatedly identifies this position of the subject with the feminine. The Hysteric has a 'feminine' structure because it symbolizes the primary dissatisfaction of castration (S17: 84). Lacan acknowledges that 'there are many more women hysterics than men – this is a fact of clinical experience – because the woman's path to symbolic realization is more complicated' (S3: 178). Conversely, the male hysteric has access to 'both phallic and the Other jouissance' (Fink 1995: 108). He is therefore still structured by reference to a masculine structure, that is a masculine relation to the phallic signifier, because otherwise he would not have access to the phallic *jouissance* which is linked to the male organ (S20: 7). The terms 'masculinity' or 'femininity' do not have content without reference to the description of bodily sexual difference.

In Lacan's account, subjects have a masculine or feminine structure, which provides a signification of anatomical sexual difference. The relation to the phallic signifier that produces the subject also gives meaning to biological body. In this theory, the socio-symbolic order assigns masculinity and femininity to particular bodies and in particular ways. That assignation may be contingent; such that *pace* Fink men can have feminine psychic structures and women can have a masculine relation the phallus. Nevertheless, Lacan does not describe those women as men, but as phallic women. Lacan's theory assumes that 'order and norms must be instituted which tell the subject what a man or woman must do' (1964b: 276), and that most commonly the normative position for men is masculinity and for women is femininity.

The power and difficulty of Lacan's concept of sexed subjectivity for feminism lie in its linking of social, psychic and corporeal sexual difference. The very ground of feminist critiques of Lacan's account is also that which makes it a powerful account of the formation of masculinity and femininity. This theory offers us, first, an explanation of the formation of sexed subjectivity, and second, an understanding of sexed subjectivity in which:

1   To become a subject is to become sexed.
2   To be sexed is to be caught within representations of sexual difference.
3   That signification is contingent and not fixed by the body.

In this account, sexual difference is both necessary and necessarily contingent.

While Lacanian epistemology presents the knower as if it were outside the field of sexual difference, the Lacanian theory of sexuation situates all subjects within that field. Zizek points out that '[o]ne of the crucial differences between psychoanalysis and philosophy concerns the status of sexual difference: for philosophy, the subject is not inherently sexualised . . . whereas psychoanalysis promulgates sexualisation into a kind of formal, a priori, condition of the very emergence of the subject' (1998a: 81). As a speaking subject, the knowing subject of Lacanian epistemology is therefore also sexed. While Lacan does not develop his work in this way, in the next section of the chapter I read Lacan's accounts of knowledge and sexuation together to develop a theory of the formation of the sexed knower and its knowledges. I interweave Lacanian epistemology and the Lacanian account of sexuation to offer a possible answer to the question: 'How, then, is sexual difference, this fundamental Real of human existence, inscribed into the matrix of the four discourses? How, if at all, are the four discourses sexualised?' (Zizek 1998a: 82).

The Knowing Master

> Knowledge from the point of view of the unmarked is truly fantastic, distorted and so irrational. The only position from which objectivity could not possibly be practiced and honored is the standpoint of the master, the Man, the One God, whose Eye produces, appropriates, and orders all difference.
>
> (Haraway 1991: 193)

~~Le~~ Maître châtré

For Lacan, the Discourse of the Master describes the production of the speaking subject in the symbolic field. The subject comes into being when it enters the signifying chain through identification with a signifier, S_1. The S_1 is a fundamental symbolic element which 'knots' signifier and signified and thereby arrests their constant sliding (S17: 219). It represents the signifier that gives the subject its symbolic coherence and situates it within language. For this reason, the S_1 marks the point of the 'origin' of the subject's speech, because identification with the *I* of speech, the S_1 that symbolizes the *I* of the master, constitutes the subject (S17: 70). In this way, identification with the *I* of the Master forms the subject in the symbolic field. The Discourse of the Master thereby inaugurates a speaking subject which is identical to its proper signifier and which 'names' it (S17: 101). For Lacan, this discourse binds the subject to the master signifier and all its illusions.

In the Discourse of the Master, the subject refuses knowledge of its formation in signifying networks. In his schema, Lacan represents this refusal to know by an arrow $S_1 \rightarrow S_2$, labelled '*impossibility*' (S20: 16). Given this structure, it is impossible for the subject to know its relation to the signifier. For this reason, Lacan represents that impossibility by his figure of the barred subject, S. He represents the subject as barred because it refuses to acknowledge the truth of its unconscious division. That lack is a consequence of its constitution as a speaking being, because castration is the price of entering the Symbolic order. The discourse of the Master hides the truth of the lack-in-being of the subject (S17: 90). The Master does not want to know, and cannot know, the truth of its unconscious. Lacan describes how, in identification with the signifier, the subject 'sees himself as constituted by the reflected, momentary precarious image of mastery, imagines himself to be a man merely by virtue of the fact that he imagines himself' (S11: 142). The subject perceives itself as an *I*, that is, as a unified subject, and hence refuses to acknowledge that it is in fact a Master that suffers castration.

This Discourse produces a subject who wishes to master its self, its others, its desire, and its unconscious. For Lacan, the Master wishes to dominate that which it excludes from its discourse (S17: 110). Fink describes how this subject 'must show no weakness, in this sense carefully hides the fact that he or she, like everyone else, is a being of language and has succumbed to symbolic castration' (1998: 32). The castrated Master refuses to believe that it is castrated. It veils over its lack with the illusion that it is whole and complete; the *méconnaissance* of a self that imagines that it is identical to itself and to its master signifier (S17: 70). It imagines that it has mastery of a 'univocal' discourse that masks its unconscious division (S17: 118).

The Master of consciousness

In his later work, Lacan differentiates between 'le sujet de la connaissance' (*the subject of knowledge*) and 'le sujet du signifiant' (*the subject of the signifier*) (S17: 53), echoing his earlier distinction between the imaginary *méconnaissance* of consciousness and unconscious symbolic *savoir*. Lacan explicitly links consciousness to mastery and to the Discourse of the Master (S17: 79). The consciousness that masters is the Knowing Master. In the subject position of the Master, the knower claims to be consciousness. The knowing subject perceives itself as a conscious self, in a defensive operation that repudiates the unconscious. In that position, the knowing subject imagines a unity of identity of consciousness, self and subject. In Chapter 2, I described this position of the knowing subject in the Lacanian epistemology of *Écrits* as the knowing subject of consciousness. The Knowing Master can be seen as a later formulation of the knowing subject of consciousness of Lacan's classical epistemology.

The Knowing Master is a position in which the imaginary order captures the knower such that it perceives its self and its objects in the mirror of the ego. The Master subject claims to be a unified subject which creates itself in an act of mastery. It imagines itself to be whole and identical to itself, and perceives its self and its others as identical to its egoistic projections. The knower constructs its relationship to its others as an objectifying identification in which the other is an object that it seeks to master. Its knowledge is an aggressive, objectifying and distorting domination of its known object. The knowing subject attempts to gain omnipotent control of itself and its world, so as to imagine itself as the 'Absolute Master' (Lacan 1955: 47, *Éc*: 33). It posits itself as omniscient, the possessor of absolute knowledge.[1]

The Knowing Master

Lacan's description of the knowing subject of the Discourse of the Master presents it as the universal, disembodied knower. However, given that the Lacanian account of subjectivity posits sexuation as its condition, then the knower is necessarily sexed. Following a feminist deconstructive strategy leads us to ask, how is sexuation inscribed into the Lacanian theory of the knowing subject? To answer that question requires the reinscription of sexual difference into Lacan's account of the production of the Master subject.

For Lacan, the Master subject is produced through identification with a symbolic term, the *trait unaire*, translated as the unitary, unary or 'single-stroke' trait. Lacan's theory draws on Freud's account in *Group Psychology* (1921) of the process of the assimilation of an aspect or characteristic of another, in which the subject identifies with a trait of another subject. Lacan argues that an identification with the unitary trait 'marks' each one of us as a singular and unified identity: '[l]'identification-pivot, l'identification majeure, c'est le trait unaire, c'est l'être marqué *un*' (*the pivotal identification, the major identification, the unitary trait, it is the being marked <u>one</u>*) (S17: 180). He links this concept of the unifying mark to the signifier of 'L'Un' (*The One*). 'The One' is the signifier that institutes the symbolic structure of the subject (S17: 12; S20: 143–144). In the Discourse of the Master the unitary trait appears as S_1, the master signifier. The master signifier functions as the signifier that represents the subject as subject.

However, Lacan also links S_1 to the phallic signifier. In his discussion of sexuation, Lacan describes the phallus as 'that which is also incarnated in S_1, which, of all the signifiers, is the signifier for which there is no signified' (S20: 80). The phallus incarnates or 'makes flesh' the S_1 of the master signifier. For this reason, identification with the phallic signifier operates as identification with the master signifier. What links these terms is the process of symbolic identification in which the phallic signifier is a master signifier that produces the subject.

Lacan does not elaborate the process of symbolic identification in *L'envers* and *Encore*. However, he does provide an account of symbolic identification in his earlier account of the paternal metaphor. Lacan argues that in the formation of the subject, the signification of the phallus 'is evoked only by what we call a metaphor, in particular, the paternal metaphor' (*É*: 220). The paternal metaphor is the attribution of procreation to the Name-of-the-Father and the signification of the paternal relation. A moment of the Oedipus complex, the paternal metaphor represents the intervention of the Symbolic order (signified by the Name-of-the-Father) in the subject's imaginary relation to the mother (and her desire). In the operation of the paternal metaphor, the desire for the mother is repressed and the phallic signifier stands in for that desire in the subject's unconscious (Muller and Richardson 1994: 213). This process forms the subject in a relation to the phallic signifier and hence as a sexed identity which has or does not have the phallus (S5: 186). In this account, the masculine subject has the phallus, a position of possessing the signifier of the phallic object, while the feminine subject does not have the phallus, a position of lack and hence castration.[2]

For Lacan, then, symbolic identification is a process of introjection of the unitary trait of the symbolic Father. For Lacan, introjection is a symbolic process which 'is always accompanied by a symbolic denomination. Introjection is always introjection of the speech of the other' (S1: 83). Lacan argues that the dissolution of the Oedipus complex involves symbolic introjection, in which 'what was the outside becomes the inside, what was the father becomes the super-ego' (S1: 169). In symbolic identification the subject introjects the signifier of the father, forming the super-ego. The subject assimilates the phallic signifier as the mark of the Father, and thereby incorporates the Symbolic father as an *I* (S11: 256–257). In the account of the four discourses, that identification with the master signifier involves the introjection of the signifying chain of discourse of which the signifier is an element. The formation of the subject therefore involves symbolic identification and the consequent assimilation of discourse.

With that understanding of symbolic identification, it then becomes possible to describe the reformulation of the paternal metaphor (and of the Oedipus complex) in the theory of the Discourse of the Master. In this discourse, identification with the phallic signifier – S_1 – of the Father produces a 'unified' subject. It is an identification with the paternal signifier because the phallic signifier is the mark of the Father, and hence of his Law. This symbolic identification 'marks' and names the subject with and by the Name-of-the-Father. Identification with S_1 involves an assimilation of the Symbolic father. For this reason, Lacan describes 'the law', that is, the Law of the Father, as dominating the Discourse of the Master (S17: 48).

This process of symbolic identification with the Father produces the illusion of a conscious self. It establishes a subjective relation of *I* and ego in which the *I* of the speaking subject appears to be co-extensive with the ego because of the operation of repression. For the Master subject, consciousness founds illusion of the transcendental I (S17: 70). Identification with the Symbolic Father who has the phallus and is not castrated structures this position of mastery, forming the master subject in terms of a psychic structure of defence against the unconscious. The identification with the Symbolic father produces a subject structured by a *méconnaissance* of its originary and ontological lack.

However, in the Lacanian account identification with the Symbolic Father operates differently in formation of masculine and feminine subjects. In the logic of castration, the model of a typical 'successful' resolution of the Oedipus complex is that of the paternal identification of the little boy because of the tie of the symbolic phallus and the real penis (S4: 209). In the third stage of the Oedipus complex, the little boy *identifies* with the father who possesses the penis while the little girl *recognizes* that he has it (S5: 196).[3] For Lacan, if masculinity and femininity both 'fail', they fail differently. The difference concerns the more or less 'problematic' assumption of Oedipal subjectivity, because the master signifier that represents the subject is masculine (S17: 107).

In Lacan's account, the masculine subject has the phallus (S20: 80). That is, the masculine subject possesses the phallus and, in this sense, is not castrated.

The male subject defines its masculine position through the exception of castration such that his 'all' is defined through an other position of 'not-being-all'. This other position is that of castration, which is the feminine position of a being that does not have the phallus. The phallus is the master signifier by which the masculine subject refuses the (lacking) body. The masculine subject structures his lack-in-being through the castration of the other. Lacan describes the masculine subject as supported by the phallic signifier and hence by S_1, the master signifier (S20: 80). The phallus 'that props him up as signifier and is also incarnated in S_1, which of all the signifiers, is the signifier for which there is no signified' (S20: 80). His ontological loss cannot be acknowledged without being symbolized as castration, for otherwise his fantasy of omnipotence, unity and universality would unravel. That displacement of ontological loss through the representation of castration in a symbolic function allows the masculine subject the illusion of mastery (S17: 144).

In that illusion of mastery, the masculine subject misrecognizes itself as a being whole and complete of itself. It is a position of (masculine) mastery. The Master's Discourse produces a masculine subject that seeks to master itself and others. It claims presence in its being as subject, and mastery of itself and its universe. In a series of punning neologisms, Lacan links the *I* (*je*) and ego (*moi*) of the subject with being (*être*) and mastery (*maître*): 'I am the master (*m'être*), I progress along the path of mastery (*m'êtrise*), I am the master (*m'être*) of myself (*moi*) as I am of the universe' (S20: 56). Lacan emphasizes the drive to mastery of its self and its universe that characterizes this subject of the conscious. For Lacan, the phallic function inscribes the masculine subject – 'man as a whole' – (S20: 79) as a being where all succeeds (S20: 56). It is a position of presence, of the universal masculine subject which is 'whole' and which does not suffer loss or lack. The Discourse of the Master describes the production of the knowing master, a masculine subject that secures its identity through identification with the Symbolic father in a repudiation of castration.

Reconceiving the knowing master as a masculine subject explains the formation of the masculine knower and its imaginary *méconnaissance*. It explains the relation between the knowing subject of consciousness and the masculine knower, showing the link between the formation of masculine subjects and knowers. In this way, it provides an account of the constitution of the knower as a masculine subject by providing the feminist deconstructive project with a means of understanding the formation of the subject of 'masculine' knowledges.

Desiring knowledge

In *Écrits*, Lacan suggests that the operation of desire produces and structures knowledge. In 'Subversion of the Subject', Lacan distinguishes between the Hegelian and Freudian theories of the relation of the subject to knowledge. Lacan criticizes Hegel's foundation of that relation upon the assumption that the knowing subject knows what he wants. By contrast, 'Freud reopens the junction between truth and knowledge to the mobility out of which revolutions come. In this respect: that desire becomes bound up with the desire of the Other, but that in this loop lies the desire to know' (*É*: 333). Lacan characterizes the psychoanalytic theory of the relation of the subject to knowledge as a relation of desire. For Lacan, desire 'envelopes the pleasure of knowing and of dominating with *jouissance*', giving it a metonymic structure (*É*: 184). The pleasure of knowing emerges in relation to desire. This formulation suggests that the desire to know is formed in a relation to the lack inherent to desire.

Desire describes that ceaseless and unsatisfied metonymic movement of lack from signifier to signifier which originates in the alienation of the subject's demands in language (*É*: 316). The desire of the subject is the desire of the (unconscious) Other. If 'man's desire is the *désir de l'Autre* (the desire of the Other)' (*É*: 345), it is as Other that the subject desires. 'Man's desire' emerges from an originary lack that the barred desire for the mother produces. This lack forms desire as a desire of the Other. Since a relation to lack constitutes and structures desire, a relation to lack also structures the 'desire to know'. For example, Lacan sees in the 'pleasure of knowing' a metonymic structure of desiring movement from signifier to signifier. Lacan depicts the desire to know as a ceaseless movement along the signifying chain. Knowing has the structure of desire because a relation to lack produces it.

If a relation to the Other of the unconscious structures desire, then a relation to the phallus as the signifier of lack must also structure it. The phallus is the mark of primary repression (*É*: 317), and functions as the signifier of desire. For Lacan, 'what surfaces in the unconscious of the subject is the desire of the Other, that is, the phallus desired by the Mother' (Lacan 1960: 94, *Éc*: 733). In this way, an absence structures the subject – the absence of the mother's body. Michael Payne argues that '[a]bsence in both Freud's and Lacan's theories – as well as those of boys and girls – is thought to generate desire, development and knowledge' (1993: 91). In Lacan's account, because lack structures knowledge (the desire to know what is not known), knowing operates in a movement of desiring lack, seeking the absence that it encircles.

If knowledge is a desire that exists in a relation to the phallic signifier, then the sexuation must also inflect the desire to know. If to desire to know is to desire the phallic signifier, then, because a relation to the phallic signifier defines sexed subjectivity, the desire to know must be structured differently for sexed subjects. In the masculine position, the desire for the phallic signifier is the desire for the barred (m)Other's body. The structure of that desire can also be seen in the masculine desire for the feminine subject, which is a desire for confirmation that he has what he has, and that he does not suffer castration. For the masculine subject, a desire for mastery, completion, unity and presence similarly structures the desire to know. The desire for the phallic signifier is an imaginary desire for the lost plenitude and unity that the mother's body represents. In this way, a repudiation of castration structures the desire to know. To know the (m)Other would be to have access to an imaginary plenitude that would fill the subject's originary lack and division.

For the masculine knowing Master, a desiring lack structures knowledge such that there is a relation between ontological and epistemological lack. From Lacan's description of the structure of knowledge, and his description of the masculine subject, it is possible to see that the structure of the knowledge of a masculine subject is predicated on lack, since it is based on the subject's desire for the lost (m)Other. For that subject, an unfulfilled desire structures knowledge, so that knowledge is understood as a negativity which an original repudiation of the (m)Other produces. The paternal law therefore always structures such a knowledge, which remains within its symbolic economy.

Therefore, in the classical epistemology of *Écrits*, the paternal order structures the knowledge of the masculine subject. However, in his later epistemology of the four discourses, Lacan argues that knowledge takes different structural forms. These different symbolic structures form discourses of knowledge. In this later work Lacan describes discourses of mastery as different structural articulations of knowledge that are ordered by the paternal law.

The discourses of mastery

In *L'envers de la psychanalyse* and *Encore*, Lacan identifies two dominant forms of knowledge in the modern social order: the Discourse of the University and the discourse of science. Lacan provides a structural and schematic description of the Discourse of the University and nominates philosophy as an exemplary University knowledge (S17: 71). In this discourse, '[s]ystematic knowledge is the ultimate authority' (Fink 1998: 33). Lacan links this form of knowledge to the Discourse of the Master, which is both its condition and foundation. Lacan perceives the function of the University as the elucidation and justification of the Discourse of the Master (S17: 172). It makes manifest the Master's discourse in the field of knowledge, positing knowing only in terms of authorization, justification and completeness.

The Discourse of the University supports the Master's desire for omniscience, justifying its insistence upon univocal conscious belief and concomitant refusal of the unconscious. As with the Master's Discourse, the knowledge of the University is caught in the repetition of the master signifier. For this reason Lacan represents the functions of $M(S_1)$ and $U(S_2)$ as 'congruent' (S17: 117). For example, the paradigmatic University knowledge, philosophy, founds its knowing upon a conscious self – '*Je-cratie*' – an *I* which believes that what it perceives of itself represents its true self, such that it can know itself and hence master itself (S17: 71). For Lacan, the transcendental and illusory *I* irreducibly designates University knowledge.

Lacan defines a Master as a subject who intervenes in an order of knowledge (1969b: 121, S17: 232). The *I* that masters founds the knowing subject of the University (S17: 70–71). The University produces a knower that is founded on the conscious self – the knowing subject of consciousness. However, that position of the knower is a position of a masculine subject. The position of the *I* that masters is therefore a position of a masculine knowing subject. For this reason, the Discourse of the University produces a masculine knower. As an institutional articulation of University knowledge, philosophy therefore also founds itself upon a masculine Master.

Lacan identifies the other dominant modern knowledge as science. In *L'envers*, Lacan considers science as being on the side of the Master in its desire to know the world (S17: 174). For Lacan, science is the most evident example of the instrumentality and totalization of the Master's Discourse, because it participates in the Master's drive for power and domination of the world (S17: 120–121). While science is a symbolic knowledge – a *savoir* – nevertheless it misrecognizes (*méconnaît*) the unconscious (S20: 139). Similar to University knowledge, science produces a knowing subject of consciousness that takes up a masculine subject position. It is a discourse of the Master and as such it produces a masculine knowing subject.

In his account of these forms of knowledge, Lacan proposes that his formalization of the discourses of the university and science distils the 'nature' of academic and scientific knowledge. For feminist epistemology, that formalization permits a tracing of the sexuation of these discourses. However, Lacan's account takes place at a level of generality seemingly removed from the institutional and disciplinary specificity and complexity of these fields of knowledge. For example, he does not specify which scientific, academic or philosophical knowledges he intends to include in his theory. In *L'envers* Lacan condemns philosophy *in toto*. However, he also implicitly exempts philosophers such as Aristotle, Hegel and Heidegger that he deploys in the service of his psychoanalysis. Moreover, the field of university knowledge is extremely broad, and the difficulty of theorizing 'academic' knowledge is indicated by debates within the sociology of knowledge and intellectual history.

A similar problem arises in relation to Lacan's theory of scientific knowledge. Throughout his work, Lacan consistently links psychoanalysis to the scientific 'subversion of knowledge (*connaissance*)', while also condemning its drive to totalization and domination (S20: 80). Lacan shifts between characterizing science as a Discourse of the Master or as a Discourse of the Hysteric, so that it is unclear as to whether science is knowledge that a drive to mastery founds or whether it is a precursor to psychoanalysis (1974: 19). Lacan does not provide a detailed description or elaborated account of its operation. Moreover, he does not address the specificity of scientific practice or of the construction of scientific theory.

However, Lacan's purpose in presenting his account of discourses is not to provide a philosophy of science or a sociology of knowledge, since his aim is not to analyse the construction of propositions that constitute a field of knowledge. Rather, he proposes a description of the symbolic structure of the discourse that produces that knowledge. Lacan's account of scientific and academic knowledge articulates the structure of signifiers that subtend them, and the symbolic relation between subjects that the signifying chain produces. This focus can be seen in Lacan's discussion of science in *Encore*, in which Lacan argues that:

> scientific discourse has engendered all sorts of instruments. . . . You are now, infinitely more than you think, subjects of instruments that . . . are becoming elements of your existence . . . it is nonetheless part of what I am calling scientific discourse, insofar as a discourse is what determines a form of the social link.
>
> (S20: 82)

Lacan's account of the discourses of mastery therefore describes how Western modern knowledge produces the knowing subject and specific forms of knowledge – namely, the University and science. In Lacan's theory, these orders of knowledge have a particular discursive structure that produces the relation between the knower and its objects, and the meaning that is given to the known object.

Lacan's theory of the discourses of mastery does not focus epistemological analysis upon the propositional content of knowledge, but rather upon the symbolic economy that produces it. This theory provides a means to understand the construction of a knowing subject and a known object in discourse, and how that symbolic structure forms knowledge itself. Importantly too, it permits an analysis of the production of knowledge in symbolic relations between subjects (that is, in social relations). For feminist epistemology, it provides a means of understanding how feminist deconstructive accounts of 'masculine' knowledge and subjects describe discourses of masculine mastery that form knowers and their knowledges in particular ways.

Knowing ~~The~~ Master

My account of the discourse of masculine mastery describes the production of a particular knower and form of knowledge. It shows the constitution of knowledge as a discourse of mastery. In the Discourse of the Master, the relation between the knower and its object takes the form of mastery of the object. 'Mastery' does not imply competence, proficiency, or reasoning. Rather, it represents a discourse that constructs knowledge as domination, as instrumentality, and as objectification, in which the subject seeks to master its object through a repudiation of its difference in an imaginary misrecognition of the identity of the object. The Discourse of the Master produces an imaginary subject which is a fictional Master, and which is never more than supposed. However, the subject that it supposes is a masculine subject. That normative subject reflects a modern Western ideal of white bourgeois masculinity. This ideal is 'The Man of Reason', with the attributes of mastery: individuality, autonomy, rationality and universality (Lloyd 1984). This account of the Discourse of the Master permits us to see how a particular structure of discourse produces a masculine knower and 'masculine' forms of knowledge.

The usefulness of this theory can be seen if we analyse two key accounts of masculine knowledges that inform feminist deconstructive theories. The first key account draws on standpoint theory by arguing that masculine knowledge reflects the social experiences of the male knower. Notable theorists of this strand of deconstructive work include Sandra Harding (1990), Donna Haraway (1991) and Lorraine Code (1991). For example, in *What Can She Know?*, Code offers an argument typical of this approach when she claims that 'knowledge is a construct that bears the marks of its constructors . . . claims to objectivity are derivative of culturally constituted male experiences. They derive out of the subjective, affective preoccupations of privileged, paradigmatic knowers' (1991: 55). In this argument, men have different social experiences from women, and hence have different knowledges of the social world. Because of their privileged social status, their knowledges and epistemic practices are also privileged.

However, theories that derive from standpoint epistemology generally conflate masculinity as a cultural ideal and men as individual social subjects. For example, that paradigm of masculinity and its social experience may differ according to the man's sexuality, ethnicity and class position. Code acknowledges (and forcefully argues) this point. Nevertheless, her description of 'male experiences' is typical of these accounts in its linking of masculine knowledges to all male knowers. This conceptual conflation derives from a more serious problem in standpoint theories. These theories propose a model of knowledge that is grounded in experiential claims. However, Marnia Lazreg points out that experience itself is a social category which linguistic and social forms construct and give meaning (1994: 51–55). Despite their emphasis upon the social construction of knowledge, these accounts do not address the formation of masculine knowledge other than as a reflection of the experience of the masculine knower. Ironically, in these models of knowledge it is as if linguistic and social forms do not effect the formation of knowledge. For example, standpoint theories explain why certain knowers are epistemologically privileged, but not why those knowers deploy particular paradigms of knowledge, nor why their knowledge takes particular forms. The material and social relations of an androcentric Western culture do privilege white, bourgeois masculine knowers and their knowledges, and feminist epistemology needs to retain this insight.

Nevertheless, it also requires a more complex account of the relation between the production of masculine knowers and masculinist knowledges.

A second key deconstructive theory argues that dominant cultural and social forms form masculine knowledge. Exemplified by the work of Evelyn Fox Keller (1985), Naomi Scheman (1993a) and Susan Bordo (1986), these theories claim that 'there is a demonstrable alignment between the ideals of autonomous reason and ideals of masculinity' (Code 1991: 117). These theorists argue that paradigms of rationality rely on a model of masculinity, which reflects its social formation and characteristics. For example, the work of Susan Bordo and Naomi Scheman studies the emergence of the Cartesian subject as the paradigmatic modern masculine knower. Bordo traces the 'Cartesian masculinization of thought' in the seventeenth century, which she characterizes as the emergence of a 'historical identification of rationality and intelligence with the masculine modes of detachment, distance and clarity' (1986: 456). Similarly, Scheman's work draws out the 'normative paranoia' of Cartesian method that attempts to posit the knower as self-constituting. She identifies the Cartesian knower as a paranoiac subject which 'goes about the task of reconstituting the world . . . under the problematic aegis of an all-powerful father. This reconstituted world is perceived as hostile – made up as it is of everything the ego has split off – and as permanently in need of vigilant control' (1993b: 156). These theorists predominantly use psychodynamic accounts of the production of subjectivity to explain how the concept of the rational knower is linked to the process of individuation of the modern masculine subject. For example, Fox Keller (1983) uses object-relations of both the English school, such as D. W. Winnicott, and the American feminist school, such as Nancy Chodorow.

However, these accounts also suffer from a reductionist analysis. For example, they present an essentialist idea of masculinity, failing to acknowledge that '[l]ike ideal objectivity, ideal essential masculinity is a specific socio-cultural construct, not a manifestation of a natural essence' (Code 1991: 54). This essentialist concept of masculinity is symptomatic of a reduction of social to familial relations. Reliance upon psychodynamic object-relations models of subjectivity reduces paradigms of knowledge to a reflection of familial object-relations, which does not acknowledge their formation in social and cultural forms. These theories present important insights as to the affective and psychic structures of masculinist knowledges, and their production in dominant familial structures. However, it is necessary to provide a more complex explanation of the relation between the production of subjectivity and forms of masculine knowledges.

My account of the discourses of mastery provides a means of retaining these insights of deconstructive theories, while also not reducing masculine knowledge to an effect of individual experience or familial objects. In the later Lacanian epistemology, different discursive social links produce particular forms of knowledges and knowing subjects. Those symbolic relations between subjects represent different forms of the social bond. In a Western culture, a phallocentric Symbolic order structures those social relations between subjects. In particular, it founds the Discourse of the Master as a dominant discourse of Western culture. The Discourse of the Master produces dominant forms of knowledge and the masculine knowing subject.

These masculine subjects need not be men. Both men and women can, and do, become knowing Masters. However, men are more likely to assume this position than women for two reasons. First, the Master is a paradigmatic knower because of the material and cultural privileging of particular forms of masculine identity. Second, the normative production of identity attaches masculinity to biologically male subjects. My account of the discourses of mastery provides an explanation for this 'demonstrable alignment' between masculine knowers and knowledges. For example, following Scheman's description of the Cartesian knower, it explains how identification with the Symbolic father forms this egoistic, defensive Knowing Master. Similarly, following Bordo's description of the masculine Cartesian subject, it explains why the knowledges of the masculine knower repudiate its feminine others (indeed, all others), the better to control their difference (1986: 452).

Rather than seeing masculine knowledges as a reflection of the privilege of men in social relations (as in standpoint theory), my account explains how those social relations produce masculine discourses of mastery. Those social relations produce discourses of knowledge that form the knower and its objects. These forms of knowing are discursive practices that do not describe the nature of 'knowledge', but rather the production of particular knowers and forms of knowing.

Knowing Otherwise

An Other to the Master

> But how can this little mechanism be stopped?
>
> (S17: 207)

For feminist epistemology, the question is how to create a political discourse that does not reproduce the Discourse of the Master. Its utopian claims posit the possibility of other discourses, citing feminist knowledges as evidence of that possibility. This project shifts its focus from the deconstruction of masculine knowers and their knowledges, to the construction of a theory of feminist knowers and knowledges.

For Lacan, the question too is how to stop the discourse of mastery (S17: 207). The possibility of a psychoanalytic discourse also subsists in the disruption of the Discourse of the Master. In the later Lacanian epistemology, that disruption occurs in the Discourses of the Hysteric and the Analyst. Those discourses unfurl the otherwise fixed structures of signification and inter-subjectivity, making them less rigid and more mobile. They disrupt and change structures of intrasubjectivity, by changing the relation of the subject to its self and its others.

Lacan argues that the discourses of the Hysteric and the Analyst create new positions of epistemological enunciation and a new relation of subject to object. Can his account of these discourses explain the new position of epistemological enunciation and relation which feminist epistemology seeks? If so, does the feminist knower occupy the position of the Hysteric or the Analyst? Or neither?

The hysterical analysand: the Discourse of the Hysteric

For Lacan, women occupy a privileged place in analytic discourse (S17: 62). 'Women' are eminent guides to psychoanalysis, both the hysterical analysand and the woman analyst who mistakes psychoanalytic truth for revolution. However, the 'true' handmaiden of psychoanalysis is the hysterical analysand, rather than the recalcitrant woman analyst.

For Lacan, the hysterical analysand opens the Master's Discourse to the Analyst's Discourse. The desire to know the Master animates the Discourse of the Hysteric (S17: 36). She asks 'what is it to be a woman?' (S3: 175). The answer to that question is a castrated being, and hence the Hysteric reveals the possibility of lack, the castration that all subjects suffer. The possibility that a castrated being exists reveals the possibility that the Master also suffers castration. For Lacan, the hysteric exposes the castration of the Father, and so the secret of the Master's discourse (S17: 110). This secret is that the subject suffers lack and loss, and this privation is covered over by repression in the Discourse of the Master. The Hysteric reveals that loss produces the Master's *jouissance*, and that his discourse finds its enjoyment in the *jouissance* of lack (S17: 112).

In Lacanian theory, female subjects are more likely to call the Discourse of the Master into question because of the structure of sexuation. The hysteric articulates primary dissatisfaction (S17: 84). In Lacan's discussion of the case history of Dora, he places the emergence of hysteria in the *Penisneid* or penis envy of the little girl, which originates in the little girl's reproach to the mother that she does not have the phallus. The hysterical demand emerges from that reproach, in which the hysteric signifies the frustration of her unanswerable demand to have and to enjoy the phallus (S17: 112). According to Nobus, hysterics 'take the Other – whether one of its concrete representatives, or society in general – unconsciously to task for tampering with their enjoyment' (2000: 29). She subjects the Master's Discourse to her unanswerable demand, and he can only reply with the assertion that she is castrated – that there are beings that do not have the phallus and that she is in that class of beings.

One strand of feminist thinking, such as that of Elaine Showalter (1987), has also understood the hysteric as a position of feminine protest, and her symptoms as a bodily rewriting of her experience of a social order that causes her psychic pain.[4] It perceives Dora, the exemplary hysteric of psychoanalysis, as its first feminist heroine who represents the limits of psychoanalytic knowledge and patriarchal discourse.[5] It interprets Dora's rejection of Freud's cure both as a refusal to be reinserted into the exchange of women, and as a protest against that exchange. In this interpretation, Dora is a metaphor for the inability of psychoanalytic knowledge, and patriarchal knowledge generally, to describe feminine sexuality in general, and female homosexuality in particular. She comes to represent a rupture of an apparently seamless masculine representation and knowledge of women.

In both these accounts, the hysteric represents a contestation and disruption of the Master's Discourse. She represents its moment of failure because she reveals its cost. However, Lacan argues that the position of the Hysteric resolves itself in a demand to the Master (S17: 150). She constructs her protests within his terms. The Hysteric desires knowledge, but the knowledge that she desires is that which the Master possesses. In this way, her position is one of symptomatic repetition that fails to contest or change the Master's discourse. The Hysteric's response to her pain is a symptomatic protest rather than resistance to the social order that produces her symptoms. She does not represent a contestation of the knowledge of the Master but is trapped within it.

Other feminist readings of the hysteric perceive her in similar terms, arguing that she does not represent a political figure. For example, Maria Ramas (1985) argues that the hysteric silently protests the oppression of women by taking up a position of inarticulate and passive resistance, thereby participating in traditional feminine protest of mute victimhood. These feminists argue that while such a position may have been the only position open to Dora, it does not provide an adequate basis for an active and interventionist politics that seeks to change the social order rather than to silently suffer its injustices.

In both Lacanian and feminist theory, the position of the Hysteric represents an important moment in the contestation of the Discourse of the Master. However, while the hysteric reveals the failure of the Discourse of the Master, she fails to disrupt its operation. The hysterical analysand exposes the castration of the Master, but she does not dislodge him from his position of mastery. The Discourse of the Master ultimately recuperates the position of the hysterical analysand. She knows that the Master is castrated, but she refuses to address him as other than Master.

In epistemological terms, the limit of the Discourse of the Hysteric is evident in relation to her knowledge. What is the knowledge of the hysteric? She knows the truth of the Master's discourse, namely that he suffers castration. Lacan acknowledges that the price she pays for that knowledge is herself. But what does this castration reveal? The hysteric's demand that she have the phallus is unanswerable. She cannot be a Master nor have mastery, and in this the hysteric must always fail. Her knowledge cannot be spoken because she cannot articulate the castration of the Master within her discourse, and hence cannot bring it into representation. Without that possibility, the hysterical analysand cannot represent the Master other than as Master. She cannot articulate a position other than that of unattainable Mastery or of suffering hysteria. For that reason, hysteria operates as a symptom, rather than as a political discourse that can change the social order that causes the Hysteric's psychic conflict and distress.

For this reason, the Discourse of the Hysteric does not produce an adequate subject position for the feminist knower. Dora the hysterical analysand may be interpreted as a nascent feminist heroine. However, her knowledge of the Master's discourse is bodily rather than political. Feminist politics implies symbolization, a representation of how we might understand gender and gender relations differently. However, the hysteric wants to evade the very possibility of representation, because it is the refusal to articulate desire that produces the hysterical symptom. The Discourse of the Hysteric is not the Discourse of the Feminist. Is, then, feminist discourse a Discourse of the Analyst?

The knowing analyst: the Discourse of the Analyst

Lacan argues that the Discourse of the Hysteric leads to a revolutionary knowledge – that of the psychoanalyst. For Lacan, the Discourse of the Analyst is revolutionary because it articulates the truth of the (unconscious) subject. As in the earlier Lacanian epistemology, psychoanalytic knowledge is a process of symbolization which acknowledges the lack of the subject and which recognizes its subjection to the signifier. The knowledge of the Analyst is *savoir*, symbolic knowledge. Psychoanalysis produces knowledge (*savoir*), rather than learning (*connaissance*) or representation (*représentation*) (S17: 32). The Discourse of the Analyst articulates *savoir*, knowledge of the laws of the Symbolic order.

For Lacan, the Discourse of the Analyst stands in opposition to that of the Master (S17: 99–100). It is revolutionary because it operates against the closure and rigidity of discourse of the Master's discourse, since 'it is opposed to all will of mastery, engaging in a continuous flight from meaning and closure, in a displacement that never ceases' (Bracher 1994: 124). In psychoanalysis, the analysand traverses the imaginary *objet a*, the fantasy which sustains its identity and which fixes the structures of its discourse in repetition. It comes to recognize 'that the Other is lacking, that the object is separated from the Other, that the Other does not have a final answer' (Adams 1996: 79). The analysand recognizes the lack in the Other – the symbolic *a*, its excluded element. The reinscription of the symbolic *a* into the analysand's signifying chain shifts the fixed structure of their discourse. Because the Discourse of the Master excludes that *a*, the inscription of that element disrupts it. The *a* is the cause of psychoanalytic knowledge. The reinscription of the excluded *a* permits the analysand to reconfigure its structure of signifiers, and, with that reorganization of signification, to produce new meaning and knowledge.

In Lacan's account, the knowing subject of psychoanalysis is an analyst and an analysand, since analytic discourse produces both. Yet the positions of analyst and analysand are not the same, either in Lacan's descriptions of their analytic roles or in their structural positions. The schema of psychoanalytic discourse does not describe the speaking position of the subject that it produces (the analysand), but that of the transferential figure that supports the production of that subject (the analyst). Lacan's schema describes the production of one subject, the analysand, not two. Logically, the analyst and analysand cannot occupy the same position, because they represent different speaking positions. Otherwise, it would not be possible to exclude 'wild analysis' from the psycho-analytic field, as it would be the figure of the analyst, and not the structural operation of psychoanalytic practice, which produced analytic effects upon the discourse of the analysand. Lacan's schema thus describes the operation of analytic discourse and the production of the analysand, rather than that of the analyst.

In contrast to the analysand, the analyst occupies an imaginary position of mastery. The analyst is structurally posited as the subject supposed to know (*le sujet supposé savoir*) (S11: 232). The analyst functions as the supposed subject of knowledge because the analysand posits the analyst as the Master who can answer the question of his desire (S11: 234). Lacan notes that if the Discourse of the Analyst opposes that of the Master, it is also its counterpoint (S17: 99). It is the analyst who is the master (S17: 38). The Analyst, both structurally and institutionally, is in the position of the Master.

However, while the analyst may have knowledge on his side, he must refuse this position of the Master. If the psychoanalyst understands him or herself as the master Clinician and Theoretician – the one who is able to 'know' the desire of the analysand and who is able to intervene in the analysand's knowledge in the act of interpretation – then he or she insists upon being the knowing Master, offering their interpretation as knowledge and that knowledge as complete, whole and comprehensive. It is this desire and enjoyment of knowledge that the analyst must refuse in order for the analysand to come to their own truth (Nobus 2000: 95). According to Lacan, the analyst must institute the analysand as master of their speech (S17: 59).

For these reasons, we should understand Lacan's schema not as describing the knowledge of the analyst, but that of the analysand. It is the analysand who must refuse a relation of mastery to knowledge, in order that he or she can recognize the truth of their unconscious desires. This relation to knowledge is a refusal of the imaginary position of the Master, with his dreams of unity and omnipotence. The discourse of the analysand provides a means of conceiv-ing of a knowledge that does not invoke mastery. If feminist epistemology is to deploy the theory of analytic discourse, that theory needs to be understood as a description of the knowledge of the analysand rather than the mastery of the Analyst. This reformulation of Lacan's theory retains his concept of the structure of analytic discourse but emphasizes the position of the knowing subject which that discourse produces. This reconfiguration shifts analytic knowledge from being a Discourse of the Master Analyst to being the Discourse of the Analysand.

Analytic knowledge/feminist knowledge

In analytic discourse, the analysand as knowing subject takes up the position of the barred subject – the subject of the unconscious. The analysand acknowledges the pain and psychic cost of entering the Symbolic order because he or she articulates the lack that all speaking subjects suffer. To know this truth is to know the lack of castration (S17: 58). The love of truth enables the analysand to know 'this weakness', to recognize the failure and limits of its knowledge. Refusing the comforts of the fantasy of a secure and securing identity, the analysand recognizes its split and contradictory self.

In her description of situated feminist knowledges, Donna Haraway argues that feminist epistemologies should privilege the notion of the knower as 'split and contradictory self'. Haraway contends that '[s]plitting, not being, is the privileged image for feminist epistemologies. . . . The knowing self is partial in all its guises, never finished, whole, simply there and original; it is always constructed and stitched together imperfectly' (1991: 193). This conception of the knower acknowledges her production. The knower recognizes herself as a speaking subject and so her formation in symbolic and social fields. In this position, the knowing subject critically articulates existing orders of representation, and the cost of entering those symbolic economies. By reinscribing that cost into the order of representation, she refuses the position of Master in her acknowledgement of her temporality, disunity and division.

However, the aim of psychoanalysis is to enable the analysand to accept its lack-in-being. Through analysis, the analysand articulates the truth of subjectivity: ontological lack. The analysand consents to that symbolic debt paid by the speaking subject because it accepts the castration that signifies its division and incompleteness. The analysand represents that loss as castration, which is rendered symbolically through a relation to the phallic signifier. In this way, the analysand sutures its fundamental lack-in-being through the signification of ontological lack as the sexual difference of castration.

By contrast, the feminist knowing subject articulates that symbolic debt but genders, politicizes and refuses it. While, *pace* Zizek, subjects may exchange common lack in the Symbolic order, feminism insists that women bear it in their signification of the ontological loss of all subjects. The 'Woman' functions as the sign of phallic lack because she comes symbolically to embody ontological (all) lack. In this way, the female subject pays the debt of the speaking subject in the Symbolic order.

In Lacanian terms, the symbolic price that is paid for becoming a subject is the giving up of the mother, and the lack-of-being of all subjects. In feminist terms, women pay this price. Ragland-Sullivan argues that 'female depression, passive aggression, and disturbed children is simply too great a price to pay', and her list is far from being a complete enumeration of the cost of such a social order (1987: 301). However, a feminist subject refuses that cost for herself, other women and other subjects. Unlike the analysand, the feminist knowing subject does not articulate the truth of the Symbolic order simply in order to come to terms with herself. Her knowing position emerges from a relation not only to herself but also to others. In this way, a political relation to others constitutes her position. With that political relation, the position of the knowing subject shifts from psychoanalysis to feminism.

In psychoanalytic discourse, the analyst stands as the cause of the discourse (in the place of the *a*). The analyst is the silent partner of the analytic process who functions as the addressee of the analysand's demand for love and knowledge. This address to another introduces the intersubjective dimension of analytic practice. Without the analyst, the analytic process could not unfold because it is through the transferential operation of demand and identification that the analysand produces a hysterical discourse that introduces his or her desire. In this way, the analysand's relation *to an other* – the analyst – as a relation *to self* structures the analytic process.

Unlike psychoanalytic discourse, a political relation *to others* structures feminism. The feminist subject addresses her desire to know and to love to others, constituting the intersubjective dimension of that address. Other women provide her discourse with its cause. This political address to others distinguishes her position from that of the analysand. Her relation to others, rather than the analysand's relation to self, produces her speaking position. In her political relation to her others, the knowing subject addresses her desire for knowledge to other women. This address inflects her knowledge, structuring it as an intersubjective negotiation of political principles. Feminist knowledge seeks to found its act of knowing in the political.

Lacan argues that it is not by accident that women inaugurate the revolutionary discourse of psychoanalysis (S17: 62). The analysand Anna O., the subject of the first psychoanalytic case history, named psychoanalysis the 'talking cure' (Freud and Breuer 1895: 83). The case of 'Anna O.' can be read as an account of the hysterical analysand, or it can be reread through Anna's own name, Bertha Pappenheim, who was a historical subject with speech, agency and knowledge. In that subjective position, the analysand Anna O. can be recast as the feminist Bertha Pappenheim.

Anna O. undoubtedly suffered as a hysteric; it was the hysterical symptom that drove her to her two doctors, Breuer and Freud. However, she also has a speaking position that is not that of the hysterical analysand. Throughout her life, Bertha Pappenheim 'was a pioneer in German social work as well as a leader in feminist and Jewish women's organisations' (Decker 1992: 136). Hannah Decker points out that, unlike Dora, 'an avocation-turned-career had been the salvation of "Anna O."' (1992: 108). Bertha Pappenheim was truly able to love and to work. We can see in her life the movement from hysteria, silence and depression to ethical and political engagement, a shift from passive symptom to feminist practice. If we consider the feminist position as analogous to that of the analysand, and the Discourse of the Hysteric as leading to the Discourse of the Analyst, then it is possible to see the relation between the 'protofeminism' of hysteria and feminist discourse (Forrester and Appignanesi 1993: 68). However, while both have discursive structures that originate in the question of sexual difference and unsatisfied demand, what distinguishes the two is the shift from symptom to signifying practice. One discourse produces a symptom; the other produces a political knowledge. This shift is evident in Anna O.'s life, shifting her position of hysterical analysand to that of the feminist, and from analytic discourse to feminist discourse.

Knowing women: what can ~~The~~ Woman know?

[W]hat we want to know is the status of the Other's knowledge.

(S20: 87)

'Does the Other know?' (S20: 89)

The question remains: who is the knowing subject of feminism? Is it a female knower, a feminist knower, or both? One view irrevocably ties these two subjects together. For example, Rosi Braidotti presents the subject of feminist knowledge as the 'female/feminist subject' (1992: 188). Yet another argument contends that there is no necessary relation between the female and feminist knower. For example, Helen Longino argues that models of feminist knowledge should not be 'exclusively gender-based' (1996: 277).

While the problem of the relation between the female and feminist subject haunts much of recent feminist theory, it is particularly acute for theories of feminist knowledge. Feminist epistemology claims that it is not possible to posit the knower as a sexually neutral subject of reason, because it is always a sexed subject. If we understand the knower as sexed, then it is not possible to simply claim that there is no relationship between feminist knowers and women. However, the task of understanding that relationship is not made easier by a common failure to distinguish between the subject of feminist theory – women – and the knowing subject of feminist epistemology – the feminist knower.

In the field of feminist epistemology, it is necessary to maintain the distinction between female and feminist subjects. There are many women who do not identify themselves as 'feminists'.[6] Moreover, there are many men who declare their allegiances to feminism.[7] For this reason, while feminism engages with the politics of the social ordering of gender, feminist knowers are not reducible to 'feminine' identity. Rather, they represent a political subject of feminism, subjects which feminist politics produces. What distinguishes the formation of female and feminist subjects is a relationship to feminist politics. The question of the feminist subject is necessarily a political question, since the feminist subject is first and foremost a political and politicized subject.

Nonetheless, it is not possible to completely sever the relation between these subjects for two reasons. First, in pragmatic political terms, feminism is ultimately a practice concerning the politics of gender (which by definition requires that its projects engage with the multiple axes of the oppression of women). For the most part, this political practice is still undertaken by women. Second, beyond that pragmatic politics, a feminist theory of knowledge that insists that the knower is sexed cannot then argue that the feminist knower does not have a sex. To do so is to reinstitute the universal knowing subject which feminist epistemology compellingly critiques.

The relation between the female subject and feminist knower therefore remains a crucial issue for feminist theories of knowledge. However, existing theories consider this issue in terms of foundational concepts of knower that fix it in already given terms. These theories begin their analysis with a concept of the knower that substantiates it as a sexed knower or as a political subject. This approach mires feminist epistemology in a series of circular debates concerning female/feminist subjects, which oscillate between arguments for and against which subject can serve as the better foundation for feminist knowledges. However, these debates do not actually put those foundational terms into question, and fail to consider the *production* of those subjects. They assume a given sexual identity (the female knower) and a given political identity (the feminist knower) so that these models do not explain the constitution of the feminist knower.

Rather than assuming the prior existence of sexed knower or the political subject, we need to explain their formation. Moreover, we need to explain the relationship between these subjects. To evade the circularity of existing debates, I begin with an analysis of the relation between the formation of the sexed female subject, and the constitution of the knower as feminist subject.

Reading femininity

How do we become sexed subjects? Butler argues that 'psychoanalysis has a crucial role to play in any theory of the subject' (2000b: 140). Feminists theorizing subjectivity have predominantly read Lacanian theory as and for an account of the constitution of 'femininity'. Those engagements with Lacan's work focus upon his account of the operation of the phallic signifier in relation to the 'feminine' subject and sexuality, particularly upon the theory of sexual difference presented in Alan Sheridan's translation of *Écrits*.

In this classical Lacanian theory, sexed subjectivity is assumed in relation to the phallic signifier. Masculine subjects are defined by having the phallus and feminine subjects by being the phallus (*É*: 320). When subjectivity is assumed in the Symbolic order, the masculine or feminine subject is sexually differentiated in its relation to the phallus. In this account, the speaking subject is always a sexed subject defined by the phallic signifier of the Symbolic order, whether it is the masculine subject that has the phallus or the feminine subject that is the phallus. For both sexes, sexuation pivots on the phallus.

Two readings dominate the anglophone feminist reading of the classical Lacanian theory of femininity. The first response, which Nancy Fraser (1992) exemplifies, refuses Lacan's account as hopelessly and irrevocably phallo-centric. The second response, which Ellie Ragland-Sullivan (1987) exemplifies, is a sympathetic interpretation of Lacanian theory that argues that it provides a compelling description of the difficulty of phallic femininity. However, these debates continually return to the problem of sexual difference that constructs femininity as either phallic or Other to the phallus, thereby defining femininity in relation to the phallus. Moreover, neither of these readings offers a theory of the female/feminist knower because they do not unpack the relationship between these two identities. Such a theory requires a closer examination of the formation of 'feminine' subjectivity. It cannot reduce the feminist knower to either her 'femininity' or her 'sexuality', because it needs to address her political as well as subjective formation. In other words, it must address the distinction 'between different notions of political identity – between the idea of a political identity for feminism (what women require) and that of a feminine identity for women (what women are or should be)' (Rose 1986: 103).

How then is it possible to provide a psychoanalytic account of these two identities that is 'beyond the phallus'? One way is to explore another reading of Lacan. The feminist reception of Lacan has been based on the 'classical' Lacanian account of the sexed subject presented in *Écrits*, rather than his later seminars of the 1970s. The focus of Anglo-American feminist theory upon *Écrits* may be attributable to the delay in the publication and translation of Lacan's later work on femininity, in particular his seminar *Encore* (1972–1973) (S20). *Encore* was not published until 1975 and, with the exception of two chapters that Jacqueline Rose translates in *Feminine Sexuality* (1982), remained untranslated until 1998.

Lacan's later work proposes a more complex account of the production of the female subject that avoids the phallocentric circularity of his classical theory of sexed subjectivity. In the next section, I examine the later Lacanian concept of the sexed subject in *Encore*, developing and redeploying it as a feminist theory of the formation of the female subject and its 'feminine' sexuation.

The not all of the **pas-toute**

Rose characterizes *Encore* as 'a turning point in Lacan's work, both at a conceptual level and in terms of its polemic. It represents Lacan's most direct attempt to take up the question of feminine sexuality' (1982b: 137). However, *Encore* is not only an examination of feminine sexuality. Importantly, Lacan also returns to, and rethinks, his notion of the female subject and of femininity.

Similarly to the earlier accounts of the sexed subject, the phallus remains the pivot of the later Lacanian account of sexual difference. Lacan's 'Graph of Sexuation' represents sexed identity in relation to the phallic function (S20: 79). The phallic function is '*the function that institutes lack*, that is, the alienating function of language' (Fink 1995: 103). A relation to the phallus structures the masculine and feminine positions, which the formulae of sexuation represent (S20: 79–80). Because it turns on the phallic function (S20: 59), 'there is no such thing as a sexual relationship' (S20: 12). For this reason, a relation between the sexes is an impossibility. Lacan claims that the 'male way' of *jouissance* produces the non-relation between the sexes (S20: 56–57). The phallic function produces the *jouissance* of the masculine subject, the enjoyment of the (phallic) organ on which 'all' turns.

Lacan argues that the phallic function inscribes the male subject 'man as whole' or 'as all' (*l'homme comme tout*) (S20: 79). Joan Copjec describes that inscription as producing 'a universe of men', a masculine universal (1994: 235). The masculine subject claims to be a man who is whole and all, a master of himself who '[b]y denying the trauma of primary Castration . . . unconsciously perpetuates the suppression of the person's own division and the belief in her or his autonomy' (Ragland-Sullivan 1987: 305). The masculine claim rests on the exception of castration – such that he defines his universality in relation to an other without the phallus. The masculine subject represents his ontological lack as the castration of the feminine other.

That other position of the subject is that of ~~The~~ Woman – a fantasy that affirms that the masculine subject has the phallus. In this fantasy, ~~The~~ Woman desires the phallus, confirming that he has it. If the whole of the sexual relation is a fantasy, it is a masculine fantasy of ~~The~~ Woman as the cause of his desire (S20: 131). The cause of his desire is the *objet a* – the originary missing object that can never be found (S20: 86). Zizek identifies that missing object as the Mother-Thing on which masculine fantasy turns (1989: 119). For the masculine subject, the feminine represents a fantasy object that can answer his desire for universality and completeness: she confirms that he does not suffer castration. In its relation to the masculine subject, the feminine is a fantasy of a castrated other that confirms that she is castrated and he is not. The operation of the phallic function produces this fantasy.

For this reason, Lacan argues that ~~The~~ Woman does not exist. She exists only as a fantasy of the masculine subject, formed in his phallic *jouissance* and in his desire. No woman can fulfil that fantasy. In this way, ~~The~~ fantasy Woman does not exist in the real, because no woman could enact the fantasy that he substitutes for her. Lacan points out in his earlier work on feminine masquerade that women may attempt to fulfil that fantasy (*É*: 321). However, while a woman may attempt to play out the masculine fantasy, in doing so she does not exist as other than in and through fantasy. Lacan indicates the impossibility of '~~The~~ Woman' by his bar through the definite article 'The'. When interviewed in 1973, Lacan formulates the impossibility of 'Woman' as 'The Woman does not exist' (1974: 38). In *Encore*, Lacan makes it clear that, by that formulation, he does not mean that women do not exist but that the masculine fantasy of ~~The~~ Woman is an impossibility (S20: 72–73).

If Lacan's later account of the sexuated subject went no further than this description of masculine and feminine subjects, then it would only be a more elaborated version of the classical Lacanian theory of sexuation. As such, the phallus would still function as a transcendental guarantee of subjectivity and the Symbolic order. Such an account would therefore remain vulnerable not only to the feminist objection of androcentrism, but also to the compelling deconstructionist critique of 'phallogocentrism' (Derrida 1980). However, in *Encore*, Lacan confronts the question of 'What does woman want?', which leads to a reworking of his theory of the female subject.

In *Encore*, Lacan describes how 'what I am working on this year is what Freud expressly left aside: *Was will das Weib?* "What does woman want?"' (S20: 80). Lacan responds to that question with some of his most misogynist statements. He suggests that women tell nothing of their body or their pleasure, and that in fact they know nothing of their bodies or their pleasures (S20: 74–75). Ultimately, Lacan reduces this mystical unknown Other to the unknowable maternal Thing (S20: 99). The question of *what do women want* implies a desire to know women, insofar as Lacan wants to know what women want. What is in question is Lacan's knowledge of women. However, what Lacan puts into question is what women themselves know. His answer? Nothing. What emerges in Lacan's discussion of what women want is a succession of gestures of rhetorical mastery, which understand this unknown object as ignorant of itself, and finally as unknowable. The drive to master that object is evident in Lacan's claimed status of Knowing Master: '[i]t's just that they don't know what they're saying – that's the whole difference between them and me' (S20: 73).

However, these gestures of mastery are at play within the same text in which the 'truth' of women is in excess of a phallic regime, and constantly threatens to breach its symbolic logic. The question of what *women* want opens the way for Lacan's conception of the female subject as '*not all*' (*pas toute*). In Encore, the position of the female subject is not rendered as nothing, but as *not all* of the phallus: 'I said "of woman", whereas in fact *woman* does not exist, woman is not whole (*pas toute*)' (S20: 7).

In this formulation, the *not all* of the female subject is a *not all* of the phallic function. Lacan argues that 'when any speaking being whatsoever situates itself under the banner "women", it is on the basis of the following – that it grounds itself as being not-whole in situating itself in the phallic function' (S20: 72). If the exception of castration defines 'all' of the masculine position (S20: 79), then the position of the female subject is that of an exception. The masculine rests on the exception of feminine (castration). It rests on her being other than the phallic all. With this exception, the phallus cannot be posited as a universal and so cannot define all, because it has the status of a universal that rests on a non-universal.

Reading the Graph of Sexuation in *Encore* from the side of the masculine subject positions the female subject as an exception to the phallic signifier and hence as a signification of its limit. The phallus does not define her sexed subjectivity, because she comes to be a sexed subject through normative identifications with a member of the opposite sex. It does not define her body, for the phallus does not symbolize her body (S3: 176). It does not represent her sexuality, since her *jouissance* is not a phallic *jouissance* (S20: 74). Lacan argues that '[a] woman can but be excluded by the nature of things, which is the nature of words and it must be said that if there is something that women complain about enough for the time being, that's it' (S20: 73). To be a woman is not to be excluded from language. For Lacan, '[i]t's not because she is not wholly in the phallic function that she is not there at all. She is there in full (*à plein*). But there is something more (*en plus*)' (S20: 74). The paradox of the female subject is that she is within the phallic law of the signifier and yet 'there is something more'.

The *not all* of the female subject should therefore be understood as the failure of the law of the signifier to represent her sexed subjectivity. The *not all* of the female subject is constituted in its failure to represent her subjectivity as other than phallic. Her position of 'Other' is then a position of being other than the phallic subject. Therefore, the phallic signifier does not define the female subject. The *not all* is not that which is Other to the phallus, but that which it does not define. The Lacanian account of the position of the female subject is the failure of the symbolic to represent that subjectivity. The Graph of Sexuation should therefore be read as a Graph of Male Sexuation and of the operation of masculine subjectivity. It does not describe the female subject other than in terms of the phallic function. For this reason, Lacan's Graph can only represent the female subject as not defined by the law of the signifier.

In this later model of sexuation, the phallus only guarantees a masculine subject and symbolic order. The subjective and symbolic structures that it supports are therefore incomplete – there is always 'something more', such that the phallic order always produces an excess to itself. The phallus fails to effect closure of what otherwise appears to be a transcendental Symbolic order. For this reason, the *not all* provides a means to reconceive the female subject.

Lacan argues that the position of exception to the phallic signifier is not that of negation or contradiction but of indeterminacy (S20: 103). The *not all* of the female subject is a position which the symbolic does not capture. As a position which the law of the signifier does not determine, the *not all* is a limit to its claim to represent an infinite set of all (S20: 103). It marks both the limit of the phallic signifier (as its exception) and the failure of that limit (as its infinite excess). The *not all* is an objection to the universal claim of the masculine (S20: 103). The *not all* of a female subject is a position of a non-universal subject, and so is a position of specificity and particularity. The logic of that position is 'one by one' (S20: 10). In the position of *not all*, the female subject is a specific and particular subject: women 'do not lend themselves to generalization. Not even, I say this parenthetically, to phallocentric generalization' (1975e: 18). For Lacan, women do not lend themselves to generalization 'since we cannot speak of more than one' (1974: 40).

Pas-toute-encore

> By epistemological shift I mean a new way of thinking about culture, language, art, experience, and knowledge itself that, in redefining the nature and boundaries of the political, at once addresses women as social subject and en-genders the subject as political.
>
> (de Lauretis 1988: 10)

De Lauretis identifies a central difficulty of theorizing the knowing subject of feminism – on the one hand, a female (sexed) subject which is produced in social relations, and on the other, a feminist (political) subject which is produced in the contestation of those relations. De Lauretis emphasizes the radically indeterminate and unstable nature of this subject, and for this reason rejects a Lacanian theory of the subject. She argues that it proposes 'a subject constructed in language alone, an "I" continuously prefigured and preempted by an unchangeable symbolic order', and so cannot address a feminist notion of the subject as 'a multiple, shifting, and often self-contradictory identity' (1988: 9).

However, my reformulation of the later Lacanian account of the sexed subject emphasizes its social *production* as an unstable subject that can therefore be engendered as political. It does not conceive the female subject as an ontological femininity, nor as founded in sexual difference. The position of the *not all* is not an ontological description of women, but rather a description of the position of the female subject in socio-symbolic relations.

This concept of the female subject locates women neither 'outside' nor 'inside' the socio-symbolic order. Rose points out that 'the former relegates women outside language and history, the latter simply subordinates them to both' (1982a: 57). Rather, resistance can be found in the faltering of the phallic function, which provides the possibility for imagining the socio-symbolic contract otherwise. This possibility is that the phallic Symbolic order does not define all (others) because it fails to know the female subject. The *not all* is a position that is neither 'inside' nor 'outside' the Symbolic order but is in excess of its phallic imaginary. It represents the failure of a metaphysics of phallic identity, and in that failing lies the possibility of an epistemological shift that is able to account for, and move beyond, its limits.

This strategy recognizes that ~~The~~ Woman is a masculine fantasy that does not represent women. As such, ~~The~~ Woman does not describe 'women', but is rather a site of feminist contestation. The female subject becomes a position of strategic engagement that recognizes that in 'feminist theory one *speaks* as a woman, although the subject "woman" is not a monolithic essence defined once and for all, but rather a site of multiple, complex and potentially contra-dictory sets of experience' (Braidotti 1992: 182). This conception of the *not all* of women requires understanding the female subject not as an ontological ground of the feminist subject, but as a political project which aims to 'bring about new forms of representation and definition of the female subject' (Braidotti 1992: 182). It thereby reveals that the possibility of the feminist knower – a knower engaging in the transformation of the failure of the phallic signifier and the socio-symbolic order which it guarantees – is contingent upon a political project of new forms of the socio-symbolic relations and subjectivity.

Female/feminine/feminist

How does that subject become a political subject? Is there a relationship between female and feminist subjects? To answer these questions, we need next to consider the relationship between the formation of female and feminist subjects.

In the Lacanian account of the production of the female subject, while the phallic function may fail to secure the position of the *not all*, that position may also resolve into normative 'masculine' or 'feminine' Oedipal identifications. These 'normative' identifications reflect norms of how to be a sexuated subject, and as such are fictional representations of 'masculinity' and 'femininity'. While these Oedipal norms may (and do) fail, they nevertheless represent mascu-line and feminine identity. Although all identifications are labile, they work to secure the otherwise 'unstable' female subject within the ideals of 'masculinity' or 'femininity'. For Lacan, all speaking beings are inscribed on either side of the Graph of Sexuation (S20: 79). Subjects are by definition sexed, and therefore have masculine or feminine structures.

The female subject can 'choose' to take up a place on the masculine side of sexuation. Lacan describes how '[o]ne ultimately situates oneself there by choice – women are free to situate themselves there if it gives them pleasure to do so. Everyone knows there are phallic women' (S20: 71). This female subject takes up a masculine position in phallic identification. This is a subject posi-tion of identification with the Law of the Father. In this position, it is not that the female subject exhibits 'masculine' traits, but rather that she refuses to recognize that she does not have the phallus. In this position, the subject accepts the terms by which the Law of the Father defines 'masculinity' and 'femininity', with a concomitant privileging of masculine identity and consolidation of the father's law.

Alternatively, the female subject can take up a feminine position. That position also requires a masculine identification, insofar as the female subject identifies with the Law of the Father and the operation of the phallus (as the mark of desire) (Evans 1996: 220). In the Lacanian account, the female subject recognizes that the father has what she does not, the phallus. She arrives at the feminine position through the desire for the phallus and its symbolic substitute, the child of the father. For that female subject, the phallus/child operates as the *objet a*, or the object of desire. Unsurprisingly, that position is arrived at with difficulty because of the absence of the threat of castration and the necessity of identification with the other (masculine) sex.

These operations of normative Oedipal identification confront the female subject with a Symbolic order that says all and nothing. In both positions, the female subject identifies with the Law of the Father, the phallic signifier becomes a masculine *all*, rendering her *not all* as a nothing. The female subject appears to be caught within a symbolic field that appears as a universal and transcendental, rather than a contingent, order. These normative identifications do not disrupt a phallocentric subject or socio-symbolic order. They do not disrupt the operation of the phallic signifier, nor contend that other signifiers could structure the subject or the Symbolic order.

However, a fundamental tenet of psychoanalytic theory is the 'problematic, if not impossible, nature of sexual identity'; the contingency of sexuation, the failure of identity, and the incompleteness of the symbolic field (Rose 1982a: 28). For psychoanalysis, 'femininity' is a symptom of that contingency, failure and incompleteness. It is a symptom because female subjectivity is an 'indetermination' of a *not all*, posited as an exception to the phallic function. For this reason, the 'riddle' of femininity has proven to be a source of much difficulty for psychoanalysis. For example, both Freud and Lacan begin by understanding the production of the female subject in the same identificatory structures as the male subject, but in their later work come to recognize the inadequacy of this account. They encounter the difficulty that the phallus 'guarantees' the masculine but not feminine subject. Phallic identification does not determine the female subject because it does not necessarily secure, nor is it secured in, her formation. How, then, do we provide an account of the identificatory instability of the female subject?

In both Freudian and Lacanian theory, the primary and secondary identifications structure the female subject in relation to the mother. Primary identification occurs prior to the object-cathexes of the Oedipus complex and involves an affective relation to the parent, who is then incorporated into the subject to form the nucleus of the ego and the ideal ego.[8] The parent is assimilated as an object 'inside' the subject, forming a prototypical self. This process is the 'individual's first and most important identification . . . a direct and immediate identification' (Freud 1923: 370). For Freud, the young girl's formation of a prototypical self 'rests on her primary affectionate attachment to her mother and takes her as a model' (1933: 168). Lacan argues that this process takes place in the mirror stage. He also suggests that this primary constitution of the subject involves identification with desire of the phallic mother (*É*: 320). In these accounts, the first and primary identification of the young girl with her mother forms her prototypical 'self'.

Secondary identification also involves the process of the incorporation of the parental object into the ego. However, in contrast to primary identification, this secondary process takes place in the context of the object-cathexes of the Oedipus complex. It marks the dissolution of the Oedipus complex, since it is a process of identification with the same-sex parent (Freud 1923: 373). For both Freud and Lacan, that identification forms the super-ego.[9] Lacan argues that this secondary identification is symbolic, a process of introjection of the paternal signifier of the father. Lacan perceives these oedipal identifications as having a secondary 'pacifying and normalising role' (Bowie 1991: 33). This outcome of the Oedipus complex is an ideal one, and represents its masculine resolution.

The resolution of the Oedipus complex for the young girl poses great difficulty for Freud and Lacan. In his later paper 'Femininity', Freud argues that the young girl turns from her mother in rivalry and resentment. However, in that paper he also argues that the young girl takes her mother as a model of femininity in primary identification, and then identifies with the mother as a feminine rival for the father (1933: 168). This description of maternal identification is in keeping with Freud's earlier description of secondary identification as taking the same-sex parent as its object. Lacan recognizes the contradictions within Freud's account and attempts to evade them by arguing that the young girl does not identify with the mother but with the paternal object the mother desires, the phallus (S3: 172). However, this argument has the effect that he faces similar difficulties to Freud, but in relation to the paternal rather than maternal identification of the young girl (S2: 262). Moreover, his account implies a maternal identification in that the young girl identifies with the mother's desire for the phallus, and so takes up a feminine position and becomes a sexed subject. Despite the contradictions within and between the Freudian and Lacanian accounts of the production of female subjectivity, central to both theories is the production of female subjectivity through the primary and secondary maternal identification of the young girl. Unlike the boy, the girl becomes a subject through a series of identifications with her mother. That relation to the maternal forms the female subject through an identificatory relation to an other woman.

Julia Kristeva and Luce Irigaray develop this psychoanalytic account of the female subject by arguing that a relation to the maternal structures the female subject. In *Black Sun*, Kristeva suggests that women are more likely than men to suffer melancholy, claiming that feminine identity has a melancholic structure (1987: 71–94). Irigaray also suggests that there is a relationship between the structure of femininity and melancholia (1974: 67–72). They link Freud's argument that identification is a mechanism by which the subject retains the otherwise lost object through its incorporation into the ego, to the Freudian and Lacanian argument that women fail to successfully resolve the Oedipus complex. Both Kristeva and Irigaray argue that women do not cease mourning for the lost object of the Mother, giving the female subject a continuing identificatory relation to the maternal object.

These psychoanalytic accounts of the production of the female subject emphasize the identificatory incorporation of the mother in both primary and Oedipal identifications. In these accounts, an incorporation of the maternal figure structures the female subject in a relation to the mother. That formation, and the resulting subjective structure which sustains that relation to the maternal figure, forms and structures the female subject in a relationship to another woman.

But what of the Father? In the Freudian and Lacanian accounts, the Father intervenes in the child's matriarchal universe to secure phallic identification, such that a 'successful' resolution of the Oedipus complex involves an incorporation of the figure of the Father. Yet, for the young girl, that resolution involves identification with the parent of the opposite sex, namely, by identifying with what she is not. Moreover, she must also identify with her mother in order to assume a 'feminine' position. Freud admits that the Oedipus complex is often not resolved as such for the girl, and her incorporation of the paternal figure is less 'successful' than the boy's. Lacan also perceives the 'successful' resolution of the Oedipus as problematic for women because of its phallic ordering (S17: 85). In these formulations, 'feminine' identification with the Law of the Father is not as efficacious or as immediate for the female subject.

Accordingly, the paternal super-ego does not work as effectively in securing 'feminine' phallic identification. Freud proposes that the super-ego is less developed in women than in men – a suggestion that he acknowledges will not please feminists (1925b: 342). Nevertheless, if we remember that the super-ego is formed by the introjection of the figure of the father, the representative of paternal, cultural authority, then that 'lesser' development suggests not a weaker morality but a weaker paternal super-ego. As the work of the psychologist Carol Gilligan (1982) on moral reasoning in men and women suggests, it may be that women follow other 'moral' imperatives besides those proclaimed by the Father. For Lacan, the paternal super-ego is the bearer of Kantian morality (S1: 102; 1958). Gilligan's critique of a Kantian moral framework suggests that, for a female subject, the paternal super-ego may simply not be the categorical imperative that the Father desires.

This description of the production of the female subject recognizes that the young girl may (and most often will) undertake paternal identification and so resolve the otherwise 'indeterminate' position of *not all* in either normative masculine or feminine identifications. However, a primary and secondary identification with the mother, and a less successful paternal identification, also forms that subject. For this reason, the female subject does not necessarily reproduce normative phallic identifications because she may not identify with the Law of the Father. An effect of the failure to secure female subjectivity in phallic identification is that the female subject has a certain identificatory mobility. Her identifications are not necessarily exhausted or made rigid by phallic identification. Rather, the formation of the female subject in maternal identification produces an identificatory relation to another woman, which has the possibility of being non-phallic. The production of the *not all* of the female subject offers the potential for a non-phallic identification, and hence for an identification with other women. How then do we understand the relationship between this formation of the female subject and the formation of feminist subjects?

Feminist identifications

What have 'we' meant to you?

(Miller 1990: 75)

I can honestly say that it has meant the world to me to be able to learn from women who were revolutionizing ideas and learning, and who in their persons represented possibilities of what I could be – strong, successful, and devoted to thinking with depth, compassion and anger about problems in the world . . . My exposure to women's studies and academic feminism convinced me that scholarship and education could promote social criticism and change. . . . I am, however, particularly interested in addressing and engaging with other women.

(Marcus 1990: 97)

In her answer to this question, Sharon Marcus, representing a new third generation of feminists, describes her identification with other women, with other feminists, and with feminism. For Freud, identification is the 'earliest expression of an emotional tie with another person' (1921: 134). 'Identification' is 'the operation itself whereby the human subject is constituted' (Laplanche and Pontalis 1973: 206). It is the process by which the subject constitutes and establishes a relation between its inner and outer worlds. Identification constructs an 'I' and an 'other' by constituting the subject in relation to *another*.

The earliest form of emotional tie to others, identification forms the social tie between subjects. In his study of the psychical dynamics of groups, *Group Psychology and the Analysis of the Ego* (1921), Freud argues that identification is the key psychic mechanism of the group. For Freud, 'social feelings for other persons rest on identifications with other people' (1923: 377). In this way, it forms a relationship between subject and others, constituting both the subject and its relation to other subjects. If this process establishes the subject and its relation to others, then what sort of identifications or 'emotional ties' form feminist subjects?

To consider the production of the feminist subject in terms of identification does not refuse the material history of feminist politics, which would reduce the social to the psychic. Nor does such an argument entail the foundation of politics in identity, or that identification is the only route to political activism, which would reduce the political to the psychic. However, we cannot simply exclude identification from politics, for while identification is political, politics is also identificatory.

Loving the other as self: the identificatory relation

Spivak points out that feminism asks 'not merely who am I? but who is the other woman?' (1987: 150). This question suggests the production of an emotional tie to another: an identification with other women. In that process, a subject recognizes a relation to other women. The identificatory relation forms an emotional tie to, and affective relation with, other women. In the affective relation, a subject identifies her self in the other woman.

This affective relation to others is a particular type of identification. According to Freud, it is 'direct and immediate', and is an operation of primary identification (1923: 370). In that operation, the ego of the subject incorporates the identificatory object. The incorporation of the object changes the structure of the ego and hence changes the self of the subject (1923: 368). Diana Fuss describes identification as 'the detour through the other that defines a self' (1995: 2). In this process, the other woman becomes part of the self, disrupting phallic identifications which otherwise constitute the subject. Using Freud's account, identification with other women can be seen as a primary identification of a feminist subject, which forms the nucleus of that subject. In that assimilatory process, the figure of an other woman is brought from the 'outside' to the 'inside' of the subject, changing the subject in terms of its relation to both self and other. The incorporation of the figure of an other woman grounds the production of that subject in an identification with other women. This identification permits the construction of ties between women. For example, Lisa Bowleg offers a typical third-wave account of the relationship between her identification with other women and her sense of feminist community. For Bowleg, '[i]f alliances between women symbolize feminism in its broadest sense, then my entire girlhood was a lesson in feminist training' (1995: 48).

It is possible to link this primary feminist identification of a relationship to other women to the formation of the female subject. I argued previously that a relationship to another woman, the mother, constitutes the female subject, which thereby structures her in relation to the maternal object. A primary identification with other women reproduces the originary relation of the young girl and her mother, because it reproduces that affective relation to the mother as an other woman. In this way, an affective relationship to other women finds its antecedent in the formation of a female subject position. Kaja Silverman argues that 'without activating the homosexual-maternal fantasmic, feminism would be impossible' (1988: 125).

This affective relation is possible because of the production of the female subject in relation to the maternal figure. I argued earlier that the identificatory relation to the maternal permits mobility of identifications. Crucially, it permits a non-phallic identification with other women, because it is possible to constitute a relation to others not through a relation to the father but through a relation to another woman, the mother. Because the paternal figure does not fix female identifications nor the phallic function define female subjectivity, the female subject has the structural possibility of a non-phallic relation to other women.

However, these primary affective relations invoke the incorporation of a relationship to another woman, rather than a loving pre-Oedipal symbiosis. This affective relationship does not reproduce pre-Oedipal maternal relations without symbolic mediation, since the subject is already produced as a subject and is therefore already within language. Rather, it reproduces the structure of maternal identification, such that the operation of primary identification constructs an affective relation to another subject. For this reason, a primary identification with other women reproduces the maternal relation in all its complexity and difficulty. That complexity and difficulty is evident in the conflict between self-described second-wave mothers and third-wave daughters (Detloff 1997).

A primary affective relation to other women does not itself produce a feminist subject. This relation does not guarantee or secure a political subject, because it does not necessarily produce political commitments to feminism. Third-waver Aminatta Forna points out that '[s]isterhood is not a natural bond or empathy, it simply requires a sufficient number of shared political concerns' (1999: 151). However, a primary identification permits a relation to other women that disrupts the operation of phallic identification, and thereby opens the subject to other possible models of the subject, including those of feminism. For this reason, it is possible to politicize that affective relation and then to reconstruct it as a political identification with feminism.

Freud's theory of intersubjective identification in *Group Psychology* provides a useful way to begin to elaborate the construction of those political identifications. In *Group Psychology*, Freud describes two forms of group identification: a vertical relation to the leader and a horizontal relation between the members of the group (1921: 124). For Freud, vertical identification secures the relation of the leader to the members of the group. Each member of the group adopts the perceived attributes of its leader, and in so doing replaces his or her ego-ideal with that of an idealized model of the leader. In this way, each member of the group comes to possess the same ego-ideal. Horizontal identification secures the relation between members of the group, as each member of the group identifies with the ego-ideal of other members.

However, the feminist movement cannot be said to have a leader of the type that Freud describes (that is, the prescribed, fixed status of a Pope of the Church or a General of the Army). Rather, it generally rejects 'leaders' because it insists upon an anti-hierarchical politics, in which 'groups' attempt to organize themselves within models of co-operative and collective decision-making. In this sense, feminism attempts to resist the vertical tie of group member to leader while emphasizing the horizontal tie between members of its communities. How then is it possible to account for the operation of identifications within the feminist movement?

Freud suggests that what he calls 'leading ideas' can serve in the place of the ego-ideal provided by the leader of a group, and as such can secure the inter-subjective relations of the members of a group (1921: 125). Drawing on Freud, Teresa Brennan suggests that a feminist 'body of writing' can serve as an ego-ideal (1986: 10). In terms of the subject, then, the 'leading ideas' of feminism can serve as the ego-ideal of the vertical tie of identification. The identification is with the political ideas of feminism. For example, bell hooks (1981) argues that many women of colour identify with and enact feminist ideas, even while disidentifying with second-wave feminism because of their perception of its racism. More recently, Rebecca Walker (1995a) put forward a similar argument in relation to her third-wave generation. Despite the complexity of naming them, there is a set of commitments or 'leading ideas' that the term 'feminism' represents. According to this model, each subject identifies with, and thus incorporates, these 'leading ideas' of feminist politics. In this way, the body of ideas that forms 'feminist politics' serves as the ego-ideal for the subject. They function as the object that the subject identifies with and 'wants to be like'. For example, Veronica Chambers offers a typical third-wave description of her encounter with feminist ideas, in which she discovers 'a context for my political existence. A vocabulary for my situation. An agenda to empower myself and others' (1995: 21).

However, Brennan suggests that this process is more complex than the assimilation of the abstraction called 'feminist politics'. Brennan perceives not only a body of ideas but also 'a person, people' as objects of feminist iden-tifications (1986: 10). For example, third-wave feminist Rebecca Walker describes how '[l]inked with my desire to be a good feminist was a deep desire to be accepted, claimed and loved by a feminist community that included my mother, godmother, aunts and close friends' (1995a: xxx). Functioning in a very concrete and literal way as role models, these people are also the objects of vertical ego-ideal identification. The subject takes both the ideas of the feminist movement and its members as identificatory objects. For example, Barbara Findlen notes in her introduction to the third-wave anthology, *Listen Up*, that many of the writers 'cite the writings and actions of older feminists as an integral part of their own development and beliefs' (1995a: xv). The vertical tie to a politics and to persons forms a feminist subject. In this way, the incorporation of those feminist politics and persons into the ego of the subject forms a feminist 'I'.

However, the feminist movement is not simply constituted by a series of identificatory ties of each member to an 'ideal'. The collective nature of a political movement implies more than each individual's commitment to a set of ideas or role model. It also implies that these individuals perceive themselves as members of a political movement and that these individuals identify with each other as members of that movement. This relation is an identification with the other members of the movement, as well as with the ideals that produce political engagement. There is, it seems, another 'emotional tie' at work in the feminist movement. How do we understand that emotional tie?

In his discussion of the psychology of the group, Freud argues that, in addition to the vertical tie of identification to the 'ideal', there is also a tie between group members. Freud argues that in this relation between group members, each member has '*put one and the same object in the place of their ego-ideal and have consequently identified themselves with one another in their ego*' (1921: 147). This horizontal tie between members of a group can be seen within the feminist movement. Members recognize others as 'feminists' because of a shared commitment to a political project. Each member identifies in others a shared ego-ideal of 'feminist politics'. In this sense, each subject has put 'one and the same object' – feminism – in the place of their ego-ideal and 'have consequently identified themselves with one another in their ego'. That identification creates a relation between subjects as members of a collective movement. For example, in the introduction to the anthology, *To Be Real*, Walker argues that 'these thinkers stake out an inclusive terrain from which to actively seek the goals of social equality and individual freedom they all share' (1995a: xxxv). These ego-ideal identifications construct both a feminist subject and its relation to other feminist subjects, forming a feminist 'we'.

Brennan suggests that the ego-ideal identification of feminists offsets the categorical imperatives of the patriarchal super-ego, which permits an evasion of the commands of the Father, and makes it possible to think 'outside' patriarchy (1986: 10). Certainly, it appears that a feminist ego-ideal displaces the patriarch's. However, the possibility of such a process also suggests that the Father's intervention may not be as effective as he would wish. If, as I have argued, the paternal super-ego is not necessarily effectively secured in, or does not secure, the formation of the female subject, its failure permits an evasion of its normative injunctions and hence creates a possibility of feminist ego-ideal identification.

In this model, feminist identifications take three forms. The first is an affective primary relation with other women. The second and third involve ego-ideal identifications with the 'ideals' of feminist politics and with others as members of a political movement. In Freudian terms, both horizontal and vertical ties form feminist subjects. An example of this process can be seen in Elissa Marder's description of the label 'feminist' as 'seemingly personally conferred (I declare myself a feminist) and collectively confirmed (I am acknowledged by others as participating in feminism)' (1992: 149). This personal conferral – 'I identify myself as' – and that collective confirmation – 'I identify myself with others and others identify me as' – produce feminist subjects and the relation between them.

If identification is 'the detour through the other that defines a self', then that process forms a feminist 'self'. Primary identification enables a feminist subject to engage with other women. It institutes a relation between female subjects, and enables a recognition of, as well as a relation to, other women. In this way, it enables feminists to identify with other women and to imagine a relation to them. Fuss describes how Fanon's psychoanalytic theory repeatedly calls for '"an ethics of mutual identifications" . . . a world of reciprocal recognitions' (1995: 144). The construction of an affective relation to other women provides the possibility of an ethics of mutual identifications with, and reciprocal recognitions of, other women.

The operations of ego-ideal identifications enable feminist subjects to recognize and imagine themselves as a political movement. After all, feminism is a movement of people, an imagined community that coheres in demonstrations, writing, meetings, actions, projects, conferences, and other forms of activism. The mechanism of ego-ideal identifications enables feminists to perceive themselves as members of a movement. The identifications of its members form this collectivity, both with the ideals of feminist politics and with other subjects identifying with those ideals. This political relation enables feminist conversations to take place, because it forms a feminist 'I' and a feminist 'we'. Therefore feminist subjects are not 'autonomous, self-making, self-determining subject[s]' (Alarcón 1994: 141). Rather, a relation to other subjects and to feminist politics produces feminist subjects.

Loving the self as other: imaginary identification

This description of identificatory relations between political subjects should not be mistaken for a second-wave 'sisterhood' of women united by their identity. Identificatory ties are a means of establishing both commonality and difference, which work to produce both unity with, and differentiation from, others. Lacanian theory provides a means of further understanding this complicated process. While drawing on the Freudian theory, Lacan's account provides a more complex distinction between imaginary and symbolic identification. This distinction enables us to understand the different identificatory processes at work in the production of feminist subjects, and to draw out the politics of feminist identifications.

Like Freud, Lacan recognizes the importance of identification in the formation of the subject, but inflects the Freudian theory through his own theory of the mirror stage. Malcolm Bowie points out that Lacan understands primary identification as being formed in the mirror stage, and accordingly emphasizes its narcissistic and egoistic aspects (1991: 33–34). For Lacan, the mirror stage can be understood '*as an identification*' which forms the ego-ideal and hence precipitates the ego (*É*: 2). For Lacan, identifications are always situated in the imaginary order because they reflect the ego's narcissistic perceptions.

This Lacanian theory is crucial to understanding feminist identifications because it describes the other side of identification – the desire of the ego that the other mirror the self.[10] Lacan argues that in imaginary identifications, the object is caught in the ego's *méconnaissance* or misrecognition of the other as self. The ego misrecognizes the other in its specular reflections, perceiving the other as identical to itself. The identificatory object is known only as the same as self, and with that misrecognition comes a refusal of difference. In a desire for sameness, the ego perceives only those qualities that are identical to it, so that it refuses difference in the object. The identificatory object functions not as an Other but as an imaginary counterpart, an other that the self imagines to reflect it.

Those imaginary misrecognitions can be seen at work in the feminist movement when a knower, while identifying with other women, does not perceive another woman's difference, but instead only her similarity. An example of a literal *méconnaissance* can be seen in Veronica Chambers's critique of Naomi Wolf's failure to 'see' the colour of her beauty myth (1995: 27). Such an imaginary identification produces the effect of a refusal to recognize the differences between women. In refusing the differences between women, imaginary relations do not recognize other identifications that women may themselves have. Rightly or wrongly, the third wave emerges from a perception of second-wave refusal of difference. It contends that feminism cannot reflect only the concerns of white, middle-class women, but must recognize 'the multiple, interpenetrating axes of identity' (Drake and Heywood 1997a: 3).

This refusal of the difference between women is symptomatic of the relation of aggressivity to, and mastery of, others of imaginary identification. In this relation to others, the self appropriates the other in an act of violence, reducing the other to an imaginary counterpart whose difference has been mastered. If the other insists upon her difference, the egoistic self greets her with hostility arising from an anxiety of difference. Such an identificatory operation 'is itself an imperial process, a form of violent appropriation in which the Other is deposed and assimilated into the lordly domain of self' (Fuss 1995: 145).

The relation of aggression to, and mastery of, the other can be seen in feminist identifications. For example, in 1981 bell hooks described how:

> as I moved from one women's group to another trying to offer a different perspective, I met with hostility and resentment. White women liberationists saw feminism as 'their' movement and resisted any efforts by non-white women to critique, challenge or change its direction.
>
> (1981: 190)

hooks's description of the aggression and hostility that greet her reveals the other side of feminist identifications. hooks describes imaginary perceptions of commonality that construct the feminist subject as 'white' and women of 'colour' as an other to the white feminist. When the 'other' insists on her difference, she is met with the aggression of an imaginary identification that seeks to master difference and reduce it to identity. Typically of the next feminist generation, Chambers (1995: 27) and Jee Yuan Lee (1995: 209) identify the aggression and fixity of such imaginary identifications as one of the most difficult problems facing the third-wave reconstruction of feminism.

However, Lee also points out that an acknowledgement of the multiple axes of oppression is crucial to the contemporary rearticulation of feminist politics (1995: 211). Because an imaginary relation to the other refuses to acknowledge the politics of the differences between women, it prevents that rearticulation. For example, Forna notes that currently 'middle-class women have the luxury and capability of deciding that feminism is over' (1999: 151). However, other groups of women cannot afford to make that decision (and indeed, one could argue that neither can middle-class women). Instead, Forna argues that a third wave of feminism 'will witness other groups of women, such as black, Asian and/or immigrant women, disabled women, impoverished women or mothers who still have concerns to be met, successfully recreating the movement in their own image' (1999: 150).

Without such a recreation, feminist politics will enact the imaginary mastery of an other which reproduces the social relations of power that enable a subject to enact that mastery. That reproduction does not challenge the operation of power within the feminist movement. Some feminists have more material and cultural capital than others, and some have racist, classist and homophobic relations to others. In her discussion of discursive competence, Sara Mills points out that 'factors (both actual and perceived) such as education, family background, age, gender, race, general self-confidence, knowledge-base, voice quality, past interactive experience, and others can lead to a person being interactionally in a position of power' (1992: 6). Of course, 'a person' includes women. The feminist movement is not exempt from the operations of power any more than the broader social world is, just as a feminist identification does not necessarily render its bearer less likely to reproduce social power. Social power enables some subjects rather than others to insist that it is their self, and not another, that constitutes feminism, and privileges certain identifications over others. In its refusal to recognize the politics of power within the feminist movement, imaginary identification condemns feminists to reproducing rather than resisting those politics of power.

A feminist identification that operates in the imaginary order thus reproduces the violence of contemporary social relations. It imagines the feminist movement as the relation of a woman to another identical to herself, rather than as formed in the negotiated relations between women. That woman treats her relation to other women with all the contempt that power gives – the power to refuse another's subjectivity. An imaginary feminist identification, which leads a subject to refuse the particularity and specificity of another subject, condemns her to participating in 'the same falsely universalizing pretensions as the masculine knowledge' (Lennon and Whitford 1994a: 3). In an identification in the imaginary register, 'feminism' shifts from being an identificatory object to being an object of idealization. It renders the discourses of feminism in the singular, feminisms as feminism, and the many feminist subjects as a universal 'feminist' subject. It fixes feminism in the narcissistic gaze of a subject, who is able to gaze at others in this way because the social order gives her the power to do so.

Such an act of aggression and mastery militates against an ethics of mutual recognitions. Without a recognition of the difference of an other, a feminist subject cannot have an ethical relation to that other. An ethical relation is not possible because the other is denied its existence as other and as such can exist only as the subject desires it to. Reciprocal relations require two subjects, not one. The other woman is not allowed to be herself, but only to reflect the self of the powerful subject. Imaginary identifications constitute the possibility of the recognition of, and relation to, others because they form relations between subjects. However, in the relation of self to other women, there also needs to be recognition of the alterity of the other woman. She must be recognized not only in her similarity and commonality but also in her difference and non-identity.

A symbolic relationship to the other: symbolic identification

Lacan proposes another form of identificatory relation besides that of narcissistic, imaginary incorporation: symbolic identification. For Lacan, identification in the symbolic register is both part of the formation of the subject, and a psychic process of the subject. As I described earlier in this chapter, for Lacan symbolic identification is a process of introjection of the *trait unaire* – the unitary trait – of the symbolic Father. In that process, the subject identifies with the phallic signifier as the mark of the Father, and thereby incorporates the Symbolic father as an *I* (Lacan 1964c: 256–257). In the later Lacanian theory of the four discourses, the phallic signifier is the master signifier – the signifier that represents the subject as subject.

However, in primary and secondary feminist identifications, there does not appear to be an introjection of the paternal signifier as a representative of the Father's Law. Therefore, either symbolic identification is absent from the production of the feminist subject, which condemns her to the narcissistic reflection of imaginary relations, or else it does operate, but not as an identification with the paternal signifier.

While Lacan proposes that symbolic identification is an assimilation of the paternal figure, he also describes it more generally as a process of introjection of a signifier. For this reason, it is possible to reformulate symbolic identification in these more general terms as the psychic assimilation of a symbolic element. That symbolic element is a master signifier, which shapes the structure of the discursive chain and produces the subject. Reformulating symbolic identification in this way permits us to understand its role in feminist identificatory relations, and to provide a fuller account of those relations. In particular, the reconception of this process of introjection of a master signifier further explains the operation of ego-ideal feminist identifications.

By using this concept of symbolic identification, we can understand how the ego-ideal identifications with feminist politics and persons are a process of introjecting the signifier 'feminism'. In that process, a subject identifies with the signifier 'feminism' and introjects it as an ego-ideal. This explanation provides a conceptual basis for Brennan's description of the feminist ego-ideal, because symbolic identification explains the process by which the subject assimilates the signifier 'feminism', thereby changing the paternal super-ego. Lacan argues that the master signifier represents the subject as a subject, both to itself and to others. Therefore, the horizontal tie of identification can be reformulated as a process in which 'feminism' functions as a signifier which represents the subject to itself and to other subjects, and by which those subjects recognize each other's signifier.

In this process of symbolic identification, the subject introjects the signifier 'feminism', and the signifying chains that attach to it. In that process, the subject enters those signifying chains of feminist discourses. By entering these discourses, a subject enters into a symbolic relation to other women. Symbolic identification permits the subject to engage in a process that exteriorizes affect in intersubjective dialogue. By incorporating feminist discourses, the subject is able to enter into a symbolic exchange between women. The signifying elements of these discourses provide the representational material for that exchange. This intersubjective dialogue renders in signification the affective identifications between women that form the nucleus of feminist identifications. Those affective relations shift from being an emotion of the individual subject to being a dialogue between subjects, and from object relations to subject relations. In this way, symbolic identification permits the subject to acknowledge the differences between herself and other subjects. It does not construct a relation between subjects as an imaginary desire for unity that entails a *méconnaissance* of others, but as the representation of the difference of an other that enables a relation to the other. Symbolic identification forms political relations that do not require that an other is loved as self, but rather that subjects engage with each other as speaking subjects.

Imaginary identification is a means of seeing the self in an other, and an other in the self. Symbolic identification marks an entry into discourse with the other. Discourse is a means of speaking with, and listening to, the other in intersubjective dialogue. Feminist discourses mediate the relations between women because they symbolize relations to others. In the recognition of the other as a speaking being, conversation can take place between two subjects who have equal entitlement to take up a position in a discursive exchange. Discursive exchange opens feminism to negotiation and thereby to change, rather than being frozen in imaginary relations.

If symbolic identification makes possible the recognition of an other woman, it also makes possible the recognition that at least two subjects participate in a dialogue. Importantly, that recognition moves past an ethics of reciprocal identification to a symbolic identification with the other as speaking subject. That shift constructs a collective that the negotiations of coalitional politics form. These intersubjective dialogues enable the articulation of new and different discursive social links between women.

If feminism is 'phantasmic', it is a phantasm that has political effect because it produces political subjects and collectivities. Feminist identifications are not established once and for all, but are constantly made and remade in the affective, imaginary and symbolic relations between women. However, this account also suggests that there is a link between symbolic relationships between women and the production of feminist discourse. In the next chapter, I explore this relationship by examining the discursive practices of feminist knowers and developing a model of feminist discourses.

4   Feminist discourses

Discursive stakes

From feminist theory to feminist discourse

For third-waver Veronica Chambers, feminism promises 'a context for my
political existence. A vocabulary for my situation. An agenda to empower myself and others' (1995: 21). This promise lies in the power of feminism to
represent our social world differently, and so to know our relation to ourselves
and our others differently. *How* feminist knowledges symbolize a different and
better world is a central question for feminist epistemology.

This question concerns the transformative 'nature' of feminist knowledge.
Drucilla Cornell stresses that '[p]art of political struggle is to shift reality
through shifting the meaning of our shared symbols. Politics is not just about
power but also about the very basis of what can become "real" and thus acces-
sible to consciousness and change' (1992: 68). If how the world is known makes
it 'real', then new knowledges permit the world to be known differently and
so potentially to change it. Feminist knowledges shift the meaning of 'our shared
symbols', politically reconfiguring those symbols and the symbolic field of
which they are a part. Feminist knowledge does not consist of a neutral process
of 'bringing' women into representation. Instead, it is a productive epistemic
practice that provides new representations.

While contemporary feminist theory has engaged with the 'discursive
problematic' (Fraser 1995: 157), for the most part it has not been taken up in
the field of feminist epistemology. Research in this area has not yet undertaken
a sustained examination of feminist knowledge as a system of signs. Such a
failure is ironic, given that feminist epistemology fundamentally concerns
women as knowers, that is, as the makers and users of signs. Many models
of feminist knowledge do not theorize signification in the sense that they
treat language as if it is a neutral and transparent representation of objects.[1] This
conception of language is surprising given that a standard feminist epistemological position is that systems of representations form the known object.
This position implies that a representational model of language is inadequate

because those systems of signs are neither neutral nor transparent. However, feminist epistemologies often do not explicitly address or develop the implications of this position.

Moreover, feminist epistemologies have yet to provide a model of feminist knowledge as a transformative practice, remaining largely prescriptive or silent on this point. Existing accounts either prescribe the normative practices which are necessary for the production of feminist knowledge, or assume that feminist work by its very nature produces a different form of knowing, rather than explicitly elucidating how feminist knowledge is able to change the way in which we know ourselves and our others. They have yet to provide a model of that practice, and of how that practice shifts how we understand the world.

Let us return, then, to a fundamental proposition of feminist epistemology: that feminist knowledge is a practice that *produces* meaning. Existing accounts of feminist knowledge commonly characterize it as a set of ideas or concepts that are practices of representation, in the sense that they give a particular meaning to the world. This formulation conceives feminist knowledge as a practice of signification. However, this formulation in turn raises four questions:

1   Do feminist knowledges represent a set of epistemic practices, and if so, do they share certain common features?
2   What is the nature of that practice?
3   How does it operate, that is, how does it have political effect?
4   How is it produced?

In this chapter, I explore possible answers to these questions by developing a model of feminist discourse. In Chapter 3, I suggested that Lacanian theory offers feminist epistemology a model of a transformative practice in its description of analytic discourse. This chapter uses Lacan's model of psychoanalytic discourse as a template to develop a theory of feminist knowledge as a transformative discursive practice.

Analytic discourse

In Lacan's model, the exclusion of 'an element of impossibility' founds and structures all discourse (S17: 50). Lacan represents that excluded term by an algebraic *a*. In analytic practice, the analysand recognizes the relation of his or her discourse to its excluded term *a*, such that the analysand recognizes the foundation of his or her discourse upon the exclusion of this term. That recognition is an act of symbolization, in which the analysand articulates the signifier of its otherwise excluded term (Fink 1999: 49). In psychoanalytic practice, the analysand represents the excluded signifier, so that it is not repressed but is inscribed in his or her signifying chain. The analysand's inscription of the signifier of the *a* changes the relation of symbolic elements in that signifying chain, so producing a new signifying chain. In this way, the analysand produces new meaning or signification. For feminist epistemology, the importance of the Lacanian theory of analytic discourse is that it provides a template that it can use to analyse other transformative discourses.

It could be argued that feminist epistemology cannot appropriate a Lacanian model of psychoanalytic knowledge because it derives from clinical practice. In this argument, any such appropriation either reduces feminist practice to psychoanalytic practice or relies on an unsustainable analogy between them. However, my use of Lacan's model as a template to theorize feminist discourse neither proposes nor relies upon an identity between feminist and psychoanalytic practices and knowledges. It does not claim that feminist knowledge is analytic knowledge in another mode, nor that feminist knowledge is able to be (or needs to be) produced in the clinical operations of resistance, transference, and so on. It is evident that the transferential relation of analyst and analysand does not produce feminist knowing. However, my use of the Lacanian model of knowledge does not rely on such an analogy between feminist and psychoanalytic practices because it reconfigures that model in the feminist field. As I argued in Chapter 2, rereading the Lacanian theory of analytic discourse through feminism positions that model within social and political relations. With this rereading, it becomes possible to use Lacanian theory to understand how feminist knowledge changes how we know ourselves and our others.

The Lacanian approach identifies three elements in an analysis of discourse:

1   the structure of signifiers of a given discourse, or, the common features of feminist knowledges;
2   the relation of the structure of the discourse to its repudiated and yet foundational term *a*, or, the nature of that discursive practice;
3   the operation of that discourse in the production of meaning, or, an account of its operation.

In the next section, I use this Lacanian model to understand how feminist knowledge operates as a discourse.

Feminist discourse

In the Lacanian account of language, the Symbolic order is that which literally orders an undifferentiated Real (*É*: 71–72).[2] An effect of that arrangement of signifiers is to 'cut' the Real, such that the Symbolic order structures signification of the Real in one way rather than another. In Lacan's later reformulation of the discursive operation of the Symbolic order, signification is structured so that it privileges certain discursive operations while excluding others. The Symbolic order delimits discursive operation because it inscribes certain subjects but not others, and certain social relations but not others.

However, it is that which the socio-symbolic order does not represent that puts feminism to work. In many different practices, feminist knowledges attempt to reinscribe the object as subject through the tropes of the 'impossible' feminine, the repressed maternal, the refused body, the banished other, a misrecognized difference, an 'unimaginable' utopia. As the third-waver Barbara Findlen describes it, feminism has named 'the problem that had no name':

> by the time that I was discovering feminism, naming had become a principle occupation of feminists. Everywhere you looked feminists were naming things – things like sexual harassment, date rape, displaced homemakers and domestic violence – that used to be called, as Gloria Steinem pointed out, just life.
>
> (1995a: xi)

In Lacanian terms, feminist knowledges represent that which the Symbolic order does not represent, and bring into the signifying order that which it previously refused.

Applying the Lacanian model, how then might we understand the structure of this discourse? In its most structural and minimal terms, we might say that feminist discourse represents the *a*, the excluded of discourse. We can represent existing discourse and its relationship to its excluded term like this:

Existing discourse: s-s-s-s-s-s | a

Feminism recognizes that the Other is lacking; that it excludes from its symbolic economy the *a*. Feminism sets the knower to work, and the product of that work is a new signifier. Feminist knowledges articulate the *a* and produce a new signifier.[3] This new symbolic element represents that which the signifying chain did not previously articulate, the *a*:

Feminist discourse: $a \rightarrow s_a$

Feminist knowledge affirms the existence of this excluded term, in an act that Freud (1925a: 438–439), and Lacan (S1: 57–58) following him, describe as a judgment of existence. By such a judgment 'we symbolically affirm the existence of an entity: existence is here synonymous with symbolization, integration into the symbolic order – only what is symbolized fully "exists"' (Zizek 1992: 136). It is possible, then, to describe a feminist act of knowing as an act of symbolization, which articulates the *a* of discourse in a judgment of existence. This symbolic affirmation gives the *a* existence, producing a new signifier.

In the Lacanian model, the inscription of a new signifier into the signifying chain produces new discourses. Because the differential relation of symbolic elements in the signifying chain produces meaning, its production is contingent upon a particular relationship of signifiers. However, the inscription of the excluded term reorders the relation of those symbolic elements. The insertion of the otherwise excluded term changes the previously closed order of these elements, creating a new discursive structure and so a new signifying chain. In this way, the analysand produces a new discourse and hence new meaning.

From this model, it is possible to understand how the feminist articulation of the *a* can produce a new discourse. In the operation of feminist discourse, the act of knowing inserts a new signifier into the existing structure of symbolic elements, and thus forms a new signifying chain:

$$\text{Feminist discourse:} \quad s_1 - s_2 - s_3 - s_4 - s_5 \;\; \leftarrow s_a$$

$$s_1 - s_2 - s_3 - s_4 - s_5 - s_6$$

The disruption and rearrangement of the prior signifying order produces a new relation of symbolic elements, and hence a new discourse. This new discourse produces new meaning, and hence a different representation of the world. This new representation of the world provides a new way to understand it. If knowing is a discursive practice, then the production of new discourses permits the creation of new knowledges by which to know the world.

My description of the structure of feminist discourse understands feminist knowledge as a signifying practice that produces meaning. It recognizes that '[m]eaning is always political . . . all meanings have implications for existing social relations, contesting them, affirming them or leaving them intact' (Weedon 1987: 138). One of the most powerful examples of this operation of feminist discourse can be found in the contestatory naming of gendered harms, such as domestic violence and sexual harassment. In the 1970s, the feminist movement began to name the sexual violence many women experienced, but which was perceived neither as a political issue nor as being related to gender politics. This naming is the signification of the *a* of discourse, because it represents a violence against women which had previously not been articulated. The naming of gendered harms produces a signifier of an otherwise unsignified *a* of social discourses. For example, in her discussion of street harassment and African-American women, Deirdre Davis argues that '[i]n order to address, deconstruct, and eradicate a harm, we must give the harm a name' (1997: 200). This naming of the *a* is then inscribed into the signifying chains of social discourses, which produces a new signifying chain, or knowledge, around the issue of gendered harms. In this way, feminism produces new discourses of gendered harms that fundamentally shift the social meaning of sexual violence.

One specific example of the creation of a new feminist discourse of gendered harms can be seen in the area of law reform. In both the US and the UK, over the last two decades feminist campaigners have achieved a number of significant changes to both substantive definitions of sexual assault, such as the legality of marital rape, and the evidential rules of the trial process, such as the admissibility of the prior sexual history of the complainant (Lees 1997: xiv). Similarly, the recent recognition of sexual assault as a war crime in international law can be traced to feminist activism in this area (Cleiren and Tijssen 1996: 265). These legal reforms reflect what Nicola Lacey calls 'a genuine change in the cultural climate' regarding sexual violence (1998: 101). The feminist naming of rape as a gendered harm changes the legal and social meaning of that act, and inscribes that change into broader cultural discourses of sexual violence.

The example of the naming of gendered harms shows how Lacan's model of analytic discourse can lead to a new understanding of feminist knowledge as a discursive practice, and how that practice produces new discourses. However, that template derives from a particular field of practice: Lacanian psychoanalysis. In contrast, feminist discourses consist of many different disciplines and methods, theories and activisms. Given the heterogeneous nature of feminism, is it possible to speak of 'feminist discourse' in the way that Lacan speaks of 'psychoanalytic discourse'? Or does such an approach reduce the heterogeneity of feminist epistemic practices to a singular feminist knowledge, thereby failing to acknowledge the plurality of the field?

If my model of feminist discourse was concerned only with providing an account of propositional knowledges, that is, with an account of the content of truth-claims, then such an argument could have merit. Given the contentious debates within feminism concerning its foundational propositions (such as the nature of gender for example), it is not possible to argue that all feminists make the same truth-claims. However, this model of feminist knowledge takes from Lacanian theory an emphasis upon the analysis of symbolic structures of discourses, not their substantive content. It focuses upon the description of the signifying structures of discourse – namely, how those structures give meaning to the known object, shape the relationship of the knower to that object, and produce the relation between the knower and other subjects.

This focus upon discourse provides a means of understanding feminist knowledge as symbolic practice. On the one hand, it permits the analysis of specific feminist knowledges as discursive practices because it enables us to examine particular instances of feminist knowledges and to analyse how they work in that specific case. On the other hand, it also permits the construction of general models of feminist knowledges. This more general approach enables the development of a theory of feminist discourse that can be applied across the diverse areas of feminist praxis. This broad application is necessary for a feminist epistemology to be useful: a feminist social worker should find a theory of feminist knowledge as useful as a lecturer in Women's Studies. Because of its focus upon the structure of discourse, the Lacanian template provides a means of developing such a model for feminism.

Discourses of knowledge

> In the final analysis, there's nothing but that, the social link.
>
> (Lacan S20: 54)

However, using the Lacanian template to understand feminist knowledge shifts it from the psychoanalytic to the feminist field. Following Freud, Lacan rejects the notion that psychoanalysis provides a world view (S20: 30). While it is not a task of psychoanalysis to provide an account of social relations, feminist epistemology needs to do so for political and epistemological reasons. First, feminism's political analysis assumes a particular understanding of social relations. Second, theories of feminist knowledge propose that knowing is both a social and a political practice. For these reasons, a feminist theory of knowledge needs to be able to provide an account of discourse as a social and as a political practice. Therefore, we need to consider whether Lacan's model of analytic discourse provides, or can be developed to provide, a theory of, first, discourse as a social practice and, second, discourse as a political practice.

For Lacan, knowing is a social practice in the sense that relations between subjects produce it. However, Lacan does not provide an account of how analytic knowledge is a social practice other than by characterizing it in this way. That is, Lacan does not provide a social theory of discourse. Moreover, we should not expect such an account, as Lacan's theory is psychoanalytic and not sociological. Nevertheless, Lacan's work presents a theory of the social, even if he does not develop it as a social theory. The issue is not whether Lacan's work has a theory of the social, since it undoubtedly does. Rather, the issue is whether it provides an adequate social theory for a feminist theory of knowledge. Therefore, it is necessary to consider, first, what notion of sociality subtends Lacan's model of psychoanalytic discourse, and, second, whether that notion of sociality is adequate for a model of feminist discourse.

In the later epistemology of the four discourses, Lacan repeatedly characterizes discourse as 'a social link (*lien social*), founded on language' (S20: 17). In his later work, discourse functions as the social link because it produces relationships between subjects (S20: 54). While the theory of the four discourses provides a complex and sophisticated exploration of relationships between subjects, it does not provide an account of social relationships. For example, he does not sufficiently explain the relationship between discourse and the social 'link', and the nature of the discursive social bond and its production remain unclear. While Lacan characterizes discourse as a form of social relation, he does not elaborate its specifically social dimensions.

This failure to elaborate the social relation in his theory of the four discourses does not stem from an absence of a concept of the social. Rather, it results from the later notion of the social bond of discourse resting on the earlier concept of the Symbolic order. For example, the Discourse of the Master reformulates the operation of the paternal metaphor described in *Écrits* (*É*: 221), in that it elaborates the production of the subject in its identification with the paternal signifier. In this way, it rests on the earlier account of the production of the subject in the Symbolic order of the Law of the Father.

The concept of the social link of discourse draws upon the earlier theory of the Symbolic order, in which the symbolic structures of language produce subjectivity and intersubjectivity. The 'social link' is not merely any social relation, but a relationship between subjects that the Symbolic order founds. For Lacan, the subject is always a speaking subject that comes into being in the social link of language. In *Écrits*, Lacan argues that '[m]an speaks, then, but it is because the symbol has made him man' (*É*: 72). 'Man' becomes a speaking being in the Symbolic order of language. Lacan repeats this thesis in his later work on discourse, where he declares that 'there's no other way to designate it once we realize that the social link is instated only by anchoring itself in the way in which language is situated over and etched into what the place is crawling with, namely, speaking beings' (S20: 54). For Lacan, the Symbolic order of language founds the 'social link' of discourse, that is, the relationship between subjects.

Lacan's theory of the four discourses therefore understands the social through the concept of the Symbolic order. However, Lacan does not develop his concept of the social relation in the later work of the four discourses, which relies on this earlier concept of the Symbolic. Given that the later notion of the discursive social relation rests upon this concept, it is necessary to return to his earlier account of sociality.

In the papers of *Écrits*, Lacan draws on the structuralist linguistics of de Saussure (1916) and the structuralist anthropology of Lévi-Strauss (1958, 1967) for his argument that the Law of the Father that founds language as a symbolic structure also founds social structure. Lacan takes the notion of kinship structures from the work of Lévi-Strauss to argue that social relations are formed in a fundamental prohibition against consanguinity. Lacan reworks that anthropological theory of culture as a psychoanalytic account of the Oedipal subject. For Lacan, this prohibition establishes the Law of the Father as the law against incestuous desire for the mother, which founds culture as structures of symbolic exchange. In the Law of the Father, the father appears as the bearer of cultural law and woman as sign of cultural exchange (*É*: 72–74). These structures of cultural, linguistic and sexual exchange constitute the Symbolic order.

Louis Althusser argues that Lacan's concept of the Symbolic order is 'the most original part of Lacan's work' because it shifts our account of the human subject from the order of the biological to the order of the signifier (1996: 25). However, if the Symbolic order encapsulates Lacan's understanding of sociality, he presents it as a series of propositions about the nature of the social rather than developing it as a social theory. Typically, Lacan expects his readers to simply accept his account, and does not provide a substantial argument concerning its adequacy. This rhetorical move does not prevent a Lacanian theory of the social world from being compelling, but it does prevent a satisfactory rendering of the nature of sociality in Lacan's work.

A typical example of the weakness of Lacan's account of the social can be seen in his conception of the Symbolic order within *Écrits* and the later seminars. In these texts, the symbolic, the social and language function as co-extensive terms. Lacan does not offer clear definitions of their distinctive content, nor does he explain their relation to each other or to other social phenomena. The operation of these terms as conceptual synonyms leaves us with a speculative sketch of three foundations of the social order. This speculative sketch collapses social order into Symbolic order, and Symbolic order into linguistic order.

One effect of the collapse of these key concepts is that Lacan's concept of the social does not address the complexities of social relations but instead presents them as homogenous. For this reason, Peter Dews rightly argues that the concept of the Symbolic order ignores the relations of domination and oppression within the social world (1987: 105–106). For example, the Lacanian account does not address the operations of power upon and within discourse. The theory of the four discourses understands discursive relations between subjects as horizontal, such that each subject is equally powerful. Yet clearly certain subjective positions are more socially powerful than others, and certain persons are more easily able to take up those positions of power.

A stronger account of the social is necessary for Lacan's notion of the Symbolic to function as an adequate social theory. For example, such an account would consider the relationship between the Oedipal family and society, as Lacan recognizes in *Family Complexes* (1938). However, this 'sociological reference' implies that a psychoanalytic social theory needs to understand those family complexes not only in terms of sexuality but also ethnicity and class. Without an account of the Symbolic order as social order, the Lacanian theory reduces it to narratives of founding myths. The Symbolic order comes to function as a foundational myth which functions as the condition of the subject and culture. Butler rightly argues that if understood as a transcendental structure, the Symbolic functions as a 'presocial law . . . the law of the Father, which sets limits upon the variability of social forms and which, in its most conservative form, mandates an exogamic, heterosexual conclusion to the Oedipal drama' (2000a: 75). Understanding the Symbolic order in this way refuses the possibility that existing social relations can shift. For example, if the Symbolic determines the social, and that Symbolic is unchanging, then can how we explain social change itself?

For feminist epistemology, a particular problem of a notion of a transcendental Symbolic order is how to explain the emergence of contestatory politics, such as feminist or queer theory. Contestation and change are evidently possible, and so an account of the social needs to address those possibilities. However, for Lacan it appears that the only escape from the Discourse of the Master is psychoanalytic practice and theoretical formalization (such as the matheme). In Lacanian theory, contestatory knowledge is psychoanalytic and subversion emerges from each individual's psychoanalysis. If we follow Lacan to the letter, then it seems a critical or collective politics outside psycho-analysis will fail. In contrast, feminism *is* a collective politics that contends that it is possible to create knowledges that do not reproduce the Discourse of the Master.

Lacan does not intend his psychoanalytic theory to be a social theory. Nevertheless, his work presents a series of explicit and implicit claims as to the nature of the social in its account of the Symbolic order. The problem for feminist epistemology is that because Lacan presents these claims rather than elaborating them as a social theory, he reduces his account of the social to the concept of the Symbolic, and this concept does not address the heterogeneous, complex and changing nature of the social world, and ignores the politics of power and resistance.

This failure to provide an adequate social theory produces a correlative problem in Lacan's theory of discourse. While Lacanian knowledge is by definition a social practice, his work presents an unelaborated concept of sociality. For this reason, Lacan does not develop the radical implications of his epistemological theory. Rather, this theory of knowledge removes the knowing subject and knowledge from their social frame and so fails to address their social and political production, a central contemporary epistemological concern (Doyle McCarthy 1996). Linda Alcoff and Elizabeth Potter argue that 'to be *adequate*, an epistemology must attend to the complex ways in which social values influ-ence knowledge' (1993a: 13). In this sense, Lacanian epistemology does not present an adequate account of knowledge as a social practice. A theory of feminist knowledge requires a more complex account of the social than Lacan's unelaborated notion of the Symbolic order.

For the Lacanian model of analytic discourse to be useful for a theory of feminist knowledge requires a reformulation of the concept of the Symbolic order in order to address its theoretical flaws and to resist its conservative implications. In the next section, I address these problems in the theory of the Symbolic order, using two strategies. The first elaborates the theory of the Symbolic order through Lacan's later concept of discursive intersubjectivity. The second develops this Lacanian theory of the social relation through a feminist theory of social relations. These two strategies represent the first part of a rereading of the Symbolic order as a social order.

Social fictions

'Who is speaking?'

(*É*: 331)

Discourses of the social

Like its more traditional forms, contemporary social theory continues to look to psychoanalysis for an account of the subject. From the 'Freud' of Critical Theory to the 'Lacan' of Althusser, Marxism has deployed psychoanalysis as a theory of the subject to supplement its materialist explanation of the social. Similarly, feminism has used 'psychoanalysis for an account of how ideologies are imposed upon subjects and how female identity is acquired' (Rose 1986: 15). This supplementary appropriation of psychoanalysis can be seen most recently in the work of Judith Butler, who draws on both Freudian and Lacanian accounts of the subject to augment Foucault's theory of social power (Campbell 2001: 41).

To develop Lacanian theory as a social theory, it is necessary to reconsider that use of psychoanalysis. Rather than regarding Lacanian psychoanalysis as a theory of the subject that can supplement an already existing notion of 'society', a more productive approach is to develop a social theory from Lacanian psychoanalysis, since the Lacanian account of the subject rests on a theory of the social. The Lacanian account of subjectivity contains within it a theory of intersubjectivity because it provides an account of the production of relation between subjects.

However, in his later work Lacan characterizes 'intersubjectivity' as an imaginary relation between subjects. By the 1960s, the concept of intersubjectivity acquires negative connotations, as Lacan associates it with the imaginary and dual relation of two selves trapped in the *méconnaissance* of their egos (Evans 1996: 90). Lacan develops his critique of this imaginary intersubjectivity from the Hegelian account of the battle for recognition between the master and the slave. Zizek points out that '[w]hat the late Lacan does with intersubjectivity is to be opposed to the early Lacan's Hegelo-Kojèvian motifs of the struggle for recognition' (1998b: 194). Zizek counterposes the intersubjective character of fantasy – the imaginary relation to the other as object – and the field of intersubjectivity of the symbolic Other (1998b: 195–196). This later account of the symbolic field of intersubjectivity differs from the Hegelian model of imaginary recognition. An example of Lacan's concept of symbolic intersubjectivity is found in his description of the transference between analyst and analysand. In the relation between analyst and analysand, there is always a third party – that of language as the order of culture which intervenes in the imaginary relation. This third party is the Symbolic order, a symbolic relation between subjects.

The Symbolic order represents a symbolic rather than an imaginary relation between subjects. The Symbolic is 'a point beyond the specular oscillation of intersubjective rivalry – a purely symbolic point' (Lechte 1996: 12). The Symbolic order forms the subject and its relations to others. In this formulation, Lacan presents a model of intersubjectivity in which language constructs the relation between subjects. In this sense, intersubjectivity implies a symbolic relation between subjects that makes possible their social relation. The theory of the four discourses is an example of such a model of intersubjectivity, as the four discourses describe the foundational discursive bonds between subjects. This formulation reflects a classical concept of intersubjectivity in critical theory, drawing upon its most minimal formulation as a relation *between* subjects.

The concept of symbolic intersubjectivity offers a means of rereading the Symbolic order through the later theory of discourse. The later theory shifts its emphasis from the Symbolic as a monolithic and closed structure to the open and incomplete nature of both discourse and the Symbolic order. For Lacan, discourse always produces a remainder, which represents its foundational and excluded term, as '[n]o matter how many signifiers one adds to the signifying chain, the chain is always incomplete; it lacks the signifier which could complete it' (Evans 1996: 96). An excluded term structures discourse because there is a lack in its foundation, the Symbolic order. With this poststructuralist inflection, we can use Lacan's later work on discourse to reformulate a concept of the Symbolic order that does not imply that it is a singular or total structure of language, and so to develop from it a feminist and psychoanalytic social theory.

The theory of the four discourses reconceives the Symbolic order as producing different discursive structures, giving more complexity to the account of the symbolic relations between subjects. It permits us to reformulate the concept of the Symbolic order as a mobile system of signifying chains – or discourses – which produce social relations and subjects. This model of the Symbolic order accepts Lacan's proposition that it founds the stable structures of discourse. However, it also proposes that these stable structures take different discursive forms, which in turn produce different symbolic forms of subjectivity and intersubjectivity. In this way, I develop the concept of the Symbolic order to describe the structure and operation of social discourses; and their production of subjects and social relations.

My reformulation of the notion of the Symbolic order retains the later Lacanian conception of discourse as constructing possible subjective positions and discursive acts. However, it emphasizes the productivity of discourses, in the sense that it emphasizes their production and reproduction in subjective and intersubjective discursive practices, rather than being fixed or frozen structures that are imposed upon the subject. In this way, it understands discourse as constitutive of, and articulated in, subjectivity and intersubjectivity; as producing and being reproduced by subjects and the relations between them.

This discursive conception of the Symbolic order permits the development of my account of feminist discourse as a social and political practice. However, to develop such an account requires the further elaboration of the Lacanian theory of discourse through the reinscription of social relations. In particular, a feminist social theory needs to address social relations of gender, sexuality, class and ethnicity as dominant social discourses of subjects and the relation between them. In the next section, I elaborate Lacanian theory as a feminist social theory by using the concept of the 'social fiction'. Nancy Fraser claims that in the Lacanian model of discourse, 'one cannot even pose the question of cultural hegemony' (1992: 184). However, by using the concept of the social fiction it is possible not only to pose the question of cultural hegemony using Lacan's model of discourse, but also to see the productivity of its answer.

Social fictions

What is a social fiction? It is a social discourse of subjectivity and inter-subjectivity. My concept of the social fiction draws upon Kaja Silverman's 'dominant fiction'. Silverman uses the term 'dominant fictions' (itself from Ranciere) to describe dominant social representations of subjectivity, using an Althusserian model of ideology to explain how they function as interpellatory identifications (1992b: 15–51). However, I do not work with Silverman's notion of the 'dominant fiction', but instead draw upon it to develop my own concept of 'social fictions' for two reasons. First, while Althusser's work informs how I understand 'social fictions', it does not ground it; not only because of the well-rehearsed problems in his work, but also because of my focus upon the Lacanian theory of discourse rather than the Symbolic order (as in Althusser's account). Second, my concern is not only with accounts of the production of the subject but also of its relationship to other subjects. My concept of the 'social fiction' emphasizes the formation of subjectivity and intersubjectivity in social discourses. This concept stresses the social and ultimately fictive nature of social discourses, which are fictional in the sense that they are contingent upon a symbolic field that gives them meaning. The concept focuses upon the discursive production of forms of subjectivity and the relations between subjects, developing the Lacanian theory of discourse as a description of the structure and operation of social discourses.

This concept of 'social fictions' describes the dominant social discourses that constitute a subject, such that the term names the multiplicity of socially produced and sanctioned ideas about how one 'is' a subject. A social fiction is a socio-symbolic representation of subjective identity. Social fictions work to produce a subject as subject, with a gendered and racialized identity. With that identity, a subject (mis)recognizes itself in particular dominant signifiers of social discourses. Dominant social fictions include discourses of ethnicity, sexuality, class and gender. As discursive formations, social fictions produce the speaking position of subjects. They represent an enunciative position, for example, 'I am Scottish', or 'I am a woman', and so on. This *I* of the speaking subject is an imaginary position of consciousness or 'self'. These social fictions produce a subject's relation to itself and its others, and so enable the subject to think of itself as a self and as distinct from, or the same as, its others. As an *I*, the subject experiences itself as a unified self that possesses identity.

However, the production of the identity of the subject in social fictions generates not only its relation to itself, but also its relations to other subjects. For example, in the Lacanian schema, the Discourse of the Master describes a relation of mastery of 'self' and others. In this way, social fictions can be understood as a symbolic relation of subject to other subjects. Social fictions represent the discursive relation of the subject to itself and to other subjects, because their discourses are socio-symbolic representations of subjectivity and intersubjectivity.

In the Lacanian model, master signifiers 'dominate' discourses, holding a discourse together and giving it a distinctive shape by ordering its structure of signifiers. The subject takes up a speaking position according to the master signifier of its discourse (in the Lacanian model, that of Master, Hysteric, Analyst and Academic). I understand social fictions as discourses, which a dominant signifier structures and gives its distinctive shape. Social fictions operate as a sequence of master signifiers that, as Mark Bracher describes, have other signifiers attaching to them in metonymic and metaphorical movement of signification (1993: 49). Every social fiction has a discursive structure, and a dominant master signifier that produces the subject.

The master signifier functions as the interpellative 'hook' of subjective identity, since it represents that moment at which the subject (mis)recognizes itself in social fictions. The master signifier enables the subject to perceive itself reflected (or otherwise) in social discourse. This identificatory and phantasmic 'interpellation' gives social fictions their power – for subjects literally recognize themselves or, in Althusserian terms, are 'hailed' by social discourses of identity. The master signifier serves as a mechanism of identification with social fictions, and so as a mechanism of psychic and social identification.

Master signifiers enable the subject to represent its self to itself and also to other subjects. As social subjects, we recognize the master signifiers of other subjects, whether similar or different to our own, because the master signifier represents the subject for another subject. In this way, master signifiers serve to anchor social fictions as discourses, both in the production of the subject and in the production of its relation to other subjects. In this way, this notion of the 'social fiction' reworks the Lacanian conception of discourse as a social bond in terms of socio-symbolic relations between subjects.

As discourses, social fictions produce meaning, as well as relations between subjects. While Lacan emphasizes the fundamental ambiguity and mobility of the signifier, he also argues that the discursive tie of signifier to signified produces meaning (S20: 30). The social bond of discourse knots together words and concepts, which enables the circulation of symbolic elements between those who speak (S20: 30). This discursive link is the social relation that fixes meaning, because it makes meaning both possible and stable. Because discourse constitutes the intersubjective structure of social relations, it enables the otherwise arbitrary symbolic element to have meaning not only to the subject but also to other subjects. In discourse, these elements come to take on meaning, because 'the signifier as such refers to nothing if not to a discourse, in other words, a mode of functioning or a utilization of language qua link' (S20: 30). As discourses, social fictions therefore momentarily 'fix' meaning by constructing a link between the signifier and signified. They enable subjects to give meaning to themselves and to their others. That meaning is secured within the discursive structures of social fictions.

However, social fictions should not be misunderstood as a neutral representation of subjectivity and intersubjectivity. Anthony Elliot argues that Lacan's account of the arbitrary nature of the sign 'fails to explain how some ideological and political meanings predominate over others in the personal sphere' (1996: 182). However, Lacanian theory reveals how the otherwise arbitrary relation between signifier and signified comes to be fixed in the Symbolic order. One of the strengths of the Lacanian account of discourse is that it draws out the relation between the Symbolic order and discourse, emphasizing that the phallic signifier structures the signifying chains of discourse. The Symbolic order is the foundational symbolic economy of a social order, and that symbolic logic produces discourses. For this reason, certain discourses dominate the multitude of social discourses, since they represent overdetermined socio-symbolic relations. These socially dominant relations are social fictions, representing the particular ways to be social subjects that the Symbolic order prescribes and regulates. Comprised of signifying networks of master signifiers, social fictions are overdetermined and powerful representations of subjects and their relations to others. Social fictions are culturally dominant representations of how to be a subject and how to exist as a subject in relation to other subjects.

Lacan links what he describes as the dominant discourse of our age – the Discourse of the Master – to the rise of capitalism and the modern ego (S17: 207), indicating that discourses are historically and culturally specific. Accordingly, social fictions can be understood as historically and culturally specific forms of the Symbolic order, which articulate particular historical and cultural discourses. Judith Butler offers a useful reading of the Symbolic order as 'a register of regulatory ideality', which includes not only sexualized but racialized interpellations (1993b: 18). For Butler, the Symbolic produces 'regulatory norms' which demarcate and delimit forms of family, identity and love (1997b: 66). It represents 'reigning epistemes of cultural intelligibility' (1997b: 24), suggesting that it is a set of cultural rules which constitute social norms. However, in this formulation, the Symbolic remains a closed and monolithic structure that produces a single normative subject. Such a conception of the Symbolic does not explain the many discourses of identity, or their historical specificity – which are precisely the grounds of Butler's critique of the Lacanian notion of the Symbolic.

'Social fictions' help us to understand the 'register of regulatory ideality' as a discursive register of social fictions, as discourses of identity that produce it through the identification with master signifiers of sexualized and racialized subjectivity. The Symbolic order also produces racialized and sexualized relations *between* subjects, operating as a register of regulatory *relations*. While the Symbolic order structures discourses in terms of the production of sexualized and racialized subjects and intersubjective relations, the 'content' of those identities and social relations will be historically and culturally articulated as social fictions. Social fictions are therefore specific to a historical moment of that social order. In this way, social fictions are contingent in the sense that they represent particular cultural and historical forms of the discursive production of identity. If social fictions are contingent and mobile, then they are open to political contestation and change.

Discourses of the subject

How do discourses produce subjective identity? In his later work on the four discourses, Lacan suggests that symbolic identification with a master signifier produces the subject. As I discussed in Chapter 3, the master signifier is a symbolic element that represents the subject to itself and to other subjects. It is the 'unifying' trait which constitutes the subject and which functions as the *signifiant-m'être*, that signifier which masters the subject. This represents, in Lacan's account, the signifier of my 'being' (S17: 178). Identification with that master signifier which 'names' the subject produces it within discourse, and so produces its speaking position. In this reformulation of the Oedipus complex, the imaginary *I* becomes the social *I* of identity in its identificatory attachment to those master signifiers which structure the signifying chains of discourse.

This account of subject formation explains how the Freudian bodily ego becomes a social identity. In Lacanian theory, a symbolic representation of the imaginary morphology of the ego of the mirror stage produces the subject as a 'self'. This symbolic representation is articulated through the master signifiers of the Symbolic order that enable the subject to experience itself as a self – as an *I* of identity. Identification with the master signifiers of social fictions produces that experience of self. Social fictions are both imaginary and symbolic. In social fictions, the Symbolic order is given content by the imaginary: 'at the level of the Imaginary, the subject believes in the transparency of the Symbolic; it does not recognize the lack of reality in the Symbolic . . . in effect, the Imaginary is where the subject mis-recognises (*méconnait*) the nature of the

Symbolic' (Lechte 1994: 68–69). Social fictions reproduce the Symbolic order because the production of the subject in identification with its master signifiers gives the fictional Symbolic order 'flesh' and so 'life'.

The discourses of social fictions produce subjects through a process of introjection of their master signifiers. If discourse produces the subject, it cannot be separate from the subject but must be integral to subjective formation. Through that formation, the subject comes to have imaginary relations of phantasy and identification to its symbolic master signifiers and hence to discourse. Psychic mechanisms operate to produce the subject in relation to discursive master signifiers and, in particular, to the social fictions of identity that they represent. Identification with the master signifiers of discourse constitutes subjects, since that is how the subject becomes a subject.

While the Lacanian model addresses the sexuation of the subject, this conception of the social fiction includes other master signifiers of identity, such as sexuality, ethnicity or class. Butler points out that it is necessary to recognize that 'the order of sexual difference is not prior to that of race or class in the constitution of the subjects; indeed that the symbolic is also at and at once a racializing set of norms, and that norms of realness by which the subject is produced are racially informed conceptions of "sex"' (1993b: 130). Social fictions represent discourses of social identity that intersect in overdetermined master signifiers. The theory of social fictions enables us to understand how discourses reproduce the racialized and sexualized subject and intersubjective relations of the Symbolic order.

As a discourse, social fictions rest on a foundational and excluded term *a*. This excluded term is a discursive construct, since it is produced by the operations of social fictions. Social fictions of identity rest on the positing of difference – 'I am a man (because I am not a woman).' The assertion of difference is itself filled with imaginary content: 'If I am a man (because I am not a woman), then I must possess this set of associated masculine qualities.' In this way, the positing of identity in social discourses is productive because those discourses describe practices which signify how 'to be' a subject. At the same time, that 'being' rests on the production of a repudiated other – 'I am not a woman' – for social fictions rest on symbolic relations of identity and non-identity. The repudiated other functions as the foundational and excluded term *a*. Social fictions themselves produce the repudiated term – for that repudiation founds their signifying structure. For example, the social fictions of masculinity rest on the excluded and foundational term of the feminine – a masculine subject defines itself in terms of another which is castrated. The 'castrated' 'feminine' functions as the excluded *a*. We can see other examples of the operation of social fictions in Drucilla Cornell's description of the production of 'white' identity that is founded on its repudiated other of 'black' identity (1992: 67), and Butler's description of a 'heterosexual' identity that rests on a repudiated 'homosexual identification' (1993b: 111).

This production of the subjective identity in social fictions is a complex process of identification and disidentification, positive and negative inter-pellation. For example, Tina Chanter points out that black, gay or working-class bodies do not comply with the dominant discourses of racially or sexually marked subjects (1997: 45). Those identities do not stand 'outside' social fictions, but instead are interpellated in particular ways in relation to identities presented by socially dominant discourses. For, although social fictions describe dominant identities, they also construct other subjective positions such as a 'black', 'gay' or 'working-class' subject in relation to those socially dominant identities.

However, it is not only dominant cultural discourses that produce identity. Within multicultural societies, there may be many different discourses of identity, which represent masculinity or femininity in different ways. Social fictions both produce dominant subjects and represent subjects of other social groups in relation to them. However, representations of identity in those social groups also form those subjects, and those representations themselves are neither homogenous nor monolithic (Patel 1998). Social fictions are not seamless and unitary, but multiple and contradictory. For example, Gloria Anzaldúa argues that for the Hispanic lesbian markers of 'identity' often conflict, and that 'self' is negotiated in those conflictual identificatory demands (1987: 77–91). Anzaldúa describes a process in which master signifiers of the subject – those markers of 'self' – produce a subject with multiple discursive interpellations. Anzaldúa's account is in clear contrast to the white bourgeois and heterosexual masculine subject whose markers of identity seem to 'match' the master signifiers of social fictions of modern Western society.

The subject is produced in both personal and social histories that are fundamentally imbricated. In this way, social fictions are discourses of both the subjective and the social, because an imaginary and symbolic relation to other subjects always produces the subject. This description of the subject draws on the Lacanian psychoanalytic insight that the psychic and the social are moments of each other, produced in the basic 'nature' of humans not to be natural. However, the concept of the social fiction does not imply the liberal idea of the social contract in which individual subjects of consciousness agree at a mythical moment of origin to enter rational social arrangements. Rather, it retains the Lacanian insistence that there is no pre-discursive reality since the world is always already inscribed in discourse (S20: 32). For Lacan, discourse 'upholds' the reality of the world, or at least the world which we know (S17: 13). The subject does not therefore emerge into a neutral social world but is inserted into already existing social relations. Social fictions exist prior to the subject and its very existence is contingent upon them.

Social fictions are discursive relations between subjects that have material effect because they are 'lived' by subjects. This material effect can be seen in the operations of fictions of gender. For example, while the Symbolic order is a symbolic relation between subjects, the phallic signifier orders that relation, positing some subjects as having the phallus and others as not having it. At this symbolic level, the possession or absence of the phallus defines subjects. However, at a discursive level, the symbolic relation is filled with content as to the 'nature' of sexed identity. The social fictions of 'masculinity' and 'femininity' attach respectively to a subject with or without the phallus. The fictions of gender interpellate male and female bodies as masculine and feminine subjects, so that it fixes the contingency of the relation between phallus and penis. The fictions of gender render penis, phallus and masculinity as male subjectivity. In the Western social world, the phallus is a signifier that proliferates in a multitude of discourses of masculinity, which in turn produce a number of recognizably 'masculine' subjects. Male subjects can recognize themselves as 'masculine', and equally importantly, other subjects are able to recognize them as 'masculine'.

Social fictions are symbolic relations that have material effects, and those material effects give substance, reality and existence to these symbolic relations between subjects. Jane Gallop points out that it is not just the referentiality of phallus/penis that produces 'masculinity' but also the social arrangements that attach power of many forms to the masculine subject (1988: 53). The social world of the fictions of gender is still riven with material and structural inequality for women. That world is one in which the fictions of gender are lived, so that women are inserted into already existing (inequitable) gender arrangements. For example, there are social sanctions against those who fail to enact their assigned fiction of gender. The social fiction of gender operates such that even if a female subject were to want to take up a 'masculine' position, she would find innumerable difficulties in doing so. These difficulties arise not only because she may not identify with the social fiction of masculinity, but also because other subjects may insist on her insertion into the social discourses of femininity, regardless of her identificatory position. In this sense, the subject is not its own creation, for it must always contend with the realities of social life. The world of the social fiction has facticity, in the sense that it is prior to the subject and has a material and psychic reality for the subject.

Positing the subject

Social fictions produce a subjective position of social identity, in which 'position' describes a temporal and spatial moment of subjectivation rather than an ontological foundation. The true subject of the social fiction, like the subject of the Lacanian account it draws upon, is empty. Fraser claims that 'Lacan's account of identity construction cannot account for identity shifts over time' (1992: 183). However, the Lacanian subject is never an 'essence', not even an Oedipal essence. Identity is fictional, for otherwise psychoanalysis could not have as its aim 'identity shifts'. The Lacanian account fundamentally engages with the spatial and temporal formation of subjectivity and intersubjectivity, and my model of the subject of social fictions takes up the Lacanian emphasis upon its continual production.

In this model of the social fiction, two key and ongoing processes of inter-pellation produce a speaking position of the subject. The first key process is the personal history of the subject, that is, its production within familial networks. However, these familial relationships are not 'outside' the symbolic net-works of social fictions, so that a personal history describes a position formed at the intersection of both psychic and social histories. In this first process of interpellation, the subject comes into existence as a 'being' which possesses a 'self'. These imaginary relations to self and others make discursive relations lived or 'real'.

That child becomes an adult, a social being that lives in and through its formative social fictions. In this second key process of interpellation, the subject 'mis/recognizes' itself in discourse, in terms of its already given 'identity' and 'self'. In this sense, identification with the master signifiers of social fictions reproduces the subject, because it reiterates the imaginary and symbolic relations which were formative of the subject and which capture the subject in social fictions. That capture is a process both of an experience of 'identity' and of an enactment of an 'identity' for others.

This subject does not simply reflect existing social identities, because it also has agency. It can 'read' social fictions for their representation of domi-nant identities and act on that reading, such that the subject can represent itself through different master signifiers of social identity and come to occupy a different position of identity. An example of this process can be seen in class mobility, in which the subject takes on the cultural markers of its aspirant class. 'Identity' in social fictions is not a social construct imposed upon a passive subject. The subject itself acts to produce its identity by reproducing or resisting fictive identities.

Nevertheless, it is not necessarily easy to attain subjective mobility, particularly in relation to sexualized and racialized bodies, since sexuality and race are read on to and mark the body itself. Transsexuals recognize that social fact in their desire to be bodily 'men' or 'women', rather than only presenting the signs of 'masculinity' or 'femininity'. The desire for surgical intervention shows how immobile gender 'mobility' can be. In transsexuality, the subject represents itself to others through master signifiers of 'masculinity' or 'femi-ninity'. In this example, the subject is concerned with its representation of its 'self' to others. However, those others may insist that the subject embody particular and 'fixed' master signifiers of sexual difference, and it is this insistence that the transsexual often seeks to evade. In its relations to others, the subject engages with the imaginary and symbolic relations of social fictions that others seek to impose upon it. Because of sexist or racist others, it may not be possible to evade another's signification of our 'selves' in discourses of social fictions. Subjective engagement with social fictions is performative in Butler's sense and is therefore open to change. However, others will constrain the mobility of that performance of identity.

The subject has agency in relation to social fictions because of their contingency. The relation of subject to social fictions is a contingent one, as it is fixed by imaginary and symbolic relations. For example, the relation between the female body and 'femininity' is conditional upon the fixing of cultural difference to bodily difference (Chanter 1997: 59). However, to argue that this relation is contingent is not to argue within a sex/gender model that has generally dominated feminist thinking. The psychoanalytic inflection of the social fiction emphasizes the production of sexed subjectivity within imaginary and symbolic relations. If the subject is always already sexed, then feminist resistance is not merely a matter of reinscribing the female body (although this may be a strategy of that resistance), but also requires intervention in the symbolic and imaginary orders that produce our relation to ourselves and others.

For this reason, my account of the social fiction should not be misread as a social constructivist account of the imposition of a social order upon a passive being, with an additional psychoanalytic emphasis on the psychic mechanisms that produce social identity. In these accounts, which have dominated sociological and feminist theories of gender, the subject reflects the social order that produces it.[4] Understood in this way, there would be little to distinguish my model from the developmental models of identity that commonly inform social constructivism – such as symbolic interactionism or behaviouralism (to name two of the most influential) – which perceive the subject as becoming socially integrated through its relation to other subjects. Nor would much distinguish it from the functionalist model of society that often informs social constructivism. In this model, the subject is part of a social totality, whose structures enable it to reproduce itself as a cohesive entity. In both these sociological models of the subject and the social, the subject is a normative reflection of the social order.

Joan Copjec points out that if the constructivist model was an accurate description of the production of subjects, the social world would create content and happy beings whose pleasures were commensurate with its normative roles (1994: 53–54). This clearly is not the case. My account of the social fiction is distinguishable from that influential sociological account by its Lacanian insistence that social integration is neither 'successful' nor complete. As a psychoanalytic social theory, the social fiction emphasizes the cost and failure of production of the subject in social (re)production. Psychoanalysis posits a moment of failure of and excess to the social that is produced in the social order itself: the unconscious. The unconscious marks the failure of the social order to complete and fix the subject.

The unconscious marks that failure of the social order to integrate the subject fully or satisfactorily into its discursive demands. However, the unconscious

also marks an excess to the social. Unconscious desires, fantasy and identification interpellate the subject in discursive formations, but they also mark
subjective demands that exceed those social discourses, as the unconscious
describes culturally repudiated desires of the subject. For this reason, Jacqueline
Rose is right to argue that a political project which is also psychoanalytically
inflected cannot reify the unconscious – for the unconscious represents what
we (and the social order) do not want as much as that which we do (1986: 8).
For example, the hysteric's dilemma is an outcome of that repudiation of desire.
In this sense, the unconscious marks that which the social order repudiates and
represses, and so represents its excess. Psychoanalysis recognizes the anti-social,
aggressive and solipsistic nature of an unconscious for which there is no
negation.

In my psychoanalytic model of intersubjective relations, the subject is
fictional and the signifier ambiguous. The subject and meaning are never
determined; where they are fixed in a monologic symbolic economy, it is always
at some cost to the subject. The psychoanalytic insight of the cost of civilization concerns the suffering of the subject that the fixity of repetition causes.
This failure of complete interpellation not only reveals the cost of securing
social identity, but also creates the possibility of its contestation. If social
integration is never complete, then the dominant fictions of our social order
cannot ever entirely succeed, and where they are secured, it is only at a cost
to the subject itself.

Most importantly, in this account a moment of failure founds social relations
themselves. Social relations as symbolic relations fail because they are structured by an order which itself suffers a limit and concomitant failure in its
symbolic logic. The Symbolic order is structured in an absence – a lack that
founds and produces that order. Rose argues that both psychoanalysis and
feminism share the position that a limit and a failure of the social order is
sexual difference – specifically, the sexual difference of women (1986: 91). In
the modern socio-symbolic order, the social stumbles upon 'Woman' which
functions as an unstable 'break' upon which it is founded and founders. If the
cost of sociality is borne by all subjects, that cost is borne differently by sexuated
subjects. Subjects may exchange a common loss which is the price of sociality,
but the bearer of that loss is the female subject who represents all subjects' lack-
in-being. For this reason, Freud is correct to see 'women' as a problem of the
social, since 'women' represent its limit as well as its ground (1930: 293).

Yet this position of women can also be reread as possibility – for the
possibility that the phallic social order fails to define all that women are produces
feminist knowledge. In this reading, women do not represent the 'problem' of
sociality, but rather that 'problem' is a symbolic and social order that would
posit women as a defining limit. This political shift is made by feminism. While
social fictions of gender may constitute female subjectivity, feminist discourse
articulates their inability to symbolize the 'not all' of women. It represents the

possibility that a social fiction is fictional, and as such it is possible to contest and change it.

Feminist discourses

> Women cannot be self-assured without language and systems of representations being transformed, because these are appropriate to men's subjectivity, they are reassuring to the between-men culture.
>
> (Irigaray 1990: 96)

Theorizing possibility

How *do* feminist discourses contest and change social fictions? This question confronts us with a difficult epistemological and political problem, namely, that the socio-symbolic field that produces social fictions also produces feminism. The dilemma is this: if we recognize the social construction of knowledge, how is it then possible to argue that feminism escapes that construction? This problem can be seen as a variant of an earlier, classical problem of the sociology of knowledge: how can the sociologist claim to describe a 'truth' of the social world if she is in fact a member of that sociality, and hence has no transcendental position outside social relations.

In terms of my account of feminist discourse, this question concerns how feminism can produce new discourses. Ultimately, this question founds the reconstructive project of feminist epistemology, which asks how feminist knowledge can effect an epistemological break that produces new ways to know the world. This epistemological break, as Irigaray describes it, requires the transformation of 'language and systems of representation' (1990: 96). To understand how feminist discourses permit the world to be known differently from its representation in social fictions, it is now necessary to consider the production of 'new' feminist discourses.

Feminist discourse

In my earlier model of feminist discourse, I propose that feminist knowledges articulate what a phallocentric Symbolic order does not represent. In this model, these knowledges articulate the symbolic *a* of discourse. By linking this model to the theory of social fictions, it becomes possible to include an account of intersubjective relations. The theory of social fictions gives social content to the concept of 'discourse', which otherwise functions as an abstract term. Feminism aims to change social relations. In my account, feminist knowledges interrogate social fictions as discourses that produce subjects and their relationship to others.

Social fictions produce imaginary identities. These identities collapse fantasies of self and the 'idealizing capital I of identification' (S11: 272), so that they operate as the phantasy that 'I am a woman' or 'I am a man' and so on. We can therefore understand social fictions as producing the self as imaginary *a* – an imaginary object filled with phantasmic content (the *objet petit a*):

Social fictions: s-s-s-s-s-s   identity (imaginary *a*)

However, Zizek points out that the *a* 'stands simultaneously for the imaginary fantasmic lure/screen *and* for that which this lure is obfuscating, for the void behind the lure' (1998a: 80). Social fictions therefore have imaginary and symbolic registers:

Social fictions: s-s-s-s-s-s   identity | symbolic *a*

That 'void behind the lure' is the symbolic *a*, that which marks the excluded term of discourse, the gap in or void of its symbolic structure.

Feminism traverses the phantasies of identities that social fictions produce, insisting that those social discourses found themselves upon a repudiated term. This recognition of the symbolic *a* of social fictions symbolizes it, so that it no longer functions as a term which social discourse excludes. Like psychoanalytic discourse, feminist discourse seeks to sustain the distance between the imaginary object and identity so that it becomes possible to articulate the repudiated *a* of discourse. Unlike psychoanalytic discourse, feminism seeks to interrogate social discourses. Feminist discourse symbolizes the excluded *a* in relation to social fictions as descriptions of social relations.

A feminist politics permits recognition of this founding lack or excluded *a* term of social fictions. This repudiated other is the *a*, the excluded and necessary term of that discourse. Feminist knowledges link that excluded *a* to women. For example, two classical themes of feminist analysis concern the exclusion of particular realities of gendered identity from the social representation of women, whether the unequal distribution of wealth between men and women, or the cost of a normative 'feminine' identity. In each case, feminist discourses identify the social discourses of gender and the reality of the social experience of women that those discourses exclude.

Social fictions represent a fictional identity that excludes from that representation the complex and specific social experiences of women. An example of this operation can be seen in sexual difference. The operation of social fictions substitutes an imaginary and fictional myth of 'The Woman' for the complexity of social experience of women. In their operation, social fictions repudiate that reality and put in its place certain fictional ways to be a female subject. For example, those fictional representations of 'The Woman' render her as 'sexuality'. Yet at the same time, those representations refuse the real bodies of women that have physical existence and functions, a refusal that manifests itself in an array of social taboos that surround the female body. This conception of social fictions does not claim that 'women' do not exist (either as fact or in discourse). However, social fictions produce their social experiences as the excluded of discourse, namely as its repudiated *a* term.

This excluded *a* of social fictions is the 'real' of women. Social fictions do not represent the 'reality' of women's experience – an experience of oppression and domination as well as pleasure and desire – of living under their reign. That reality takes many forms: bodily, affective, cultural, material and social. Social practices produce that 'reality', which represents the particular social relations experienced by women because they are gendered subjects. This formulation does not indicate that all women have the same social experiences because they are women, but rather that sexuation inflects social experience. Social experience is discursively produced, since it is 'specifically and materially engendered' in social relations (de Lauretis 1988: 9–10). However, the discourses of social fictions produce it as an excluded term in their symbolic economy. That excluded term, the symbolic *a*, is an effect of discourse, just as much as the social fiction is. Social discourses produce it as a term that is excluded from a hegemonic ordering of representation.

The production of the excluded 'reality' of women is evident in, for example, the case of sexual harassment. Before feminist activism in this area, social discourses did not represent the 'experience' of sexual harassment. Sexual harassment existed as a social practice, but it was not possible to articulate that experience as such within the symbolic economy of existing social discourses. These experiences were literally 'not spoken of'. Yet at the same time, the sexual harassment of women is a social practice that is produced by gendered social relations. The social discourse produces both the practice and its disavowal.

The exclusions of social fictions can be traced to the operation of a phallic Symbolic order that produces discourse as discourse and subject as subject. In Lacanian terms, the production of the real of women as an excluded term of discourse is linked to the impossibility of symbolically rendering women in a phallocentric Symbolic order. The Lacanian position links the excluded real of women to the symbolically repudiated female body of the Mother in a phallic Symbolic order. In feminist terms, this symbolic economy renders 'women' as either the phantasy of ~~The~~ Woman or as an excluded term. In this formulation, feminist discourses articulate the founding symbolic repudiation of the excluded real of women.

Unlike social fictions, feminist discourses render the real of women not as lack but symbolize and reinscribe it into the signifying chain. This reinscription shifts the relation of symbolic elements within the chain, producing a new chain of signifiers. This reinscription produces a new discourse and thus a different representation of women. If we return to the example of sexual harassment, it is possible to trace the operation of feminist discourse:

Social fictions: s-s-s-s-s   identity | symbolic *a*

  s-s-s-s-s   femininity | ~~sexual harassment~~

Feminist discourse articulates this gendered social practice within social discourse, thereby changing, first, the representation of that social practice, and second, the social discourse itself.[5]

Feminist discourse: a $\rightarrow$ s_a

  ~~sexual harassment~~ $\rightarrow$ sexual harassment

  s_1- s_2- s_3- s_4- s_5 $\leftarrow$ sexual harassment

New discourse: s_1- s_2- s_3- s_4- s_5- s_6

In this way, feminist knowledge operates as a transformative discursive practice. If discourse produces social subjects and the relation between them, then creating new discourses produces different subjects and social relations. If social fictions produce racialized and sexualized subjects, then feminist discourses permit the articulation of new discourses of subjects and their relation. Feminist knowledges operate as radical discourses of subjectivity and intersubjectivity because they produce new discourses of how to be subjects and how to exist in relation to other subjects.

The unspeakable real

This conception of feminist discourse evades a politics that bases itself upon what Butler calls the 'metaphysics of substance', which stakes feminism on two positive and representable terms – masculine and feminine (1990: 28). It contends that feminist discourse does not rely on the imaginary figure of 'The Woman' for its transformative effects but rather engages with the 'real' of women. Feminist discourse engages in a signification of the female subject in discourse. That signification does not and cannot rely upon a pre-discursive femininity or female body. For this reason, my account does not found feminist knowledge upon the marked body, emphasizing bodily sexual difference, but upon the voiced body, emphasizing the female speaking subject.

My model of feminist discourse attempts to evade the trope of woman as the unconscious bodily underside of patriarchy. Reading femininity as the social unconscious traps us within the metaphysics of sexual difference. To render the real of women within the trope of 'Woman' as unconscious 'Truth' is not politically productive, since it reduces women to the mute body and the unspeakable real. Rose points out that such a reading places women *outside* of culture and language (1982a: 56), whereas feminism wants women *within* culture and language (just not in its existing forms).

In contrast to such readings, my model of feminist discourse does not classify the repudiated of discourse as the unconscious other. In the Lacanian theory of discourse from which this model derives, it is incorrect to describe women as the unconscious of discourse. Lacan conceives discourse as operating in real, symbolic and imaginary registers. It does not operate in only one register, but in all three. It is therefore mistaken to understand discourse as conscious articulation and the *a* as its unconscious other. Rather, the *a* founds and structures discourse. This can be seen in Lacan's diagrams of the four discourses, where *a* is a term which is a necessary part of discursive structure. It is not 'outside' discourse, as it is the operation of discourse that produces it as an unrepresented term. By not conceiving the real of women as an unconscious other, the model of feminist discourse avoids the error of assuming that it is possible to simply transpose psychoanalytic concepts of the psyche to the social. To do so leads to the problematic assertion of a collective or social unconscious.

The repudiated real of women should therefore not be understood as the other of the social unconscious, although the discursive operations of social fictions may be unconscious or may render the *a* as unconscious in the strict psychoanalytic sense of a signifier which is subject to repression. Instead, the *a* should be understood as analogous to the Lacanian concept of the Real. This concept is one of Lacan's most difficult and complex, as he uses it in many linked senses and its meaning changes over the course of his work. Nevertheless, it is possible to understand this term through its key conceptual elements of a psychical, material and signifying reality (Evans 1996: 160–161). For Lacan, there is a psychic real that represents the subject's experience of reality: the 'grimace of the real' (1974: 6). The real in this sense describes the subject's relation to the material Real. Lacan posits the Real as excess, impossibility and lack. In Lacan's earlier work, it is a material plenitude which exceeds the Symbolic order, and in which nothing is lacking: '[t]he real is without fissure' (S2: 98). In Lacan's later work, the real is impossible ('le réel, c'est impossible') (S17: 143). It is a logical obstacle that cannot be represented within the symbolic (S17: 143). For this reason, the Real is also lack in language, because it marks that which the Symbolic cannot symbolize. No signifying chain can represent it in its totality – hence its impossibility. Something must always fall out of discourse, which is its excluded *a*. In this way, the Real can also be understood as the hole in the Symbolic order, the impossibility on which that order is predicated and the absence that it encircles.

In the Lacanian model, knowledge is understood as a description of a signifying relation to the Real, rather than as an idea that corresponds to an objective reality. It is not the matching of a signifier to its correlative signified, because there is no metalanguage able to tell the truth about truth and no transcendental signifier that can fix meaning as a correlate of reality (Lacan 1965: 16, *Éc*: 867–868). Knowledge is a discourse of the Real, diffracting it through the prism of discursive structures. The production of a new signifying chain represents a different relation to the Real, and with it a new 'real'.

My account of feminist knowledge does not understand the Real as a fixed entity that the act of knowing passively uncovers. Rather, it is the constitutive 'outside' of the *existing* limits of discourse. An effect of the excess plenitude of the Real is theoretical and political possibility. If the Symbolic order does not represent the totality of being, then language can take a different form, can represent a different relationship to the Real, and can represent a different Real. It becomes possible to signify the Real differently. Such a conception grants a utopian dimension to knowledge, for if it is not immutable, then the world that it represents is not given, and it can describe a different Real. Accordingly, knowledge exists in both a present and a future signifying relation to the Real.

If the Real is an impossible plenitude, it becomes possible to accept that we can never fully know or represent it, while also accepting that it offers a multiplicity of possibilities. There can be other symbolic exclusions from discourse, such that the operations of discourse are less costly to those excluded others of the Symbolic order. We need not conflate the lack in the symbolic with a Symbolic that represents femininity as lack. To claim that it is possible to change a signifying relation to the Real (and with it the signifying relation to object, self and others) is not to claim that it is possible to obtain a mystical fusion with the plenitude of the Real, in which language is adequate to its all and the speaking being suffers no loss. My conception of feminist discourse assumes that there is no knowledge that can ever provide a full and adequate representation of the world. Rather, knowledge is necessarily incomplete, situated and partial, such that it cannot ever represent all, or be a transcendental Truth.

Feminist discourses

In this model, feminist discourses do not have (or need) the status of an ahistorical and universal 'Truth'. Because of their structure, instead they have the status of knowledge-claims. This formulation characterizes feminist knowledges as signifying practices or processes that give meaning to the known object. Feminist discourse is not a knowledge that can be complete or final, because it continually articulates and reinscribes the excluded terms of social discourses. For this reason, context and change are important to the operation of these discourses. With this understanding of feminist discourse, it is possible to understand why Donna Haraway, together with many other feminist episte-mologists, describes feminism as a 'situated knowledge' (1991: 188). For Haraway, feminist knowledges are 'partial, locatable, critical knowledges' (1991: 191). Feminist knowledge has this characteristic because, in each specific moment of its production, it engages with the particular operation of the dis-course that produces it, and identifies the excluded term of that discourse. In this way, it interrogates the *a* of the particular social discourse from which it emerges. For this reason, feminist knowledge occurs in a multiplicity of forms, with each form emerging within a particular discursive context (hence the diversity and interdisciplinarity of feminism).

For example, feminist discourse can symbolize the real of women through narratives of experience. Feminists such as Catherine MacKinnon (1982) and bell hooks (1991), or more recently Mari Matsuda (1996) and Patricia Williams (1993), nominate narratives of experience as an integral part of the construction of feminist knowledge. It can also symbolize that real in empirical research, such as social research that analyses the differential and disadvantageous distribution of material resources to women, or scientific research that examines the different ways in which drug treatments affect men and women. Alternatively, it can represent women through conceptual or aesthetic work, such as Irigaray's analysis of philosophy in *Speculum of the Other Woman* (1974). Each of these knowledges articulates the real of women in discourse.

It is important to recognize that the real of women that feminist discourse articulates does not have a pre-ordained content, but rather is specific to the particular operation of the discourses of social fictions. For this reason, this model of feminist discourse does not rely on a unified or singular feminist project, because it is produced wherever feminists are at work in the particular moment of their practice. As social fictions take on a multiplicity of forms, so too does the 'real' of women, which entails a multiplicity of feminist projects. Nor does its operation rely on a unitary identity of a knower. Because the specific, contingent and historical moment of her discourse produces the speaking position of the feminist knower, it necessarily engenders a heterogeneous subject of feminism.

In this model, while feminist discourse renders the real of women in many practices, it understands those practices as discursively mediated. Feminist knowledge is a discursive act, and so discourse produces its critical object – the real of women. Because discourse structures these knowledges as symbolic acts, symbolic structures mediate the form they might take. However, if discourse articulates the real of women, then the question remains as to how feminist knowledge can itself be transformative – since there is no innocent place which is outside discourse (and social relations) from which to posit a feminist politics. If feminist knowledges engage with social fictions, and symbolize the real of women within discourse, then how can those knowledges be transformative when they emerge from the discourses of social fictions?

Feminist discourses do not negate social fictions, since feminism cannot stand outside them. Instead, feminist discourses restage and resignify those existing social discourses and hence produce a new signifying chain. The symbolization of the otherwise repudiated real of women, and the reinsertion of that signifier into existing symbolic structures, produces a new discourse. Feminist discourses disrupt the established possibilities for signifying acts, and, by producing new discourses, open new possibilities for discursive acts. With these new possibilities, feminist discourses create the potential for different speaking subjects and new forms of relations between them.

This conception of the power of feminist discourse does not entail a reduction of the political to the epistemological. The political necessarily involves action, and we need to recognize that there are many acts that signification cannot perform. For example, we may not have the power to enact our discourse. We are unlikely to be the only speaking subjects or the only agents of power. We are unlikely to occupy positions of state or institutional power. For example, while feminist discourse may inscribe a recognition of the harm of domestic violence into social discourses, it may not be able to prevent, criminalize or punish it. To paraphrase Butler, there is no necessary continuity between the intention of the knowing subject, her utterance in discourse, and the political act (1997a: 92).

Following psychoanalysis, a discourse exceeds the will of the subject that produces it, and may have unacknowledged or unintended consequences. One recent example lies in the increasing use by men of equal opportunity laws intended to redress the inequality of women. These litigants frame their claims in terms of 'equal opportunity' for men as a class of people who allegedly suffer discrimination. This illustrates the complex relationship between political discourses and action.

Part of that complexity is that political action produces feminist discourse. For example, to provide refuges from domestic violence is to shift existing social discourses about it. However, another part is that political action also presupposes feminist discourse. Spivak points out that '[s]ince practice is an irreducible theoretical moment, no practice takes place without presupposing itself an example of some more or less powerful theory' (1984–1985: 176). It is here that we might identify the power of feminist discourse: the representation of another relation to the real, another symbolic order, another social order.

The real is rational

However, this formulation of the power of feminist discourse returns us to an epistemological problem that I raised earlier in Chapter 2. This problem concerns how psychoanalysis can be a discourse that transforms how we know ourselves and our world. How is it that the Discourse of the Analyst does not reproduce the Discourse of the Master, the discourse of the conscious self? The articulation of psychoanalytic theory necessarily involves a conscious knower, speaking of his or her conscious thoughts. In terms of the Lacanian model, this articulation places psychoanalytic theory within the *méconnaissance* of the knowing subject of consciousness. To write theory is to produce a discourse of concept and reference. Psychoanalytic theory is thus situated in the paradox of its conscious articulation of the laws of the unconscious that are by definition resistant to conscious representation. That representation subjects the unconscious to the imaginary captations of the analyst/theorist.

As I discussed in Chapter 2, Lacan resolves this through his strategy of the symbolization of the laws of the unconscious. From the 1960s, he increasingly emphasizes that symbolization must take place through the mathematical formalization of those laws (S20: 119). He argues that mathematical formalization offers a pure signifying relation, whose terms do not themselves have content, as they do not represent signifieds. Instead, these terms have meaning only in the differential relation between signifiers, as in the unconscious. In Lacanian terms, the mathematical equation is the only rendering of the unconscious that can avoid the depredations of the conscious. In his later work, Lacan argues that he intends the matheme to produce neither metonymic signification nor metaphorical meaning, but to indicate operations in the Real (S20: 118). They are a writing of the Real. For Lacan, this formalization allows psychoanalysis to find its method and justification for its claim of *savoir* or symbolic knowledge of the unconscious. Although there are significant problems in this account concerning the extent to which mathematization can formalize understanding of the unconscious (especially as 'pure' signification), this formalization offers an important strategy for thinking through this epistemological paradox.

The first difficulty that the Lacanian paradox raises for feminist discourse concerns how it can evade *méconnaissance*. Like the ego-psychology of which Lacan is so critical, feminist knowledge often relies on empiricist ('in my experience') or positivist ('studies have shown') justifications for its knowledge-claims. As both these forms of justification rely on a conscious knower, feminist knowledge exposes itself to the operation of the misrecognitions of the conscious, and hence to its radical error. The second and related problem emerges from the formulation of feminist knowledge as a discourse. If knowledge-claims are discursive practices, then how is it possible to posit a normative methodology of knowing or justification for knowledge? By conceiving knowledge as a discursive practice, there is no criterion or position 'outside' discourse to appeal to, because discourse will always construct what we understand as methodology and justification. How, then, is it possible to justify feminist knowledge-claims?

In my model, feminist discourse evades the *méconnaissance* of the Master because it undertakes an act of symbolization of the 'laws' of discourse. Similarly to analytic discourse, it is situated in the field of the signifier because it is a practice of the symbolization of the real of women. In the Lacanian sense, it is a symbolic knowledge. Its undertaking of the symbolization of the *a* of social fictions situates feminist knowledge within the field of signification. In its disruption of the Discourse of the Master, feminist discourse produces a different speaking position for the knowing subject. As I discussed in Chapter 3, feminist discursive practice can produce a different speaking position of a knowing subject from that of the Master of consciousness. Occupying a speaking position analogous to that of the analysand, a feminist knower accepts her 'split and contradictory' subjectivity and the finitude of her knowledge, and so repudiates mastery (Haraway 1991: 193). In this way, a knowing subject refuses the speaking position of the Master through her epistemic practices.

If feminist discourse is a symbolic knowledge, it does not then follow that feminist epistemology should reduce its project of symbolization to mathematical formalization, and reduce its discursive practice to mathemes. Lacan's mathematical formalization of itself does not resolve the epistemological paradox. A tension can be seen in Lacan's work between clinical practice, with its reliance on empiricism and a form of (positivist) scientific method; Lacan's own textual practice, with its aesthetic insistence on the excess and difficulty of the unconscious and language; and his project of the formalization of the unconscious. Formalization is unable to represent (and in fact refuses) the other dimensions of the unconscious that can be found in Lacan's work – namely, its manifestation in the clinic and the text. On the one hand, Lacan specifically invokes formalization as a refusal of empiricism and positivism. On the other hand, its rigid structure fails to capture the insistent excess and mobility of the unconscious at work on his couch and in his writing.

However, if Lacan defines the Real as an impossibility, as a truth which is impossible to articulate in the symbolic register, then in the Real we encounter the representational limits of discourse, and hence its capacity to represent Truth itself. This formulation of the impossibility of the representation of Truth as such suggests a different way to understand feminist discourse as knowledge. Following Lacan, Theresa Giron suggests that psychoanalysis:

> allows the place of truth to be marked, that is, to be formalized or symbolized; this place will always be marked as an impossibility but what psychoanalysis nevertheless contemplates is nevertheless the possibility of this marking . . . what is symbolized in psychoanalysis is the place of truth, insofar as that place can only be marked as an empty place. Once the place of truth then is held open – that is to say, marked in the symbolic – then it can be variously occupied from moment to moment by different objects.
>
> (2000a: 6)

If we sustain this Lacanian distinction between truth and knowledge, then we understand feminist discourse as holding open the place of truth, such that its knowledges represent the different objects that occupy that place from moment to moment.

Accordingly, feminist discourse cannot (and need not) take up the status of universal Truth, but instead needs to be understood as a knowledge which occupies that place in that moment, and which is therefore, *pace* Haraway, 'partial, locatable, critical' (1991: 191). For this reason, my model of feminist discourse requires a new emphasis upon the regulatory practices of feminist knowledge. If questions of method and justification need no longer be posed in the universal and the transcendental, but instead become local and particular to the context of discursive production, then these regulatory practices take on a new importance. For example, Helen Longino argues that '[t]he complete set of regulative standards, inclusive of theoretical virtues, guiding a community's epistemic practices could be called its epistemology' (1997: 33). These 'theoretical virtues' constitute the criteria of members of the feminist community of inquiry 'that will advance our cognitive aims' (34). Longino suggests five feminist theoretical virtues: 'empirical adequacy, novelty, ontological heterogeneity, complexity or mutuality of interaction, applicability to human needs, and decentralization of power or universal empowerment' (1997: 21). Refiguring the 'virtues' as practices, it is possible to suggest that feminist discourse requires new ways of both conceiving and enacting these regulatory practices. In this model, knowledge-claims are epistemic practices that are regulated by communities of knowers.

Communities of knowers: feminist epistemic communities

> Women as political beings, aware of the articulation of the politics of knowledge with the politics of gender, can transform 'the epistemological project'.
>
> (Code 1991: 262)

Theorizing epistemic community

Two leading feminist epistemologists, Lorraine Code (1991, 1995) and Helen Longino (1990, 1997, 2002) posit communities as the primary producers of knowledge. In her examination of philosophical knowledge, Code argues that the relations of knowing subjects to others produce philosophy. In her analysis of science, Longino argues that the contextual values of the scientific community produce scientific knowledge. Both theorists propose that epistemic communities produce knowledge. Unlike traditional accounts that posit the knower as an autonomous individual, both Code and Longino insist that the intersubjective relations of knowers produce knowledge.

Code and Longino also analyse the production of feminist knowledges, arguing that a relation to feminist politics forms these knowledges. For example, Code deploys the concept of 'epistemic responsibility' that she characterizes as 'responsible cognitive practice' (1991: 270). A responsible cognitive practice is one in which the knowing subject acknowledges that it exists in relation to other members of its epistemic community and that its knowledge has political effect for which the knower is responsible (1991: 264). Longino's formulation of feminist knowledges also utilizes a similar concept to Code's 'epistemic responsibility'. Longino describes a practice of accountable knowledge, in which feminist scientists include their commitments to their political values in their production of knowledge (1990: 197). In a later development of her notion of epistemic accountability, Longino (1995, 1997) turns her attention from scientific to feminist knowledge. Longino argues that feminist epistemology identifies a set of 'theoretical virtues' that regulate the accountability of knowers, such that epistemic practices continue to promote the 'cognitive goals' of feminist politics (1997: 26).

Code and Longino argue that epistemic communities produce knowledge, and that a relation to feminist politics produces and regulates feminist knowledges. However, neither theorist develops the relation between these two strands in her theory of knowledge. In particular, neither develops a theory that links the production of knowledge in epistemic communities and feminist politics. For example, Code develops a normative model of epistemic community based in a model of friendship as well as ecological theories of community. Her work convincingly argues that communities of knowers produce knowledge. However, Code does not consider feminist communities of knowers, and so does not develop a model of such an epistemic community. This omission is surprising, given that Code's discussion of her normative model of epistemological community focuses upon how that model can be useful for political practice.

In contrast, Longino assumes the existence of a feminist epistemic community in her description of its practices and cognitive goals. However, Longino's work focuses upon the development of a normative model of feminist epistemic practice rather than a descriptive model of feminism as an epistemic community. Longino does not address the specificity of the feminist community of knowers, but uses her earlier theory of the scientific community of knowers to develop her model of feminist epistemic practice. Her theory of social knowledge focuses upon science rather than upon feminism as its model of epistemic community. One important consequence of Longino's failure to specifically address a feminist epistemic community is that her consensus model of knowing does not reflect the production of knowledge in feminism (Lennon 1997: 46). Moreover, that conception of consensus within a community requires a unity of identification and identity between its members, and so does not address the fact that, in a feminist community, consensus is and must be negotiated across differences. This negotiation is imperative for a movement that not only must engage with internal debates, but also finds some of its most productive moments in them. For example, the second-wave debates concerning the politics of difference have profoundly shifted feminism in the last decade.

Despite their promise, neither Code's nor Longino's theories of knowledge develop an account of feminist epistemic communities, as they do not address the relation between epistemic community and feminist knowledges. However, if we follow Code's and Longino's argument that communities of knowers produce knowledge, then epistemic communities must also produce feminist knowledges. Therefore, to give an account of feminist knowledge requires the development of a model of feminist epistemic community.

Political identifications: reconceiving epistemic community

However, a theory of the intersubjective nature of feminist knowledge cannot just assume that this epistemic community already exists. Rather, it first needs to explain the formation of that community in terms of its members and the relations between them. Therefore, to theorize a feminist epistemic community requires a theory of the production of the forms of subjectivity and inter-subjectivity that construct it. Whatever content is given to the term, a commitment to feminist politics distinguishes its subject as 'essentially different' from other subject positions, and its movement from other political movements (de Lauretis 1994: 1–2). In Chapter 3, I argued that identification with feminist politics enables the subject to take up a position as a speaking subject in feminist discourse, and to identify with others as members of a political movement. In this account, a series of secondary identifications with feminist politics and people as ideal objects, and with other members of the feminist movement, produces the subject.

Elissa Marder argues that 'when one "speaks as a feminist", in the name of the feminist project, one must say "we"' (1992: 163). To speak as a feminist is to speak as a member of a political movement, and is to speak in a relation to other feminists. It is to shift from being an individual political subject to being a member of a collective movement. My account of feminist identifications shows how these political identifications produce an intersubjective and collective relation. It describes the processes by which affective, imaginary and symbolic identifications construct the relation between subjects of the feminist movement. In these identifications, women identify with other women, with feminist politics and with other members of a political movement. Feminist identifications construct the intersubjective relations between subjects, and in turn produce a political movement.

As I argued in Chapter 3, feminist discourses articulate those intersubjective relations. They represent a symbolic exchange with other subjects identifying with 'feminist politics'. That symbolic relation between the subjects and communities that comprise the feminist movement produces feminist discourse. Code characterizes knowledge-claims in epistemic communities as 'forms of address, speech acts, moments in a dialogue that assume and indeed rely on the participation of (an)other subject(s), a conversational group' (1991: 121). Feminist knowledges are forms of address to feminist communities and speech acts within its discourses. They are dialogues with other politically committed subjects, which the conversational groups of the feminist movement form. Feminist discourses represent these dialogues between feminist subjects. For this reason, we can understand the political movement of feminism as constituting a feminist epistemic community.

However, the term 'feminist movement' implies a political collectivity in its broadest sense of a group of people who identify with feminist politics (rather than the narrower sense of the second-wave women's liberation movement). It is a collective noun that indicates the many communities that comprise feminism. The term 'feminist epistemic community' is therefore always in the plural, since it represents the many diverse communities of the political movement. Those communities constitute a *socius* and a *polis* which constantly form and reform. It does not imply an organic community, which nostalgically dreams of unity, nor a normative prescriptive 'community' which defines what a political community should be. Rather, the term describes the epistemic communities that the relational nature of feminist politics and movements forms.

With this formulation of feminist epistemic community, Code's and Longino's descriptions of epistemic communities become very useful for understanding the production of feminist knowledge. In particular, their respective concepts of 'epistemic responsibility' and 'epistemic accountability' permit us to understand how feminist communities function as epistemic communities that negotiate cognitive goals and practices. In these negotiations, the knowing subject is responsible and accountable to the feminist movement. She negotiates her responsibility and accountability within feminist discourses, so that feminist knowledges are contingent upon the relations between subjects and the dialogue between them. However, those dialogues are themselves produced in relation to a feminist politics. Each knowledge-claim describes not only a relation between members of the political movement, but also their relation to a feminist politics.

The structure of feminist epistemic communities charges knowers with an accountability to, and responsibility for, other subjects and feminist politics. The relations between these subjects, and in turn their relation to a feminist politics, constitute this epistemic community, thereby structuring the negotiations of feminist knowledges by the criteria of responsibility and accountability. For example, the challenge of the politics of difference has led third-wave feminism to call 'for a "new subjectivity" in what was, up to that point, white, middle-class, first world feminism' (Orr 1997: 37). Whether or not this is a correct description of the second wave, the power of the third-wave call for new forms of feminist subjectivities lies in the operation of the feminist epistemic community, in which knowers are accountable to feminist politics and ethically responsible to others. The knowledges that emerge in the dialogue between these subjects therefore are never simply (or only) epistemological. They are also political in their production in relation to feminist ideals, and ethical in their constitution in intersubjective relations. This does not mean that these knowledges are necessarily or inevitably satisfactory by political and ethical criteria. They are not, as evidenced by the racist and classist knowledges which some feminists produce. However, the explicit construction of feminist knowledges as accountable to feminist politics and as ethically responsible to others entails that political and ethical values become part of epistemic practice.

This description of feminist epistemic communities should not be understood as excluding the role of other epistemic communities from the construction of feminist knowledges. For example, feminist scholars work in many academic disciplines, and draw on the knowledges and practices of those communities of knowers. Moreover, other political movements, such as anti-racist or queer movements, necessarily constitute feminist epistemic communities. What defines feminist epistemic communities is their responsibility to the politics of gender, and that accountability determines the relation of their knowledge-claims to 'feminist politics'. The production and definition of the terms 'feminist' and 'politics' are continually negotiated because 'feminist thinking has paradoxically defined itself in response to those questions of who or what' (Marder 1992: 149). This ongoing process negotiates and renegotiates who is named by the term and what such a naming implies.

Practising community

This account of feminist epistemic communities explains their construction from political identifications and intersubjective relations. It proposes that the symbolic exchange between members of those communities produces feminist knowledges. The ethical and political relation of their members to each other and to others structures this epistemic practice in terms of normative ethical and political practice.

However, this theory of feminist epistemic communities does not imply that they fulfil the requirements of a Habermasian 'ideal speech' situation. For example, Code and Longino recognize that some speaking positions of knowing subjects are more powerful than others. Longino's work in particular is concerned with the inequitable granting of authority within an epistemic community. The constitution of epistemic communities from already existing social practices creates that privileged position of the knower. For example, in her 'Lessons from a Young Feminist Collective', Tiya Miles describes the gradual disintegration of the feminist collective to which she belongs because of its reproduction of racist and classist assumptions and privileges (1995: 173). A feminist epistemic community is as vulnerable to the operations of social power as other communities of knowers.

In order to understand epistemic communities, it is therefore necessary to acknowledge not only *internal* operations of power, as Code and Longino do, but also how *external* operations of power form those 'internal' relations.

We need to address this social formation of epistemic community so that our attempts to construct democratic communities of knowers do not reproduce existing inequitable social relations. To not address this issue gives rise to a problem that can be seen in Longino's model of dialogic communities. This prescribes four conditions to ensure the formation of such a community:

> a) the provision of venues for the articulation of criticism, b) uptake (rather than mere toleration) of criticism, c) public standards to which discursive interactions are referenced, d) equality of intellectual authority for all (qualified) members of the community.
>
> (1997: 26)

In her later work, Longino describes these conditions as 'social norms for social knowledge', arguing that these are 'features of an idealized epistemic community' (2002: 128, 134). In her studies of scientific communities, Longino argues that these criteria presume that there is a diversity of members within an epistemic community. She clearly implies that the same condition is necessary for the production of a dialogical feminist community (1997: 26). Longino's position is compelling because a feminist epistemic community requires diversity of membership for political *and* epistemological reasons. If many different knowers do not compose that community, then the conversations between its members will simply reflect the homogenous identity of its members rather than the plurality of women. For example, Miles (1995) argues that, without a plurality of women members, feminist collectives will fail (as her own did). In political terms, a diversity of knowers is necessary if only for the reason that a feminist politics requires an engagement with all women. In epistemological terms, it is also necessary for the production of a plurality of symbolic exchange, and a concomitant plurality of knowledges which that exchange produces.

Moreover, Longino's argument that a diversity of membership in a feminist epistemic community is meaningless without parity of epistemological authority is convincing. Equality between those who speak, such that its members have equal standing, is necessary to ensure that all women are able to engage in negotiation as to the constitution of feminist politics and its collective movement. This equality is both an ethical imperative of feminism and an epistemological imperative for its community of knowers. Without such equality, feminist knowledge can only reflect the knowledges of privileged members of society, and reflect existing inequitable social relations.

However, Longino's construction of epistemic parity confines that equality to those knowers who already have material and cultural privilege. We cannot construct a feminist community of knowers by conferring epistemic authority only upon middle-class, university-educated 'experts' and technocrats who 'know' better. Nor does a liberal model of diversity and equality of knowers guarantee feminist exchange. For example, the scientific epistemic community that Longino describes claims that it is a meritocracy, which comprises 'diverse' groups of people, and that it grants all knowers equal epistemic authority. Nevertheless, it is unlikely that we would consider the scientific community to be a representative or democratic community of knowers.

Our account of these communities must address the material and discursive practices which also construct them. Because Longino's account does not explicitly address knowledge as a discursive practice, it separates knowledge and representation, treating signification as a neutral practice outside social relations. However, discursive practices have epistemological and political effect because they delimit what is sayable or unsayable within their signifying structures. One example of that effect can be seen in Ann du Cille's characterization of Joan Scott's phrase:

> '*women, African-Americans, and various others* . . .' I am left by accident of language to question both my own identity and the category of 'women'. I know that the intention here is not to *exclude* women of color, but the fact is that language like this does not *include* us either.
>
> (1990: 92)

For this reason, we need to recognize how discursive practices construct the knower and its relation to others, thus also constituting epistemic communities.

Material practices also form a feminist epistemic community, since material resources sustain its production of knowledges. Those resources include access to sites for the exchange of discourse, such as libraries, journals, publishing houses, and conferences. Longino acknowledges this point in her argument that dialogical discourse requires 'the provision of venues for the articulation of criticism'. However, she does not acknowledge that access to these venues will form an epistemic community itself. She presumes that all knowers within an epistemic community will have access to those sites of discursive exchange, rather than considering how that access may determine who will become a member of that community. For this reason too, Longino does not consider how time, financial security and other personal resources (such as child care) permit the knower to engage in discursive exchange, and hence will also affect who will become a member of an epistemic community. Without this recognition of the importance of material practices, feminist knowledge risks becoming a conversation between women academics, who have the contemporary equivalent of five hundred pounds a year and a room of their own, and hence becoming a privileged possession of a material and cultural élite.

For these reasons, a model of feminist discourse needs to recognize the social, discursive and material practices that constitute an epistemic community. If epistemic communities construct knowledges, social relations also produce those communities. So the social, material and discursive practices that reproduce inequitable social relations also form feminist epistemic communities. However, a political practice that produces a critique of that social order also constitutes these communities. Drawing on this politics, feminists have developed a number of material and discursive practices which attempt to resist the reproduction of existing social relations. Those practices, including equity of access, a politically aware use of language, redistribution of resources, and non-hierarchical relations, actively work to construct a democratic epistemic community.

This account of feminist epistemic community does not conceive it as a Kantian community of rational, autonomous knowers. Rather, the community is produced affectively and symbolically in political identifications, materially in already existing social practices, and discursively in the signifying practices of its knowers. Yet that community is also constituted in a political relation to the emancipatory and democratic projects of feminism, and in an ethical relation to others. The challenge for feminism is to ensure that the constitution of epistemic community is always a political and ethical act.

Feminist knowledges

This theory of feminist epistemic community permits a further elaboration of my account of feminist knowledge. It reconceives feminist knowledge as epistemic claims that the discursive exchanges of communities produce. In this reformulation, those knowledges are discursive practices that communities of knowers constitute. In this way, they form a medium of relation between members of the feminist movement. These knowledges function as the practices by which knowing subjects engage in symbolic exchange. In this model, knowers participate in discursive exchange and are able to recognize each other as speaking subjects. Feminist knowledges are discourses that articulate the symbolic relation between feminist subjects.

In these discursive practices, forms of feminist subjectivity and collectivity are constantly (re)negotiated in the consensus and dissent of the feminist movement. The dialogic structure of feminist epistemic communities constitutes the productivity of feminist knowledges, for the negotiation of political forms of subjectivity and intersubjectivity grounds their continual articulation and rearticulation. In this way, feminist epistemic communities give content to 'feminist politics' and 'feminist movement', since they define the constitution of those terms in relation to the politics of that given moment.

This description of feminist knowledges characterizes them as discursive practices negotiated in the feminist movement. Feminist knowledges are therefore both provisional, insofar as they are contingent upon their moment of production, and strategic, because they are conditional upon the definition of the aims of the feminist movement. They also have a particular ethical and political form. Their production by a knower who is accountable and responsible to others gives them an ethical structure, and her relation to feminism gives them a political structure.

This reconception of feminist knowledge provides a means of explaining why feminist epistemologists appear to characterize particular models of knowledge as 'feminist'. For example, feminist epistemology typically characterizes the knower as a provisional, partial and intersubjective position, and 'truth' as situated, contextual and political knowledge (Braidotti 1991: 270–273). These theories do not characterize feminist knowledge as a transparent and universal methodology but as a practice or process which the situated relations of the knowing subject and its known object produce. My account of feminist epistemic communities explains why feminist knowing takes these forms. First, it describes how the production of the speaking position of the feminist knower in an identificatory relation to feminist politics and to others constitutes that position as provisional, partial and intersubjective. Second, it describes how the formation of these knowledges within feminist epistemic communities constitutes them as strategic, contingent and situated discursive practices that have an ethical and political structure. In this way, my account of the production of feminist knowledge reveals the constitution of its discursive structure and the forms of its discursive practice.

Feminist discourses

With this conception of feminist knowledges, it is possible to further develop my earlier account of feminist discourse. In that account, I argue that feminist knowledges represent new discourses of subjectivity and intersubjectivity. To understand how those knowledges represent new political discourses, we need to return to my model of discourse. This model conceives discourse as a social bond that constitutes subjects in a symbolic relation to others. Feminist discourse (re)presents a new symbolic relation between subjects in its articulation of that relation in terms of a politics and an ethics. It inscribes a different relation between subjects from that of the social fiction, because it articulates the political and ethical intersubjective relations of the feminist movement. Unlike social fictions, this discourse does not represent social relations between men, but social relations between women as speaking subjects. In feminism, the subject enters a discursive relation to other women. These symbolic relations between women form feminist discourses, and permit the symbolization of new intersubjective relations. This articulation in turn produces new signifiers of feminism, which when inserted into its existing signifying chains then produce different discourses.

In this way, feminist discourse can produce a different representation of the relations between subjects. It resignifies the discourses of social fictions, because it symbolizes a political and ethical relation that is formed in the feminist movement. The power of feminist discourse lies in its production of another way to articulate the social link between subjects and so another way to articulate the social order. If discourse constitutes the social link, then the production of feminist discourse constitutes a new social bond and hence different relations between subjects.

Butler argues that, given that discourse produces speaking subjects, '*[t]o move outside the domain of speakability is to risk one's status as a subject*' (1997a: 133). While to speak as a feminist moves outside the domain of 'speakability' of social fictions, feminist discourse describes other ways to be speaking subjects and other forms of intersubjectivity. A feminist epistemic community produces discourses that open the domain of 'speakability', and shift the construction of 'acceptable' speech by offering a different representation of our relation to ourselves and our others, a new discursive social bond.

Feminist politics

This model of feminist discourse relies on a conception of feminist politics that understands it not as representational, but as coalitional. In this account, many communities form the feminist movement. The relation between these communities is coalitional, since it is an engagement between different groups who act to secure their feminist goals.

This notion of the coalitional nature of feminism can be seen in third-wave feminisms, which 'embrace the notion of coalitions and affinities' (Arneil 1999: 218). Third-wavers call for the necessary 'work of coalition' (Lee 1995: 210), for the creation of 'a new kind of sisterhood, based on pragmatic aims' (Forna 1999: 151), and for 'structures and networks which will allow women from all classes of society the possibility of meeting and communicating' (Michael 1999: 166). The notion of a coalitional feminism entails understanding it as a collectivity. Many communities, which are not themselves homogenous, constitute the coalitional movement (Hammonds 1997). The relation between these communities is coalitional, since it is an engagement between different communities who act to secure their shared feminist goals.

Defining the feminist movement as a coalition, rather than as a unified community, envisions the possibility that its members may act together to achieve certain political ends, but may also choose not to participate in other political projects. For example, feminists of equality and of difference (to use Irigaray's categories) might find coalitional aims in resisting restrictions on women's reproductive rights, even while their idea of the meaning of feminist politics remains quite different. This shift to a concept of a coalitional movement permits the making of strategic decisions to pursue particular projects, while negotiating with others as to the meanings of the signifier, 'feminist politics'. The reconceptualization of the feminist movement as coalitional provides the possibility of the negotiations of politics and the enactments of practice that are produced in strategic and contingent alliances between feminists.

By conceiving the feminist movement as political alliances between its members, those members can undertake collective action that recognizes the differences between women. A coalitional politics permits strategic action that engages many women, thereby opening the political movement to the many identifications that produce feminist subjects without a demand for a unifying identification with a singular politics. In this way, the feminist movement can engage those women who identify with its politics but who do not identify with the movement itself. Feminism can constitute and reconstitute itself by constantly negotiating and renegotiating feminist subjectivity and intersubjectivity.

This shift to a coalitional politics is also epistemologically necessary because, as Kathleen Lennon points out, we cannot and should not confine the production of feminist knowledges to feminism. Feminist epistemic practices necessarily involve the destabilization of both their own and other epistemologies, and an expansion of the horizon of its community of knowers. Lennon argues that 'we need normative engagement outside of the communities she [Longino] describes', so that feminist knowledges can move outside the stability of their epistemic community (1997: 52). This process involves 'understanding across difference' and does not rely on Longino's problematic consensus model (Lennon 1997: 48). It understands an engagement with differences within and without the feminist movement as constructing coalitional politics.

Third-wave feminists recognize the difficulty of this work of forming political coalitions, for '[w]e realize that coming together and working together are by no means natural or easy' (Lee 1995: 211). Part of that coalitional work is the recognition of the importance of feminist practice. Third-waver Gina Dent argues that 'evidence of the continued impact of feminism' lies 'not in the women's movement but AIDS activism, rape crisis centers, discussion of unequal health care, and even more importantly . . . the smaller things we do on a daily basis that form the patterns of our lives' (1995: 72). A coalitional politics is always a politics in process.

From that reworking of the notion of 'feminist politics', we can reconsider how 'feminist politics' functions as an identificatory signifier. If 'feminist politics' functions as the pivot of political identifications, it is only because it functions as an open term. As Marder describes, '[t]he term "feminist" is not a proper name. It denotes no precise group, race, class, or even gender' (1992: 149). As an identificatory signifier, 'feminist politics' has a shifting and contingent signified and no referent, unless that referent is considered to be a future utopian possibility. The operation of 'feminist politics' as a shifting signifier can be seen in feminist symbolic identification. This identification involves a process of identification with the signifier 'feminist politics'. It functions as a symbolic element whose conceptual content is contingent and changing, and which has different meanings for different subjects.

To claim that this signifier does not have a referent does not mean that it signifies nothing or that it is meaningless. Rather, it redefines the signifier 'feminist politics' 'as an impersonal, performative pronoun whose political force is neither dependent upon, nor derived from, a knowable link to a particular referent' (Marder 1992: 164). In this way, it is an identificatory signifier that is an open term, representing a contestatory project to those who identify with it, which is momentarily fixed in its content in relation to its enactment. Butler offers a useful definition of a performative as 'one which brings into being or enacts that which it names, and so marks the constitutive power of discourse' (1995b: 134). 'Feminist politics' performs the action it describes in the practices of its subjects and their movement. These practices name and enact the signifier 'feminism', marking the constitutive power of feminist discourses. In this sense, feminism comes into being in feminist practice.

The importance of this conceptual shift can be seen in Butler's discussion of the term 'homosexual'. Butler argues that the term 'homosexual' has no referent, but instead is a performative term. It is a practice. Butler argues that this formulation of the term 'homosexual' provides a space to resist closure by acknowledging the instability of the term, which in turn enables its future rearticulation (1997a: 107). Restating Butler's point in terms of feminism, feminist discourses can be seen as sustaining the difference between 'feminist politics' as a performative term and as a referential term. Feminist epistemic communities constantly renegotiate the content of the term 'feminist politics' and hence what that term might mean, allowing the reformulation of political objectives. By sustaining the difference between the reference and the performance of 'feminist politics', feminist discourses resist the closure of that term, and so allow for the possibility of its future rearticulation.

This conception of 'feminist politics' as an identificatory signifier permits a new understanding of the operation of 'feminism' itself as an identificatory signifier. This signifier can also be understood as an open term. Like 'feminist politics', we can reconceptualize the feminist movement as a performative defined by its practice. As Marder describes, 'the feminist "we" is defined in each moment of feminist thinking by its answer to who is named by the term "feminist" and what such a naming implies' (1992: 149). As feminist politics shift, so too does the 'we' of the political movement. It changes according to that set of politics with which women choose to identify. This feminist 'we' has a phantasmic and shifting status. However, as Butler points out, '[t]he radical instability of the category sets into question the *foundational* restrictions on feminist political theorizing and opens up other configurations, not only of genders and bodies, but of politics itself' (1990: 142). The 'phantasmic and tenuous status' of feminist politics and intersubjectivity as identificatory objects entails that feminist epistemic communities constantly form and reform, just as the feminist movement itself constantly forms and reforms.

5   Feminism's time

Third Wave Agenda presents a generational perspective, gathering the voices of young activists struggling to come to terms with the historical specificities of our feminisms.

(Drake and Heywood 1997a: 2)

How do we understand the historical specificities of feminist knowledge? While feminist epistemologists often understand knowledge as socially and therefore as historically specific, many fail to follow this argument through to its logical conclusion that feminist knowledges are also historically contingent (Tanesini 1999: 16). Feminist epistemologists who consider this issue generally do so in terms of philosophy, such as Susan Hekman's (1990) examination of whether feminism should use modern or postmodern philosophies. However, also typically, this discussion already rests on an implicit assumption of modernity. How then might we understand the historical specificity of my model of feminist discourses? Given that I develop this model from Lacan's account of modern psychoanalytic discourse, is it a model of modern feminist discourses? My questions do not concern the relationship between feminist and modern epistemologies, but rather the relationship between modern feminist discourse and social relations.

In classical social theory, 'modernity' typically indicates 'modes of social life or organization which emerged in Europe from about the seventeenth century onwards and which subsequently become more or less worldwide in their influence' (Giddens 1990: 11–12). Those modes of social life include the emergence of democratic politics and industrial capitalism. My understanding of the modern, then, accepts the founding tenet of social theory that modernity inaugurates fundamentally new forms of social relations. However, following Judith Butler (1998), it also insists that those new forms of social relations are discursive as well as material. Characterizing modernity in this way emphasizes the production of modern discursive forms, those symbolic structures that also constitute modern subjectivity and intersubjectivity. In this chapter, I explore the relationship between modern feminist and social discourses.

Lacanian modernity

Modern readings

Lacan is not usually read as a theorist of modernity. A persistent complaint against his work is that it presents an ahistorical account of subjectivity. In particular, theorists such as Elizabeth Grosz (1990) contend that Lacan posits the Symbolic order as a transcendental social form which is timeless and therefore unchanging. Teresa Brennan points out that such a reading derives at least in part from the presentation and reception of Lacan as a structuralist, since he is most often read as an ahistorical structuralist rather than as a historical thinker (1993: 7). Both critical and sympathetic readers of Lacan's work have put forward this argument, and there are structuralist aspects of Lacan's work that support this view. However, this interpretation of Lacan focuses upon his most structuralist period of the 1950s and mid-1960s, and looks to the more conservative moments of his work. It ignores those other aspects of Lacanian theory, such as his later theory of discourse, which offer another interpretation of the concept of the Symbolic order.

There are an increasing number of historicist readings of Lacan's work. For example, Mikkel Borch-Jacobsen and Élisabeth Roudinesco argue that Lacanian psychoanalysis includes an account of the modern. Borch-Jacobsen (1991) traces the notion of the modern Oedipus within Lacan's earlier writings, while Roudinesco (1997) argues that a concept of modern sociality informs Lacan's body of work. Teresa Brennan's *History After Lacan* (1993) and Juliet Flower MacCannell's *The Regime of the Brother* (1991) are two important examples of persuasive feminist readings of a Lacanian account of the modern. Lacan's theoretical heir, Jacques Alain-Miller, suggests that such readings are not only possible, but also necessary, for an understanding of Lacan's work. For example, Miller's explanatory note to the 'Classified Index of the Major Concepts' of *Écrits* suggests that Lacan theorizes a modern ideology – the ideology of the modern ego (*É*: 362). These readings suggest that Lacan's work contains at least an implicit historical model, even if it is neither explicit nor elaborated.

However, Lacan's work needs to be read closely for an account of modernity, since Lacan is neither a historian nor a social theorist, and modernity is not the object of his study. Such a reading is necessarily strategic and treats Lacan's psychoanalytic theory as a body of work, early and late, rather than as simply comprising *Écrits*. While the classical concept of the Symbolic order of *Écrits* represents Lacan's most structuralist engagements, an important series of references to modern social forms is scattered throughout this text. These references form a coherent, if not fully elaborated, account of modern discourses when read with Lacan's early work and later seminars. In particular, the later seminars, *L'envers de la psychanalyse* (1969–1970) (S17) and *Encore* (1972–1973) (S20), return to Lacan's earlier concern with the emergence of modern socio-symbolic and subjective forms. This reading of Lacan's work permits the development of a Lacanian theory of modern discourses.

Because Lacan is a psychoanalyst and not a historian, he does not address the history of modernity. Similarly, because Lacan is not a social theorist, his work does not provide a systematic or developed account of modern sociality. Rather, his aim is to provide a psychoanalytic account of the modern subject and he derives his account of modern sociality from the evidence of psychoanalysis (1969b: 127, S17: 239). However, the psychoanalytic foundation of Lacan's work raises the issue of the legitimacy of his claims, and his movement from the psychoanalytic to the social field without sufficient differentiation between the two exacerbates this problem. This problem leaves Lacanian theory more vulnerable to Nancy Fraser's dismissive comment that 'I will note only that Lacan himself was remarkably unconcerned with empirical confirmation' (1992: 185). While Lacan's account of modern discourses ultimately derives from clinical material, it clearly does not constitute an empirical study of social life in the sociological sense.

These problems in Lacan's account of modern discourses are endemic to his theory generally. However, they are also endemic to any social theory, insofar as it makes certain broad claims about the 'nature' of the social world and then proceeds to construct a theory of that sociality. As Bryan Turner comments, 'theoretical speculations have always been highly prominent in sociology [and] this commitment to theory is closely related to the problematic nature of the social as a topic' (1996: 2). Despite these difficulties, a theory of modernity requires a theory of the social. Moreover, Jurgen Habermas reminds us that psychoanalysis 'allows the *systematic generalization* of what would otherwise remain pure history' (1972: 259). While Lacanian psychoanalysis does not provide a complete or developed theory of the modern social world, it permits particular questions to be asked of modern social relations and of the discourses that found them. In particular, it focuses upon subjectivity and intersubjectivity as symbolic relations that permit an interrogation of these representations of the subject and its relationship to other subjects. Lacan's work does not offer a theory of historical modernity, but rather an account of the emergence of modern subjective and socio-symbolic forms. His work describes the formation and operation of modern discourse, which provides us with an important account of the modern discourses of the subject and intersubjectivity.

Teresa Brennan argues that Lacan's work is important because '[i]t provides us with a lever (not an elaborated theory of history, not at all) but a lever for thinking through the trajectory of modernity' (1993: 7). I develop Lacanian psychoanalysis as a theory of modern discourses in order to reconsider the relationship between modern and feminist discourses. Following Brennan, I use Lacan as a lever for 'thinking through the trajectory of modernity', and in particular the twentieth-century trajectory of feminist discourse.

In the name of the father

> But a large number of psychological effects seem, to us, dependent upon
> the social decline of the paternal imago; a decline conditioned by a return
> of extreme effects of social progress onto the individual; a decline above
> all marked in our times by those collectivities who have most strongly felt
> those effects, economic concentration and political catastrophe.
>
> (Lacan 1938a: 200, *FC*: 72)

In *The Family Complexes in the Formation of the Individual* (1938b), Lacan
argues it is possible to see the most marked effects of the social decline of the
paternal imago in those who suffer most from the cultural, political and economic turmoil of French society in the 1930s. He links this decline to the earlier
rise of the conjugal family, a familial form that emerged from a Christianity that
combined patrician ideals of marriage with an emphasis upon the individual.
This shift in familial relationships 'realized itself in the fifteenth century with
the economic revolution that produced the bourgeois society and the psychology
of modern man' (1938a: 198, *FC*: 69).

It is unsurprising that modernity should emerge as a key theme of Lacan's
work of the 1930s. He was writing in a France which had suffered the
destructive agonies of the First World War and the Depression, and which was
experiencing extreme political instability coupled with the rise of a deeply
reactionary politics. Roudinesco describes *Family Complexes* as 'a theoretical
study . . . of the crisis of modernity' (1997: 146). Both this and his earlier doctoral thesis (subsequently published as *On Paranoid Psychosis and its Relations
with Personality* (1932)) engage with the question of modern subjectivity.
In these early works, Lacan's theory of the subject turns on the relation between
the paternal function and modern shifts in social and symbolic forms. In
particular, it explicitly concerns the modern function of the paternal.

In *Family Complexes*, Lacan dismissively characterizes Freud's account of
the primal horde of the pre-history of modernity in *Totem and Taboo* as biologist
(*FC*: 54). Thirty years later in *L'envers*, Lacan takes up his earlier discussion
of *Totem and Taboo*. For the later Lacan, it is a distorted myth. However, it is
also central to understanding the Freudian Oedipus (S17: 128–129). The later
Lacan rereads the psychoanalytic fiction of the murder of the primal father of
Totem and Taboo as a collective myth, perceiving it as a story that represents
a collective narrative of a pre-history of Oedipal modernity.

Lacan regards the Freudian myth of *Totem and Taboo* as a phantasy of origin,
reading it as a cultural narrative that is both anterior and interior to modern social
forms. In that narrative, patriarchy exists as a powerful cultural form. This
cultural form posits the father as the bearer of social power, such that the father
functions as the figure of the social ideal and of repressive authority (*FC*:
67–68). For Lacan, that cultural phantasy continues in modern social forms.

Lacan's reading of *Totem and Taboo* centres on the Father of pre-history, the father of the primal horde. Unlike Freud, Lacan does not perceive the primal Father as a real being whose existence continues in phylogenetic memory. Rather, he argues that the primal father is an imaginary figure that exists as part of a collective myth or social phantasy. In this narrative of a 'traditional' patriarchy, the father rules the social world. This 'collective myth' of the pre-history of modernity describes a social order that the Father's Will founds. The primal father forbids his sons *jouissance*, while claiming its pleasure for himself (S17: 143). This myth imagines the father of pre-history as claiming and enjoying an unlimited pleasure of the mother, and hence as being an uncastrated father (S17: 115). He is the forbidding father who has all pleasure and who suffers no lack, while commanding his sons: 'do not enjoy'.

From his earliest work, such as the *Family Complexes*, to the later *L'envers*, Lacan explicitly links the mythical murder of the primal father of the horde to a new social order and form of 'family complex'. Lacan takes Freud's myth of traditional patriarchy, and rereads it as a mythical narrative of the emergence of a new and different socio-symbolic order. In this cultural phantasy, the sons unite against the fearful primal father, murdering him in order to establish their access to sexual objects (namely the bodies of women) that were previously reserved for the father's enjoyment, and in doing so establish a new form of sexual exchange and social order.

For Lacan, the murder of the father is a narrative of the emergence of the modern Oedipal structure of the subject. Lacan argues that the Oedipus complex is contingent on the symbolic murder of the father because it establishes the interdict against the desire for the mother (S17: 139). Lacan describes the familial structure that produces this subjective complex as the conjugal-patriarchal family. He characterizes this familial order as the structure of the modern family. The structure of familial desire is classically Oedipal (and Freudian) insofar as the child desires the mother, while facing the father as the rival for, and bar to, that desire. The modern family remains a patriarchal family because of the primacy of the paternal figure, where the figure of the father represents a rival for the mother's affection as well as being a representative of the social world. That father must be symbolically murdered for the resolution of the Oedipus complex.

While the paternal figure is the pivot of the modern family complex, Lacan repeatedly insists that the decline of the paternal function and the failure of the Oedipus complex characterize modernity. From his early work of *Family Complexes* to *L'envers* thirty years later, Lacan argues that the rise of modernity coincides with the increasing failure of the Oedipus complex. In 1938, Lacan describes the father as having both sexually repressive and identificatory functions in the paternal family. For Lacan, because the real father acts as the agent of the paternal function, the real father is too often inadequate to his function as Father. Lacan argues that the personality of the father is 'always in some way deficient – absent, humiliated, divided or false' (1938a: 200, *FC*: 73). Lacan echoes this description of the failing father in his later paper, 'On a Question Preliminary to Any Possible Treatment of Psychosis' (1958), where he argues that the father's position as legislator often reveals him to be a hypocrite or a fraud (*É*: 242). Lacan claims that the modern father is inadequate to his paternal function because he occupies the dual position of being a figure of repression and sublimation.

In the Lacanian account, modern society suffers a decline in the paternal function because of the failure of the modern father. Because the father fails to secure the paternal law, the subject fails to identify with the father's interdict. The subject does not identify with the father as the agent of repression, and so does not properly form the paternal super-ego. As part of that formation, 'the paternal imago is invested by repression [and] it projects its original force in the very sublimations which should overcome it' (1938a: 197, *FC*: 66). Lacan claims that this process is the source of the creativity of modern Western culture because it does not accept paternal authority but instead constantly subjects it to 'creative subversion' (1938a: 199, *FC*: 70). However, this identificatory process also fails to properly secure and maintain the paternal function. In Lacan's account of the modern family, the paternal figure is subject to constant attack. For this reason, he perceives 'the social decline of the paternal imago' (1938a: 200, *FC*: 72). Lacan's argument in his later seminar *Le sinthome* (1975–1976) (S23) (1975d) echoes this claim that the father is a position which must continually be upheld, as there is no support for the paternal function, no Other of the Other. Roudinesco argues that '[t]he story is that of modern man, man in our modern civilization, marked by the ineluctable decline of the ideals of the paternalistic family' (1997: 215).

Accordingly, the mark of modernity is not a normative, integrating Oedipus complex that succeeds; but rather one that fails. The decline of the paternal function structures the modern subject in a failure to surmount its Oedipus complex. The failure of this complex should be understood as the failure of its resolution. A 'successful' resolution of this complex involves a repression of the desire for the mother, and the concomitant formation of the ego-ideal and super-ego in paternal identification. When Lacan describes a 'failure' of the Oedipus complex, his argument is not that the complex itself fails, but rather that there is a failure of its paternal resolution.

Lacan argues that in the failed modern Oedipus complex the structure of subjective identification shifts from that of traditional patriarchy to its modern form. In making this argument, Lacan develops the otherwise blurred distinction in Freud's work between the super-ego and the ego-ideal (Borch-Jacobsen 1991: 37). Lacan draws out two aspects of the paternal function, one that forms the imaginary ego-ideal – 'be like me, the father' – and the other which forms the repressive super-ego – 'do not be like me, because you cannot have the mother'. Lacan's description of the 'failed' Oedipus complex posits a successful sublimation of the imaginary ego-ideal with its injunction 'be like me', but also a failure of the formation of the repressive super-ego with its categorical imperative of 'do not be like me'. The subject does not repudiate maternal desire because the father says 'no', but rather because the subject gives up that desire in order to be like the father.

If we reconsider Lacan's account of paternal identification in relation to the modern subject, then we can develop that account to clarify the role of the father in subjective formation. Reformulating Lacan's account, identification with the socially privileged paternal figure rather than the repressive patriarchal father produces the modern subject. In the modern familial complex, the subject sacrifices the mother for paternal identification, and receives in return the power and prestige that the father offers. In the modern social world, the father represents (and has) social power and prestige in the parental relationship (Brennan 1993: 58). This symbolic and material economy privileges the bearer of the phallus, which the father claims or is given. For this reason, the child perceives the father as having power, prestige and privilege. Teresa Brennan describes this operation of paternal identification as a process of the recognition of power, where the masculine subject recognizes the father 'as a shaper and acknowledged recognizer, a namer, into whose dominating kingdom he will one day come' (1993: 53). With paternal identification, the masculine subject accepts the Law of the Father – 'I cannot have the mother' – in return for the power of the father and access to other women.

By developing Lacan's account of paternal identification in this way, it is then possible to describe the relationship between the structure of symbolic paternal identification and the symbolic murder of the father. Mikkel Borch-Jacobsen points out that 'the modern form of the Oedipus, characterized by an ambivalent and "devouring" identification with the real father', produces a subject that engages in aggressive rivalry with the father (1991: 40). This father is the symbolic father, the paternal legislator whose position the son usurps in his incorporating identification, as he cannot do in reality. With that identification, the son commits a symbolic murder of the father. The symbolic father comes to represent the real father of the subject, who can then incorporate the paternal figure as ego-ideal. This process is an identification of the order of 'wanting to be like'. That identification incorporates what Lacan describes as the single mark (*trait unaire*), the unifying trait of the phallus of the father, which functions as a representative of the Law of the Father and of a cultural order which privileges him.

For Lacan, the modern Oedipal structure of identification has two 'resolutions'. As Borch-Jacobsen describes, Lacan's position is that, 'normative, the Oedipus is also, like it or not, potentially "neurotic" and "psychotic"' (1991: 38). One possible resolution of the Oedipus is a paranoid structure of the subject. Lacan's early studies of paranoia concern failures of the paternal function and take as their object psychotic women.[1] In his later study of paranoid psychosis, which focuses upon the Schreber case, Lacan identifies paranoia as the outcome of a foreclosure of the paternal function and a failure of the paternal metaphor. In his discussion of Schreber, Lacan argues that the subject can have a paranoid structure, but may not become psychotic until he confronts the function of being a father (S3: 293). For Lacan, Schreber cannot accede to masculinity because he cannot take up its 'normative' position of having the phallus. Unsurprisingly, Lacan renders the paranoid position of the subject as a feminine position, first as literally feminine in his early studies of paranoid women, and then as metaphorically feminine in the case of Schreber.

The other possible 'resolution' of the Oedipus complex is prevalent in the formation of the modern subject. Like Freud, Lacan argues that the failure of the Oedipus complex generates subjects who suffer neurosis. For both Freud and Lacan, the neurotic is the modern subject. However, Borch-Jacobsen argues that Lacan perceives the inadequate resolution of the Oedipus complex as symptomatic of the decline of the paternal function. For Lacan, this 'deficiency comes to exhaust (*tarir*) the instinctual impulses and to damage (*tarer*) the dialectic of sublimations', such that the modern structure of the Oedipus complex represents 'the kernel of the greatest number of neuroses – where one can recognize the great contemporary neurosis' (1938a: 200, *FC*: 73). The modern Oedipus is the neurotic Oedipus: 'the Oedipus of the modern *crisis* of identification' (Borch-Jacobsen 1991: 40). This crisis of identification is a crisis of paternal identification.

In the name of the son

Lacan develops his account of the modern subject in his later seminars, *L'envers* (1969–1970) (S17) and *Encore* (1972–1973) (S20). While he frequently refers to modern sociality in his work of this period, these seminars represent a sustained return to this theme. In these seminars, Lacan reworks his conception of the foundation of the modern subject, the conjugal family, through his account of discourse as a social bond. This return to the theme of modernity is unsurprising given the historical period in which Lacan presents these seminars. In the late 1960s, French society again experienced a period of political and cultural turmoil, involving a rejection of not only traditional French culture with its legacy of collaboration, but also a modern France with its shadow of colonialism. In a famous exchange in 1968, Lacan told the restless students of Vincennes University that 'what you, as revolutionaries, aspire to is a Master. You will have one' (1969b: 127, S17: 239).

For Lacan, the Discourse of the Master is the horizon of the Modern. The advent of the social order of modern capitalism stabilizes the Discourse of the Master (S17: 207). It is the discourse of capitalism and its other face, imperialism (S17: 104). Lacan does not specify the historical period of the emergence of the Discourse of the Master. However, he argues that this discourse fully develops in the discourse of the capitalist and in a curious conjunction with science (S17: 126). In earlier texts, Lacan places the emergence of modern science in the seventeenth century, with the Cartesian philosophy of the cogito (1965: 5, *Éc*: 856), and the birth of modern physics (S11: 8). By linking the emergence of the Discourse of the Master to the emergence of science, Lacan indicates that it emerges in the sixteenth and seventeenth centuries. Similarly, Lacan's earlier seminar, *The Ego in Freud's Theory and in the Technique of Psychoanalysis* (1954–1955), dates the emergence of the modern ego (which the Discourse of the Master produces) to the sixteenth and seventeenth centuries (S2: 7). While Lacan perceives the modern subject as emerging with the conjugal family of the fifteenth century, his later work ascribes a later emergence of the Discourse of the Master to the sixteenth and seventeenth centuries.

Linking these accounts of the emergence of the modern form of the family and the Discourse of the Master, it seems that this Discourse emerges in the earlier social shifts of the fifteenth century before it stabilizes and then fully develops with the rise of modern imperialist capitalism and media society. For Lacan, the Discourse takes on a new purity in contemporary life, which he claims is evidenced by the experience of politics of his time, and embraces everything (S17: 99). For Lacan, this is a contemporary social discourse of mastery, control and domination.

In *L'envers*, Lacan characterizes the Discourse of the Master as that of the modern subject. This subject is a universal, self-generating, autonomous Master. It predicates itself as universal because it perceives all others as identical to itself. It repudiates the difference of others, including their sexual difference. Powerful and dominating like the Father, it seeks to control its objects and its self. Above all, it is a subject that disavows its lack. As Lacan describes it, the Master subject renounces *jouissance*, so that it does not expose the limit of his mortality to him. In doing so, he places himself within the Hegelian dialectic of the master and slave (S17: 123).

Lacan links the formation of the modern subject in paternal identification to the Discourse of the Master. In *L'envers*, Lacan condemns the modern society that the Discourse of the Master founds. In this condemnation, Lacan describes the agent as the vehicle of advertising and publicity, which spreads the contemporary society of the spectacle (S17: 146). However, the agent is also the father, in his function of the agent of castration. The father is 'the double agent' – an allusion to the earlier description in *Family Complexes* of the two faces of the father as loving and repressive (S17: 147). In *L'envers*, then, Lacan retains his earlier argument that the dual function of the real father as the agent of sublimation and of repression produces the irresolution of the modern Oedipus. The real father functions as both the imaginary father (the father of identification) and the symbolic father (the father of repression) (S17: 159). Lacan's description of contemporary society, with its imaginary allure, deception and trickery, emphasizes its participation in the imaginary order. He suggests that the imaginary identification with the father facilitates 'the spreading' of the Discourse of the Master, rather than the repressive formation of the super-ego. In this way, we can see the link between the modern form of paternal identification and the modern predominance of the Discourse of the Master.

Lacan proposes that the modern Oedipal form inaugurates a new form of the social tie. This social tie takes the form of a fraternal relationship, in which a relationship between brothers founds the social order. Lacan argues that an analysis of the Oedipal myth reveals the phantasy of the brothers of the primal horde and of the fraternal social relation (S17: 131). He suggests that this symbolic murder of the father founds modern fraternal social forms (S17: 131–132). For Lacan, the Oedipus complex is contingent on the murder of the father, because it establishes the interdict against the *jouissance* of the mother. The brothers are the murderous sons, who after killing their father enter into the pact between them that will constitute the Symbolic order. In *Family Complexes*, Lacan argues that the fraternal complex (the imaginary relation between siblings) involves the subject's recognition of the other as another with whom he will either fight or contract (FC: 46). In his later seminar, *L'envers*, Lacan describes the Discourse of the Master as a founding myth of Western (capitalist) culture (S17: 207). Lacan suggests that the fraternal social relation is a social and symbolic tie between brothers, forming the modern social bond with its founding discourse of equality, liberty and brotherhood (S17: 131–132). The sons of the primal father inaugurate a new cultural form – that of fraternity. They are no longer the sons of the father, but brothers.

Lacan's work does not provide a theory of fraternal sociality. However, his account of the fraternal tie permits us to trace the relationship between the fraternal social bond and the pact of the Symbolic order. It enables us to understand how paternal identification produces the fraternal tie. In the fraternal order, the brothers imagine a relation to each other through their relation to the murdered father. They represent this relationship through the symbolic father, so that they imagine the dead, primal father to be the symbolic father – the father that does not know that he is dead. The paternal identification of each of the sons and their recognition of each other as brothers through the paternal line produces the fraternal bond. This relationship between paternal and fraternal identification thereby founds the Symbolic order and the Law of the Father. Unlike the primal horde, the Law of the Father is not a law of brute force, but a symbolic law that describes a cultural order of the exchange of women between men.

The pact of the Symbolic order founds the fraternal tie. It represents a symbolic law that forms the fraternal social bond. The Symbolic order is the social pact between subjects that forms their relationship as social subjects.[2] This Symbolic structures the social order, because it produces subjects and the relation between them. In this sense, the Lacanian Symbolic order, and its later reconception as 'discourse', describes the pact that founds the social tie between subjects and which produces the social order. This pact is not a neutral agreement of social existence but represents a particular arrangement of the social order – a fraternal form of sociality. It describes a culture founded in a phallic representational economy that differentiates 'masculine' and 'feminine' subjects. The symbolic father – the symbolic function that represents the murdered father – is the pivot of this social order.

Identification between masterly brothers forms the fraternal social tie. Freud's *Group Psychology and the Analysis of the Ego* (1921: 124) permits us to understand this identificatory process as a recognition by each of the brothers of their introjected paternal ego-ideal. This reciprocal process of recognition is grounded in an imaginary perception of similarity. However, it is also an aggressive rivalry, which views each brother as a hostile master who seeks to dominate. In the fraternal relation, the imaginary relations of fraternal rivalry structure social identification. In *Family Complexes* (1938b), Lacan describes the jealous competition between siblings as the archetypal social feeling (*FC*: 46). For this reason, a discourse of mastery structures the fraternal discourse or social tie. The brothers speak the Discourse of the Master. Despite the murder of the father, the fraternal social order does not indicate the end of patriarchy, because it does not represent a post-patriarchal order. Rather, it represents a different form of a phallic social order.

In this social order, the masculine subject functions as the universal subject. In Chapter 3, I argued that the masculine subject claims presence and universality, such that it posits its identity as a whole and complete self who is the universal representative of all being. In Lacan's terms, the masculine universal is a being where all succeeds (S20: 56). However, the universality of the masculine subject defines itself in relationship to a non-universal, the 'feminine' position of a being without the phallus. The masculine subject displaces his lack-in-being to a castrated other, which enables the construction of his fantasy of being a unified, omnipotent and universal subject. The Discourse of the Master produces the universal masculine subject. It produces a masculine subject that masters itself and its others. Paternal identification secures that Master subject. Imaginary identification with the phallic unitary trait (*trait unaire*) of the Symbolic Father produces the masculine subject. In the position of mastery, the subject identifies with the Symbolic Father who has the phallus and is not castrated. This identification allows the subject's misrecognition (*méconnaissance*) of its originary and ontological lack.

For this reason, the Discourse of the Master produces a masculine subject and establishes a social relation of masculine intersubjectivity. The fraternal social order is not a relation between siblings, that is, between brothers and sisters or between sisters, but a relation between brothers as the male children of the father. Accordingly, the social pact of the Symbolic order, and its Discourse of the Master, is a social contract between masculine subjects. It is not a contract between men and women, since women function in its symbolic economy as objects of exchange rather than as social subjects. It is a social link between those who recognize themselves (and each other) as masculine subjects. The fraternal subject is a masculine subject, which paternal identification constitutes and which founds his relation to other subjects.

The fraternal social tie is therefore a homosocial tie in which men are bound to each other through the libidinal relations of identification. This relation is not homosexual, since it is not a relation of desire between two men. It is identification between those of the same masculine sex that produces a social bond.[3] Juliet Flower MacCannell, drawing on a Lacanian account of modernity, succinctly characterizes this social order as the 'regime of the brother', in which '"fraternal objects" are eroticized' in a sublimating identification between brothers (1991: 52).

In her analysis of social contract theory, Carole Pateman rightly argues that 'in the modern world women are subordinated to men as men, or to men as a fraternity. The original contract takes place after the political defeat of the father and creates modern fraternal patriarchy' (1988: 3). My account of the fraternal social bond permits us to understand the formation of the fraternal social bond, its constitution through masculine paternal identification, and its production of the masculine social subject and relationship. A sexuated socio-symbolic order founds the modern fraternal pact. The liberal social contract, with its call of 'liberty, equality, fraternity', is a social contract between brothers. The modern fraternal bond is a Discourse of the Master. This discourse produces masculine subjects and social ties. The fraternal discourse therefore forms a sexuated social relation. By understanding the operation of modern fraternal discourses, we can explain why the fraternal social contract functions as a masculine socio-symbolic order that produces a masculine social subject.

However, it does not explain the formation of the other sexed subject – the modern female subject. This account of modern fraternal discourses addresses the fraternal order as a social bond that produces masculine subjects as social subjects. Similar to the theory of female subjectivity described in the 'Graph of Sexuation' in *Encore*, it provides a theory of the production of the modern masculine social subject, and not the modern female social subject. It does not explain the production of female subjects as social subjects, other than to imply that this form of social bond excludes them.

In *This Sex Which Is Not One*, Luce Irigaray describes a 'hom(m)o-sexual' order, in which the masculine subject only recognizes other masculine subjects (1977: 172). In a key essay, 'Women on the Market', Irigaray argues that the 'hom(m)o-sexual' order is founded upon systems of material and symbolic exchange between men, and specifically upon the material and symbolic exchange of 'wives, daughters, and sisters':

> [t]he use of and traffic in women subtend and uphold the reign of masculine hom(m)o-sexuality, even while they maintain that hom(m)o-sexuality in

speculations, mirror games, identifications, and more or less rivalrous appropriations, which defer its real practice.

(1977: 172)

Margaret Whitford's compelling reading of Irigaray suggests that this critique of a 'hom(m)o-sexual' order of exchange should be understood as a critique of a patriarchal social contract (1991: 174). Whitford argues that Irigaray's work fundamentally concerns 'a single problem, in its multiple aspects: the absence of and exclusion of woman/women from the symbolic/social order, their representation as nature' (1991: 170).

Irigaray's description of 'the between-men culture' reveals the sexuated socio-symbolic order that founds the forms of fraternal sociality (1990: 96). It politicizes Lacan's concept of the social pact of the Symbolic order and provides a feminist description of the symbolic economy of a masculine social order which produces women as social objects. However, Irigaray does not explicitly address the fraternal social contract and certainly does not provide a theory of its emergence or operation (Whitford 1991: 175). In this sense, her work provides a diagnostic description rather than a theory of the fraternal social order. Nevertheless, her analysis of the 'hom(m)o-sexual' order permits a re-reading of my account of modern fraternal discourses as a theory of the production of masculine and feminine subjects.

This rereading reveals the sexuated nature of the fraternal social bond. The social contract is an agreement between masculine subjects as brothers. That agreement forms a fraternal social bond, which produces feminine subjects as social objects of exchange, rather than as social subjects who participate in the social relation. Modern fraternal sociality thereby excludes women because it represents a social tie between masculine subjects. The exclusion of women from the social pact of the Symbolic order founds fraternal sociality, which is therefore a sexuated social form. This social bond excludes feminine subjects as social subjects.

This analysis of the sexuated nature of the fraternal social relation permits us to explain the relationship between fraternal sociality and the discourses of social fictions. In Chapter 4, I argued that the discourses of social fictions produce dominant forms of subjectivity and intersubjectivity and that a phallic Symbolic order structures those social fictions. However, the Symbolic order represents the social pact between masculine subjects. Given that that order structures social fictions, these discourses represent 'between-men' culture. Social fictions are discourses of relationships between masculine subjects, which represent masculine subjectivity and social relations. They represent the fraternal social bond, and for this reason produce the real of women as their excluded term. By linking the concepts of the fraternal social relation to the discourses of social fictions, it is possible to see that social fictions are discourses of a fraternal social order. As the fraternal social tie is a modern discourse of subjects and social relations, so too social fictions are modern discourses of masculine subjectivity and intersubjectivity.

This description of modern fraternal sociality draws out the reconstitution of a patriarchal culture in a modern fraternal form, which Lacanian psychoanalysis reveals is a crisis of traditional patriarchy. Jardine explains that in the context of the Western crisis of legitimation:

> [i]t is widely recognized that legitimacy is part of that judicial domain which, historically, has determined the right to govern, the succession of kings, the link between father and son, the necessary paternal function, the ability to decide who is the father – in patriarchal culture.
>
> (1985: 24)

This delegitimation centres on the 'loss of the paternal fiction, the West's heritage and guarantee' (Jardine 1985: 67). Similarly, Pateman also argues that the figure of the traditional patriarch no longer functions as the guarantee of the social order (1988: 88). However, the modern paternal figure of social power serves in his place and paternal identification still produces the masculine subject. The social order remains a masculine order. My account of the shift from a traditional patriarchal order to a modern fraternal order explains how the loss of the patriarch produces a new fraternal form of social order, discourse and subjectivity.

This description of a shift from feudal patriarchal to modern sexist social forms traces the continuing operation of the paternal function and its signifier, the phallus, in the production of the social and the subject. In *History After Lacan*, Brennan suggests that, while there is a 'shift from a genuinely patriarchal feudal society to a sexist capitalist one', modern social forms are born of, and precipitated in, patriarchy (1993: 167). Brennan does not develop this argument, but it is possible to do so by using my account of modern fraternal discourses. That account reveals that the decline of traditional patriarchy does not result in the dissolution of an androcentric Western culture, but instead founds its modern forms. It articulates the shift of discourse from traditional feudal society to its modern bourgeois and capitalist form.

Flower MacCannell argues that these fraternal forms represent a post-Oedipal order. In her important elaboration of the Lacanian theme of the fraternal tie, she argues that '[w]hat we have in the place of patriarchy is the Regime of the Brother' (1991: 3). For Flower MacCannell, a relationship to fraternal members of the social group forms the subject, rather than a relationship to parental figures, and, in particular, the paternal figure. However, I argue that the fraternal social form does not represent a post-Oedipal social organization, because the decline of the paternal function and the failure of the Oedipus complex are a function of the shift from traditional, patriarchal familial forms to the modern Oedipal family. This does not entail that the Oedipus complex was ever satisfactorily resolved in a pre-modern patriarchal time, because the same modern moment produces both the Oedipus complex *and* its failure.

In this modern identificatory structure, paternal identification remains dominant. However, its identificatory object is not the dominating father of the primal horde, but the Symbolic Father as the bearer of social and cultural prestige. This position creates the possibility of the failure of the real father, who may or may not be able to fulfil his paternal function. My description of the modern fraternal subject and discourse traces the relationship of the modern fraternal form to traditional patriarchal culture. Through this account of the fraternal social form, it is possible to perceive how modern social forms follow patriarchy and reconstitute the differential and disadvantageous sexed arrangements of a social order that a phallic Symbolic founds and forms.

The knowing master of modernity

In Lacanian theory, then, the Discourse of the Master is a modern discourse. As such, it produces modern forms of knowledge. Lacan argues that the shift from the discourse of the classical master to the modern capitalist master modifies the place of knowledge (*savoir*) in discourse (S17: 34). As I explored in Chapter 3, the Discourse of the Master constitutes knowledge as mastery. It produces the discourses of mastering knowledge – those of the University and of Science (S17: 172–174). If my account of modern discourses is read with this Lacanian epistemology, then it is possible to explain the relationship between these modern knowledges and the Discourse of the Master, the dominant discourse of modernity. In this way, my account of modern discursive forms places Lacan's model of knowledge within its historical frame.

Lacan characterizes the Discourse of the Master as a modern, capitalist and imperialist discourse, which implies that it produces particular historical and cultural forms of knowing. For example, Lacan identifies two predominant discourses of knowledge in the modern social order, the University and Science. Within his theory, the philosopher and the scientist are pre-eminent modern masters of knowledge. However, because the modern Discourse of the Master founds these forms of knowledge, Lacanian epistemology must describe modern discourses of knowledges. For this reason, it does not provide an account of universal Truth but of modern forms of knowing, knowers, and their relation to their known object.

However, these modern discourses of knowledge do not function outside the field of sexual difference. The dominant discourse of modernity is that of the Master, which produces a masculine subject and social bond. This Discourse of the Master founds modern fraternal discourses. However, as I discussed in Chapter 3, the Discourse of the Master also founds masculinist knowledges and knowers. A desire for power and dominance structures their epistemological imperatives. In this way, modern fraternal discourse produces the 'masculine' knowledges and knowing subjects that the deconstructive work of feminist epistemology repeatedly critiques.

The Lacanian crisis

Jardine argues that contemporary French theorists, including Lacan, constitute 'the first group of Western writers after the Frankfurt School to try to come to terms with the threatened collapse of the dialectic and its representations which is modernity' (1985: 22). In terms of my Lacanian theory of modern discourses, it seems plausible to understand Lacanian psychoanalysis as engaging with the lack in the modern socio-symbolic order. Jardine also suggests that these theorists are important because their response to the crisis of modernity has been 'to look to the future, to *affirm* and *assume* that loss' of the paternal fiction (1985: 67). However, while Lacan may affirm the lack in the paternal order, he does not assume it.

Lacan consistently argues throughout his work that the subject must accept both its lack and the Symbolic order as the price of being a speaking and social subject (*É*: 352–353). The subject must accept its lack-in-being which the Symbolic order produces. For example, an ethics of desire is a position in which the analysand comes to know and accept its desire. In his seminar, *The Ethics of Psychoanalysis* (1959–1960), Lacan argues that to act ethically is to act in accordance with one's desire. However, in that same seminar, Lacan argues that the object of desire is the impossible, unattainable object of the M(O)ther – *das Ding* (S7: 68). The acceptance of desire therefore involves accepting its impossibility, such that the subject comes to know that it desires the mother but also that it can never have her. The subject must accept that the mother is forbidden to him. This is an ethics of castration that entails an acceptance of the Father's Law. It accepts the paternal in its repressive function, an acceptance of the father of the interdict who forbids the subject access to the mother, and thus of the phallic order of the Father.

Lacan links the crisis of modernity to the decline of the patriarchal social order, and hence to the decline of the repressive paternal imago. While the modern Oedipus is the source of social creativity, it is also the source of the neurosis and psychosis of the modern man. In his later seminar of 1975–1976, *Le sinthome* (S23) (1976), Lacan asks how one is to become a subject in the face of paternal deficiency. This question is crucial for Lacan, because the foreclosure of the Name-of-the-Father results in psychosis. For Lacan, the answer is to follow the example of James Joyce, who in facing the paternal failure creates a paternal name and so is able to make his own proper name (1976: 15). Unlike the neurotic who uses the standard of the Name-of-the-Father, Joyce invents a name of the father, a symbolic nomination, for himself: the *sinthome* (Morel 2003: 141).

Zizek describes the *sinthome* as 'a signifier as a bearer of *jouis-sense*, enjoyment-in-sense . . . the binding of our enjoyment to a certain signifying, symbolic formation which assures a minimum of consistency to our being-in-the-world' (1989: 75). Rereading Zizek's description in terms of sexuation, we can perceive that 'binding' is the masculine subject's relation to the paternal name as it is rendered by 'a certain signifying, symbolic formation' that is the Symbolic order. In creating a paternal name, the subject is able to make a name for himself as the son of the father in the face of the loss of the paternal fiction. In this way, the modern masculine subject can give the father existence by engaging in the production of a name of the father, and hence creating another discourse. By creating such a discourse, the son gives meaning to and brings into discourse (that is, signifies) his relation to the father. Such a signifying act enables the father to exist, and saves the subject from psychosis, since the father's existence prevents a foreclosure of the real. Lacan's modernist project does not ask for the disruption of a phallic Symbolic order, but rather its more successful rewriting.

Ultimately, Lacan calls for the Father. The Oedipal structure of the subject does not shift, because the son comes to be a subject through the reconstruction of the paternal fiction. The relation to the phallic father is not brought into question, nor is the relation to the (m)other. Lacan calls for the father to be given symbolic existence, so that the father of modernity can exist. Behind this call, it is possible to hear a nostalgia for the traditional father of patriarchy, for the father who says 'no' to the subject's desire for the incestuous object – the terrifying and devouring 'alligator-mother'. In Lacan's terms, these alternatives run 'from the father to worse' (1974: 46).

The importance of Lacan's work is that it enables us to understand the constitution of modern fraternal discourses in the phallic Symbolic order and so to describe the relationship between traditional patriarchal and modern fraternal sociality. It permits us to describe the patriarchal 'crisis' that accompanies the emergence of those discourses, while also tracing the continuity of a masculine symbolic economy between the two social orders. In this way, Lacanian psychoanalysis does not refuse the crisis of modernity, but reveals it. However, it also presents that crisis as a crisis of paternity, which it attempts to resolve by a reinscription of the Father. In contrast, my Lacanian account of modern fraternal discourses understands the loss of the paternal fiction as a productive crisis that feminists can exploit. Because this account shows the sexuation of modern fraternal socio-symbolic forms and their exclusion of women as social subjects, it provides another way to understand the emergence of modern fraternal discourses.

Modern women

The shift from traditional patriarchy to modern sexism represents a crisis of traditional forms of masculinity. However, in her discussion of the crisis of Western legitimation Jardine points out that '[t]he crises experienced by the major Western narratives have not . . . been gender-neutral. They are crises in the narratives invented by men' (1985: 24). In this sense, the problematic of modernity is a crisis of masculine fraternal discourses of the subject and the social.

The very socio-symbolic forms that form modern fraternal sociality also institute the so-called 'crisis of modernity'. The fraternal social form produces both the masculine subject and its crisis; the masculine intersubjective relationship and its crisis. The production of this crisis can be traced to the structure of fraternal discourse. Like all discourses, fraternal discourse produces an excluded *a* which is also fundamental to its operation. The *a* structures that discourse, yet it is also a term which this symbolic economy cannot represent. This exclusionary operation can be seen in the fraternal discourses of subjects and the relation between them. For example, discourses of social fictions represent how to be a masculine subject. At the same time, social fictions produce that subject through a process of differentiation from, and repudiation of, its others. The social discourses which form the masculine subject also form its excluded others: the knowing subject of consciousness and its unconscious; the masculine and its feminine other; the white and its black other; the heterosexual and its homosexual other. In this way, the repudiation of other identities founds the fraternal subject, such that the fraternal discourse produces both this masculine subject and its refused others.

This operation can also be seen in modern fraternal intersubjectivity. This discourse posits a social relation between rational and autonomous subjects, who are 'free' subjects possessing equality in relation to other subjects. It constructs the universal citizen subject. Yet, as discussed earlier, the fraternal social bond is a relation between masculine subjects. The universal citizen subject is in fact a masculine subject that claims universality. Fraternity only recognizes a relation to other masculine subjects, that is, to those who are bourgeois, white, male. For example, that construction of the universal citizen can be seen in battles for universal suffrage; in France, the home of the Rights of Man, women did not gain the right to vote until 1944. Judith Butler points out that '"universality", "equality", "the subject of rights" have been constructed through unmarked gender and racial exclusions' (1995a: 55). Paradoxically, the fraternal order produces an emancipatory discourse that a refusal of universal emancipation founds. In effect, the fraternal discourse is a universal that a non-universal founds.

The structure of the fraternal social relation produces its crisis because it produces a claim of universal emancipation and at the same time a repudiation of that universality. While that fraternal discourse of universality founds itself upon the exclusion of 'others', it also creates the possibility that those 'others' will claim universal emancipation. For example, the rise of the feminist and civil rights movements reveals how those whom the fraternal social contract excludes, whom it constructs as other than social subjects, can claim those modern fraternal discourses. In these movements, those who function as the non-universal and asocial grounds of the symbolic and material economy of the fraternal contract claim the right to be social subjects. Those constructed as other to fraternal sociality claim this right in the name of the universality of emancipatory modern discourses. An example of this process of the reappropriation of the fraternal discourse is given by Patricia Williams's rejection of critical legal theory's critique of rights discourses, on the grounds that

> '[r]ights' feels new in the mouths of most black people. It is still deliciously empowering to say. It is the magic wand of visibility and invisibility, of inclusion and exclusion, of power and no power. The concept of rights, both positive and negative, is the marker of our citizenship, our relation to others.
>
> (1993: 164)

These subjects experience the problematic of modernity differently from the fraternal masculine subject, because modern discourse produces them as subjected others while also creating new discourses of universal emancipation.

'Feminism, as a concept, was inherited from the humanist and rationalist eighteenth century', argues Jardine (1985: 20). However, we should add 'fraternal' to this description of eighteenth-century thought. From the modern fraternal social forms emerge the emancipatory discourses of 'liberty, equality, fraternity' of the French Declaration of the Rights of the Man and Citizen of 1789. First-wave feminism emerges with the modern fraternal citizen, a concept that links universal man and citizenship rights. In this sense, the genealogy of modern feminism begins with the emancipatory discourses of the Enlightenment. With the granting of the rights of citizens to men, feminists began to demand those rights for women.[4] In 1791, Olympe de Gouges wrote her *Declaration of the Rights of Woman and of the Citizen*, and in 1792 Mary Wollstonecraft her *Vindication of the Rights of Women*. Women began to claim the right to be universal social subjects.[5]

The modern fraternal tie between masculine subjects produces a discourse of equality which women then appropriate, arguing that equality exists not just 'between men', but also between men and women. In the twentieth century, the first- and second-wave feminist movements fought for (and largely won) formal equality of citizenship, such as the right to vote or to education. These political demands claim the right to participate in the social contract. They produce a symbolic crisis (at least) in the fraternal social form, symptoms of which can be seen in the reactionary politics which face the third wave, such as claims of the 'feminization' of society or the oppressiveness of 'political correctness', as well as in the increasing backlash against civil rights legislation.

To describe the relationship between modern and feminist discourses in this way does not pose modern discourse as a condition for all feminisms. Feminist historians have shown that throughout history different feminist discourses have been present. Moreover, there can be no simple relation of linear causality between modernity and feminism. Rather, the argument is more limited. It contends that particular to modern sociality is a fraternal social contract that produces a social discourse positing universal rights, and a universal subject possessing inalienable rights. With this shift, a new discourse of universal emancipation becomes available to women to rearticulate modern social fictions. In this sense, Braidotti's claim that Western '[f]eminism is THE discourse of modernity' is particularly compelling (1991: 10).

However, the problematic of modernity for feminists emerges from this appropriation of these emancipatory discourses. It is particularly acute following the so-called 'feminism/postmodernism' debates, which centre on the paradox of a feminism which uses modern discourses of rights and emancipation but which also generates a compelling critique of those discourses (Lennon and Whitford 1994a: 1). A key example can be seen in the difficulty of contemporary feminist engagements with the question of universality. The issue of the universality of equality and the particularity of difference has repeatedly emerged in different forms in feminist debates in the last twenty years, from the fraught discussions of essentialism and identity (Schor and Weed 1994) to more recent debates concerning universal women's rights (Alston and Steiner 2000).

This theoretical and political problem is especially evident in feminist legal theory, because of its engagement with the question of universal rights in the context of legal practice (Scott 1988). For example, Zillah Eisenstein's study *The Female Body and the Law* shows the difficulty that sexualized 'differences of the body', such as the pregnant body, 'pose for notions of equality' (1988: 4). Similarly, Mari Matsuda's work describes the difficulty that racialized 'bodies' pose for notions of legal neutrality. Like other legal theorists, Matsuda argues that this modern 'paradox' is a political and legal resource for critical race feminisms (1996: 6).

However, as Matsuda recognizes, the 'problematic' of these modern discourses lies in their unfulfillable promise – the promise of formal equality. Pateman argues that feminism now perceives 'the juridical equality and legal reform so central to contract doctrine . . . as a matter of women acting like men' (1988: 227). This promise of equality is impossible because it offers no more than the right to be the same as masculine subjects. This formulation of social equality does not disrupt modern fraternal discourses because it requires women to enter the social contract as either masculine social subjects, or as their other. Women cannot be sexually different (and so will face the difficulties of sexually 'neutral' treatment, such as those of working mothers), or alternatively can only be sexually different (and so will face the difficulties of being sexed, such as discrimination and sexual harassment in the workplace). Women continue to suffer substantive social inequality, despite increasing participation rates in education, employment, politics and other social institutions. The structure and terms of a social contract based in the fraternal relation between masculine subjects remain intact.

How, then, can feminists engage with the problematic of modernity? Judith Butler suggests that the feminist appropriation of the modern fraternal discourses must rearticulate and resignify those discourses. As Butler conceives it, that strategy:

> insists *both* on the exclusionary effects of the modernist narrative and the reviewable and rearticulable status of that narrative as a cultural resource that has serviced a collective project of extending and enhancing human freedoms . . . treating the narrative of modernity as a cultural resource, a resignifiable tradition.[6]
>
> (1995b: 128)

To undertake such a strategy is to accept the promise of the social discourses of modernity, insisting that they fulfil their emancipatory, democratic ideals even while rewriting what those norms might mean. This rewriting is necessarily political because it addresses the modern fraternal contract of the rights of man, the exclusions that found that fraternal contract, and the political effects of those exclusions. The scope of that rewriting must be significant – Chantal Mouffe argues that feminism needs to build a 'truly different idea of what it is to be a citizen and to act as a member of a democratic political community', which is a project of 'radical and plural democracy' (1992: 377).

However, such a political rewriting of the modern emancipatory discourses requires more than the resignification of the discourses of modernity, and more than the rearticulation of the fraternal social contract. For example, while Mouffe argues against a 'sexually differentiated model of citizenship' (1992: 377), if the existing model of citizenship is a relationship between masculine subjects, then a 'sexually neutral' model does not disrupt those fraternal discourses but simply reproduces them. In order to think the 'truly different conception' of the citizen which Mouffe calls for, it is necessary to rethink social discourses that are not just 'between men' but are also between women, and between men and women. This strategy requires rewriting the modern socio-symbolic order that founds the fraternal social contract. That feminist rewriting involves the production of a new socio-symbolic order, which represents different ways to be a subject, and different ways to represent social relations between subjects. Such a symbolic order would move beyond an exclusionary relation between masculine subjects. Women would not represent objects of social exchange, but instead could be social subjects able to represent their relation to their self and their others.

However, that project faces the difficult task of effecting an epistemological break in existing socio-symbolic structures so as to create new symbolic orders. Without this break, feminist knowledges will continue to rework modern discourses without shifting their symbolic economy. Such a break requires new feminist thinking, and hence a radical feminist epistemology. Braidotti points out that feminist knowledge 'implies the transformation of the very structures and images of thought, not just the propositional content of the thoughts' (1992: 184). A rewriting of modern fraternal discourses requires a transformation of models of knowledge, the contemporary reconstructive project of feminist epistemology.

Realizing such a project is not a utopian impossibility. The crisis of modernity is also a crisis of the masculine subject and its knowledges. Contemporary theorists (including feminist epistemologists) identify such a crisis in modern foundations of knowledge: reason, the universal and autonomous knower, and transcendental truth. Elizabeth Grosz describes it as 'reason's inability to come outside of itself, to enclose and know itself from the outside: the inadequation of the subject and its other' (1993: 189). The crisis of modern discourses of knowledge reveals that a repressed unconscious, repudiated others, and a refused materiality found modern forms of knowing.

The 'crisis' of masculinist knowledges represents the possibility of the production of other knowledges. In its deconstructive project, feminist episte-mology reinscribes the sexed knower and reveals the production of sexuated knowledges. It thereby challenges the epistemological foundations of modern paradigms of knowledge, by revealing that the universal knower is a sexed subject and that transcendental Truth is an act of social meaning. Grosz identifies the possibility offered by this deconstruction of masculinist knowledges for feminist thinking:

> the crisis of reason does not represent an impasse but rather a path for women to explore and judge for themselves . . . facing up to the implications of this crisis – to know (as woman, as other) the knower (as man has been and woman is now becoming).
>
> (1993: 210)

From its deconstructive project, feminist epistemology moves to its recon-structive project that aims to produce other models of knowledge. This project attempts to articulate other models of knowing which do not reproduce discourses of mastery. These new forms of knowing shift the position of women from being the objects of knowledge to being feminist knowers. They under-stand knowledge as a political practice, connecting the production of knowledge to the transformative democratic aims of feminist politics. These models of knowing offer new feminist knowledges which can change our relation to our 'selves' and our 'others', and so produce new social discourses of subjectivity and intersubjectivity.

Third-wave feminist epistemologies

Another Symbolic order?

How do we reconcile this project of change with the insight of psychoanalysis as to the difficulty of change, whether personal or social? In particular, Lacanian psychoanalysis presents the subject as ontologically riven in (and by) its very production as subject in the Symbolic order. Because the signifying structures of the Symbolic order produce a speaking subject, it has 'existence' only in that order, and will always suffer ontological loss in its production in language. For Lacanian theorists such as Charles Shepherdson (1993) and Zizek (2000), the Symbolic order is the unalterable and necessary condition of speaking subjectivity. These readings of Lacan maintain that to be a subject is always costly, and sociality is always founded on a sacrifice. In psychoanalysis, there is always a price to be paid for becoming a social subject: we will never be whole or complete.

If the cost of sociality is borne by all subjects, nevertheless that cost is borne differently by sexuated subjects. The female subject pays the debt of the speaking subject in the Symbolic order. Zizek argues that with the exchange of the signifier between subjects in the Symbolic order 'subjects pass to each other a common lack. In this perspective, a woman is not complementary to man, but she embodies his lack' (1989: 172). In this formulation, while all subjects suffer 'a common lack', the woman 'embodies his lack'. 'She' comes to embody the ontological loss suffered by the social subject by embodying lack. As I argued in Chapter 3, the masculine subject is posited 'as all' (*comme tout*), because there is another subject who is 'not all' (*pas toute*) – a subject who is castrated. The representation of the masculine Master as universal, unified and 'whole' is contingent upon the representation of the female subject as lacking and as castrated. Her 'castration' symbolizes his ontological lack-in-being. If to be a subject is always costly, then in the Symbolic order she embodies the cost of the sociality. If sacrifice founds sociality, that sacrifice in the Symbolic order is the mother and then the woman. In feminist terms, women pay the cost of a sociality that founds itself upon a phallic Symbolic order.

The psychoanalytic question is not therefore whether all subjects suffer ontological loss in becoming subjects, as according to the Lacanian (and Freudian) accounts they do. Rather, the feminist questions concern the representation of that lack-in-being in a symbolic order and sociality, whether certain subjects suffer more from that representation than others, and whether other social orders are possible. Against conservative readings of Lacan's work such as Zizek's, the repression of the m(O)ther is not the only way to represent the social subject and the order that produces it. While Lacanian theory describes a modern Western Symbolic order, there is the empirical, logical and political possibility that there are other social arrangements that do not require that the sexual difference of 'Woman' represent the cost of becoming a subject, nor that she should be the signifier of social exchange.

A feminist psychoanalytic argument for the possibility of such a different social order that continues to be extremely influential derives from the work of two feminist object-relations theorists, Dorothy Dinnerstein (1976) and Nancy Chodorow (1978) (Elliot 1991: 99). These theorists argue that the social fact that women, and not men, are the primary carers of children produces and reproduces the sexism of Western social relations. Both perceive joint parenting by men and women as a means of preventing the reproduction of sexism. Although few feminists would argue against the practical necessity of such changes for an improvement of women's lives as primary care-givers, the possible contestation of the Symbolic order does not simply lie in 'better' (less sexist) parenting arrangements, or in a more equitable reconstitution of the heterosexual model of parenting. The crucial insight of Lacanian theory is that the child's parental figures exist in a symbolic relation to the child. To disrupt that symbolic relation of parent to child requires an intervention not only in the real but also in the symbolic and imaginary registers.

In terms of a feminist politics, there also must be different representations of the social sacrifice of the subject – its ontological loss. Lacan's account of sexed subjectivity rests on the premise that the Symbolic order signifies the material body as a sexed body, and thus that sexual subjectivity is contingent. If sexed subjectivity is contingent, then it is possible to change it. However, that change requires intervention at the level of signification because it is the order of representation – the Symbolic order – that produces sexual difference. This does not entail that we should or could reduce feminism to a symbolic politics, but that a rewriting of the fraternal contract requires intervention in the symbolic register. This intervention stakes itself on the possibility that the phallic signifier is not the transcendental foundation of an order of representation, and that a symbolic order need not be phallogocentric. Kaja Silverman points out that '[n]o social or psychic imperative dictates that the symbolic Law be synonymous with the Name-of-the-Father; that the phallus stand in for the subject's "very life"; or that castration be represented only by certain members of the socius' (1992a: 114).

My contention that the symbolic law that founds existing forms of subjectivity and intersubjectivity is not a transcendental condition of their formation rests on a distinction between a symbolic order, which is the necessary ordering of symbolic relations, and the Symbolic order, which is the arrangement of signifiers in relation to the phallic signifier. It distinguishes between the structure of language as the differential organization and articulation of signifiers, and the Law of the Father, which structures signifiers in relation to the phallus. The Symbolic order represents one arrangement of linguistic and social orders, and so a different order of signifying and social structures is at least in principle possible. Employing this distinction permits the possibility of other symbolic orders that represent different forms of socio-symbolic relations. By undertaking this possibility, a post-Lacanian feminist epistemology reads the *not all* of female subjectivity not as a representation of castration (and hence of the cost of sociality), but as revealing the failure of the phallic signifier to represent her. It undertakes to transform the failure of the phallic signifier to represent 'all' into a political project for the production of new forms of the social and symbolic.

This task of the production of new forms of the socio-symbolic order represents a post-Lacanian project of challenging the symbolic structures of the existing social order. One important example of such an undertaking can be found in Irigaray's work. Whitford summarizes this project as the construction of 'a female sociality (*les femmes entre elles*), a female symbolic and female social contract, a horizontal relation *between* women' (1991: 79). Irigaray calls for a horizontal relation between women because she argues that the Symbolic order represents a horizontal relation between men, and a culture 'between-men' (1990: 96). While Irigaray accepts the Lacanian description of the symbolic economy of the modern social order, she provides a feminist critique of its sexuated nature. In calling for a new symbolic order, Irigaray accepts that a symbolic order is necessary for the production of a speaking subject. However, she rejects the positing of the modern Symbolic order as an ontological condition for all subjects at all times, characterizing it instead as a necessary condition of the masculine subject and its social relations. Against a conservative reading of Lacan's work which holds that the modern Symbolic order is the only possible symbolic structure, Irigaray raises the possibility of a different socio-symbolic order in her suggestion that women create a new language and systems of representations that are appropriate for them (1990: 96).

Irigaray proposes two key strategies for a rewriting of the socio-symbolic order. The first is a deconstruction of masculinist philosophical discourse as the master discourse of modern Western culture, a strategy exemplified by *Speculum of the Other Woman* (1974). The second is a reconstructive project that calls for the creation of a female imaginary and symbolic. One important example of this constructive project in Irigaray's work is her creation of different representations of the female body, such as the 'two-lips' metaphor of *This Sex Which Is Not One* (1977). A second important example is the creation of a maternal genealogy for women through the figure of a female divine in order to ensure adequate female sublimation, as can be seen in *Je, tu, nous: Towards a Culture of Difference* (1990).

In terms of a rewriting of the fraternal contract, these strategies for the creation of a female imaginary and symbolic are both important and useful. However, those strategies also limit their intervention to the representation of the female subject. These strategies do not directly intervene in the symbolic representation of intersubjectivity, because they do not challenge the representation of sociality in the symbolic contract. In order to form new representations of the female speaking subject, it is also necessary to create a new representation of intersubjectivity, because the symbolic representation of the relation between subjects produces the speaking subject. For example, in Chapter 4 I argued that feminist discourses produce not only new representations of the female body, but also new representations of the female social subject. That project requires intervention in social discourses of subjectivity and intersubjectivity. For this reason, while Irigaray's strategies are important, they do not constitute the effective rewriting of the Symbolic order that she proposes.[7]

Julia Kristeva more explicitly takes up the same question as Irigaray: *'what is our place in the social contract?'* (1993: 212). Kristeva argues that a reconsideration of the place of women in the social contract requires a reformulation of the subject itself. For Kristeva, that project requires 'an *interiorization of the fundamental separation of the socio-symbolic contract*' in an acknowledgement of difference and heterogeneity within the subject itself (1993: 223). As a result, '[r]ather than love the other as himself, the ethical subject-in-process will love the other *in* herself' (Oliver 1993: 186). Kristeva argues that this project founds a radically new way to conceive the subject of the socio-symbolic contract. Because of her reconception of the subject and its ethical relations to others, Kristeva's work has been interpreted as providing a means of transforming subjectivity, and hence intersubjectivity (Edelstein 1993).

However, Kristeva's project does not call into question the structure of the socio-symbolic contract itself. The sacrifice that Kristeva would interiorize in the subject is the sacrifice of the mother – a maternal sacrifice that forms the founding phantasy of both traditional and modern patriarchal structures. This sacrifice to a phallic socio-symbolic contract has the effect of positioning women in symbolic (and real) exchange as symbolic (and material) lack. In this way, Kristeva's strategy leaves the sacrificial structure of the Symbolic order untouched.[8]

Knowing the mother

If the social contract of the Symbolic order is to be rewritten, then we need to represent the relation to the mother as other than a founding sacrifice. Similarly to Irigaray, Kristeva argues that women are vulnerable to depression because of an unfulfilled mourning for the mother (1987: 71). For Kristeva, the depressive position reflects a mourning for the mother, which has the effect that the subject perceives a failure of the signifier and an emptiness of language. However, as I argued in Chapter 3, the failure of the signifier occurs prior to an unfulfilled mourning for the mother. The lack of a symbolized relation to the mother precipitates a failure of representation and hence the experience of the emptiness of language, and its symptom, melancholia. The question of how to represent the maternal relation remains.

As I discussed in Chapter 3, primary feminist identifications with other women reproduce the maternal identification of the daughter in all its ambivalent complexity. However, the structure of primary maternal identification alters in its (re)production in feminist identifications. Feminist identifications do not merely replicate the personal relationship to the maternal, because political identifications with feminist politics and communities reconfigure that relationship. These identifications rearticulate the relation to the maternal figure because that affective relation is brought into discourse. This discourse enables the representation of the relation between mother and daughter because it provides the signifying material necessary to symbolize the maternal relation.

Importantly, this symbolization reworks the maternal relationship in terms of a political relationship between women. It does not reproduce the mother as a maternal object, but produces her as another woman and as another speaking subject. Feminist discourse posits the mother as a social subject. In maternalist mythologies, and the more recent communitarian versions of these mythologies, women are first and foremost mothers, and the mother is always and only a maternal object. She is not a social subject who has other social relations besides that of her maternal role. These maternalist myths have always been untrue for working-class women, and are untrue for the increasing number of women who are workers *and* mothers, who are the heads of households *and* primary carers, or the many women who do not have children. By contrast, feminist discourse represents women as social subjects rather than as maternal objects. Because of this representation, feminist discourse permits the representation of the maternal relation as a relation between two speaking subjects, rather than between a subject and an object, and so it is not predicated on the sacrifice of the maternal object. Feminist discourse can operate as a symbolic mediation of the relation between mother and daughter because it enables a symbolic relation to the mother. Feminist identifications can thereby shift the structures of maternal identification for the next generation of feminist daughters.

This discursive shift has radical epistemological implications. In Chapter 3, I argued that the Discourse of the Master produces a particular relation between knower and known object. In my reading of Lacanian epistemology, the desire for the lost (m)Other structures the knowledge of the Knowing Master, such that the knower desires the repudiated mother to 'complete' his lack-in-being. In the Discourse of the Master, knowledge is predicated on lack, and so is structured in the negativity of desire. However, in feminist discourse the knowing subject has a different relation to the maternal object. Unlike the masculine subject, a maternal identification that does not negate a relation to the mother produces the female subject. This structure of identification offers the possibility of bringing into representation the relation to the mother. Crucially, feminist discourse symbolizes that relation between mother and daughter – whether it is structured as differentiation or unification. Productive identification forms the structure of the epistemological relation of knower to what is known, rather than a desiring negativity that founds the repudiation of the maternal.

Feminist discourse produces a knowledge which (re)presents the relation of the knower to the mother. This relation is symbolized in the daughter's representation of her relation to the mother, and the restructuring of that relation in feminist discourse, which provides the signifying material for its representation and reworking. The symbolization of the maternal relation makes it possible to represent women as other than maternal figures, and to represent women as social subjects (and not only as maternal objects). Feminist discourse does not posit the mother as the subtended fertile ground of knowledge, nor as the object of the paradigmatic modern epistemological relation – because it does not pose her as the phantasmic and repressed condition of representation. It disrupts the phallogocentric relation between ontological and epistemological lack, and so the paternal law does not structure the epistemological relation of knower and known object. In this disruption, another discourse of knowledge beside the Master's becomes possible.

The discourse of women

The production of other discourses of knowledge creates new discourses of subjectivity and intersubjectivity. For women, the possibility of a different representation of female subjectivity from that of the fraternal social fictions is of crucial importance. The importance of the representation of new forms of subjectivity and intersubjectivity in feminist discourse can be illustrated through a further exploration of the 'female melancholia' that Kristeva and Irigaray describe.

Female melancholia derives from the exclusion of women from the fraternal symbolic law, which fails to represent her as a social subject. This description of depression locates it in the symbolic register. However, Ellie Ragland-Sullivan argues that depression is 'a principally female Imaginary reaction [which] attests to an identificatory loss of prestige and power' (1987: 269). She locates depression in the imaginary order, arguing that women do not have a socially powerful maternal identificatory figure. Unsurprisingly, she proposes creating new maternal roles, a similar strategy to that of the feminist object-relations theorists. Ironically, Ragland-Sullivan ignores the effect of the symbolic law. The female depressive confronts more than a problem of the imaginary order, as Lacan suggests in his argument that melancholia is situated at the level of the Symbolic (S8: 458–459). Kristeva's conception of depression as a disavowal of the Symbolic clarifies why women are particularly vulnerable to melancholia (1987: 43–47). Depression represents a melancholic disavowal of the Symbolic. It is a reaction to a social order in which the Symbolic order is structured by the phallic signifier, the phallus conflated with the penis, and the bearer of the phallus/penis privileged in the social world. If a female subject disavows the Symbolic, it is because she confronts a Symbolic order that says all and nothing. She confronts a symbolic economy that fails to represent her sexed or social subjectivity as other than phallic.

A discourse that is able to represent the female subject as a sexed and social subject can enable her to evade melancholia. She requires a discourse of sociality other than the fraternal phallic social bond. In *New Maladies of the Soul*, Kristeva argues that Mme de Staël's intellectual engagements permit her to evade 'the melancholic woe that is so tempting and threatening for the second sex' (1993: 162). In her discussion of Mme de Staël, Kristeva proposes that '[t]heory contemplates depression and protects us from it' (1993: 162). For Kristeva, de Staël sought '[t]he mastery of psychic space . . . by these words, judgements, or logical and novelistic constructs' (1993: 171). In Kristeva's account, 'theory' (that is, the act of representation) protects de Staël from depression because it enables the representation of her affect (1993: 162–163). Taking up a classical psychoanalytic position, Kristeva argues that 'theory' functions as a system of representation that can provide necessary signifiers of affect. In her argument, women require a discourse to protect them from melancholia, whether it is an intellectual or a psychoanalytic discourse. However, there is a further question as to whether existing discourses, including intellectual and analytic discourses, can provide the signifying material necessary for the psychic and social representation of female subjectivity. If the existing Symbolic order represents women as lack, then where is the female subject to find a symbolization that will not construct her as lacking? Where is she to find a symbolization that can address the failure of phallic representation? It cannot be found in the Discourse of the Master, which does not protect her from melancholia. The protection against melancholia requires the possibility of an other discourse.

This possibility can be found in feminist discourse. Rather than succumbing to melancholia by falling into a depressive position in which the symbolic says all and nothing of women, feminist discourse 'bring[s] about new forms of representation and definition of the female subject' in order to produce new symbolic and social forms (Braidotti 1992: 182). Feminist discourses resignify existing social discourses through their representation of the real of women, and so produce new discourses of what it means 'to be' a subject. In this way, feminist discourses articulate new discourses of subjectivity, and, in particular, of female subjectivity. However, in this context we should not confine 'discourse' to aesthetic, intellectual or psychoanalytic practices, but instead conceive it more broadly as those practices which resignify existing social discourses, and so produce new discourses to represent other ways to exist as subjects and in relation to other subjects.

Feminist discourse

Feminist discourse produces new discourses of subjectivity and, crucially, of intersubjectivity. In Chapter 4, I argued that feminist epistemic communities produce feminist discourses. My model of feminist discourse conceives it as symbolizing the relation between feminist subjects, functioning as the discursive medium of that relation and hence as its mediation. In this way, feminist epistemic communities produce discourses that articulate a relation between women. In this model, feminist discourse symbolizes women's intersubjective relations in terms of feminist politics. Feminist discourses articulate a relation between women as speaking subjects. In Irigaray's terms, feminist discourse constructs a female sociality in its symbolization of a horizontal relation between women – 'les femmes entres elles'. Feminist discourses produce a social contract between female subjects and hence a new discursive social bond.

However, the ethical and political practices of feminism construct that social bond. Those practices form the intersubjective relations of feminist subjects because an ethical relation to other women and to feminist politics constructs those intersubjective relations. Feminism constructs the relation between subjects in terms of politics and ethics. For this reason, feminist discourse represents intersubjectivity as a political and ethical relation. As I argued in Chapter 4, feminist discourse rearticulates discourses of intersubjectivity because it constructs the relations between subjects as ethical and political relations. Unlike other intersubjective discourses, such as the social fictions of the fraternal social contract, feminist discourses articulate the relation between subjects as ethical and political practices. This does not entail that the relation between feminist subjects is necessarily ethical or political, but that a commitment to feminist politics constructs those relations in terms of an ethics and a politics. If discourse articulates social bonds, then feminist discourses articulate a different form of social bond because they produce a new representation of social relationships. Feminist discourses represent a different intersubjective relation because they articulate it as a political and ethical act.

This new social bond does not posit women as objects of exchange, but rather as social subjects. This symbolic relation posits women as speaking subjects, and accordingly as subjects within the social order. Feminist discourse produces a new ordering of sociality that does not render the ontological loss of all subjects as the symbolic castration of women. If the fraternal relation is a discourse of the relation between men, feminist discourse articulates the relation between women. This discourse fundamentally shifts the relation between all subjects. It produces a new symbolic order that represents all subjects, men and women, as having a relation to both parents – both mother and father. In this symbolic order, all subjects experience *jouissance*, suffer ontological loss and the ravages of the death drive. This discourse is a new socio-symbolic contract that articulates a different representation of our relation to ourselves and our others.

This new socio-symbolic contract represents women as knowers, as the makers and users of signs. Irigaray calls for the female subject of enunciation to become an epistemological subject, as she argues that women must become knowing subjects. Whitford suggests that, for Irigaray, 'the women's movement, in drawing attention to the male subject of enunciation, has staked a claim for the right of the female subject to be an epistemological subject too' (1991: 49). Feminist epistemic communities create this possibility of the female knowing subject by the production of feminist discourse. Feminism creates 'the female subject of enunciation' by positing women as speaking subjects. The feminist epistemic community posits women as knowing subjects. It constitutes the feminist subject of enunciation through identifications with the feminist movement and politics. This position of enunciation in turn creates the feminist epistemological subject – the feminist knower. In positing women as knowers, feminist knowledge produces new discourses in its representation of the real of women, and in its articulation of the relation between women as speaking subjects. In this way, feminist discourse creates new orders of knowledge and new practices of knowing.

Feminist knowledges offer new representations of the female subject, and new representations of that subject to herself and to her others. In the production of new discourses of women and their relation to each other, feminist discourse undertakes a radical reconstructive project. The contestation and disruption of the Symbolic order are undertaken to create a different symbolic order. This feminist project posits its aim in both present and future tense. It concerns the necessary political engagements of the 'now' of the present, but it is also predicated upon the possibility that other ways to represent socio-symbolic relations can exist. In their (re)presentation of sociality as an ethical and political relation, feminist knowledges represent the possibility that discourses other than those of mastery can found intersubjective relations.

Radical knowledges

These feminist discourses produce another socio-symbolic contract. This new social contract does not refuse women as the Other of lack, but instead posits them as speaking and social subjects. This new socio-symbolic order permits a different representation of subjects and their relation to other subjects, such that it produces new discourses of subjectivity and intersubjectivity. Those discourses create new forms of subjectivity and intersubjectivity that do not reproduce the fraternal discourses of social fictions.

In the fraternal order, the discourses of social fictions represent social subjects and relations, and those representations have material effect. They have material effect in terms of the symbolic economy of the production of the subject and its relation to others, as well as in terms of the material relations between subjects. The production of a new discourse, such as a feminist discourse, rearticulates existing relations of subjectivity and intersubjectivity in its representation of other possible forms of subjective and social relations. If the fraternal discourses of social fictions create subjects and their relations to others, then feminist discourse both forms and transforms subjectivity and intersubjectivity.

Feminist discourse is a productive signifying practice that intervenes at the level of the signification of the existing symbolic order to produce another socio-symbolic relation. For example, if the discourses of social fictions prescribe a certain fantasy of 'Woman', then feminist discourses represent new forms of sexed identity. In this way, feminist discourse is a political discourse that can create new socio-symbolic forms. Its transformative power can be seen in the immense social changes that women have achieved over the last twenty years. Feminist discourse has transformed how we know ourselves and our others, and will continue to do so.

In a world that empirically and institutionally engenders knowledge as masculine, feminist knowledges seek to know otherwise in order to change that world. If we cannot conceive other ways to be social beings, the hegemonic socio-symbolic order will continue to replicate itself. Without new systems of representation, its symbolic economy will continue to structure forms of subjectivity and intersubjectivity. Without new ways of thinking, its discourses of mastery will continue to reproduce its epistemological regime.

The importance of the reconstructive project of feminist epistemology lies in its symbolic and imaginary intervention in existing structures of representation of subjectivity and sociality, and its production of a new socio-symbolic contract. The radical power of feminist discourse lies in its potential for the production of a new socio-symbolic order. For feminist knowledges, the radical task of epistemology involves the production of a new social bond and another symbolic order. In this project, the task of a third-wave feminist epistemology can be found.

My account of feminist discourse reconceives feminist politics as a social and discursive practice, and reveals the politics of discourse. This reconception of feminist politics creates new projects for third-wave feminism. One task is the resignification of the female subject, which posits her as a speaking subject and represents the real of her social experience. This task is part of a broader undertaking of the creation of discourses of women as social subjects. This broader project involves the production of new discourses of intersubjectivity that represent women as members of a sociality. That representation requires the creation of a new form of sociality through the construction of new ethical and political discourses of the social. This model reconceives third-wave politics as the production and enactment of feminist discourses of subjectivity and intersubjectivity. This challenge for the third wave involves a renewed activism and coalitional action that produces and performs new social discourses. The making of that utopian moment in the present is the task that remains before us.

From this One to an Other

The symbolic structures of a sociality order subjectivity and intersubjectivity, because they represent what it is to be a subject and what it is to exist in relation to other subjects. These structures order a relation to mortality and *jouissance* in that they structure the representation of death and pleasure. These symbolic laws order a relation to language, since they structure the limits of representation. These symbolic networks form the production of the subject and its relation to other subjects.

In his seminar of 1959–1960, *The Ethics of Psychoanalysis* (S7), Lacan poses Antigone as the exemplary ethical figure. Antigone's ethical act is to move outside the symbolic laws that order her community, and so to put her symbolic identity and community at stake. In Lacan's account, Antigone reveals that there is no Other of the Other in her refusal to be subject to those laws. At the cost of her life, she undertakes an act that reveals the ultimately fictional nature of the symbolic order. She reveals that the Law does not have to be obeyed. A decade later, in his seminar of 1968–1969, *From an Other to the other* (S16), Lacan admits that '[t]he Name of the Father is a rift that remains wide open in my discourse, it is known only through an act of faith: there is no incarnation in the place of the Other'.[9] The feminist ethical act refuses to undertake this act of faith. If the Symbolic order is a fiction that forms the subject (and its relation to its objects and its others), a feminist ethics refuses to sustain this fiction. That act reveals the possibility of another representation of symbolic identity and community.

A third-wave feminist epistemological project that undertakes the production of another symbolic order embarks upon a transformative ethical act. That ethical act represents a movement from this One of the Discourse of the Master to other Discourses, a discourse of others. Those other discourses seek to articulate a social bond between subjects other than mastery. In this social bond, the female speaking subject takes her place in a social order which constitutes her relation to her self and her others as an ethical and political relation. She is not the mute Antigone who lies in her tomb dying, but the Antigone who 'speaks well' of her ethical obligation. This speaking well is the production of another symbolic structure for a sociality that moves from the One of the Master subject to the Other of relational subjects. This task cannot be undertaken with a naive acceptance that our work is done (as in a postfeminism), nor with the fatalism that nothing is to be done (as in a revisionist second wave). This third feminist generation must undertake the ethical act of making feminisms' time now.

Notes

Introduction

1 For an extended discussion of third-wave feminisms, see Arneil (1999: 186–223). Typical examples of third-wave texts include: Baumgardner and Richards (2000), Drake and Heywood (1997b), Findlen (1995b), Walker (1995b) and Zita (1997b).

1 Feminist epistemologies

1 For a fuller exposition of Pierre Bourdieu's concept of 'field', see *An Invitation to Reflexive Sociology* (Bourdieu and Wacquant 1992: 94–115).
2 Compare, for example, Harding and Hintikka's earlier definition of feminist epistemology (1983a: xix) to the Lennon and Whitford rejection of a 'female' way of knowing (1994a: 13).
3 This analysis follows Spivak's argument that feminist theory should not confuse these concepts of ontology, axiology and epistemology (1989: 206–223).
4 I discuss this question of the relation between female and feminist subjects further in Chapter 3.
5 For an overview of these arguments, see Hartsock, Harding and Hill Collins in Allen and Howard (2000).
6 In this emphasis upon the production of knowledge, feminist epistemology can be seen as part of a broader movement in contemporary theories of knowledge, such as postfoundationalism within philosophy and constructionism within sociology and history and philosophy of science.
7 Alessandra Tanesini's paper concerns theories of language in relation to feminist practice, but does not address the production of feminist knowledge (1994: 203–216).

2 Lacanian epistemologies

1 For a history of the women's movement in France, see Duchen (1986).
2 See Marini (1992: 82) and Roudinesco (1990: 511–526). Catherine Millot and Françoise Petitot also note this connection in Hoffman Baruch and Serrano (1988: 89, 106).
3 These debates concern the issue of co-authorship of those seminars by Lacan's legal and theoretical heir, Jacques-Alain Miller, and the accuracy of transcription and the legitimacy of Miller's editorial preparation of the seminars: Roudinesco (1997: 305).

For a discussion of the complex political and theoretical history of the publication of the seminars, see Roudinesco (1990: 689–692).

4 To date, thirteen of the twenty-seven seminars given by Lacan have been published. Of the twelve published seminars, three have been published in the Lacanian journal *Ornicar?* Only six are fully translated into English.

5 For example, Muller and Richardson conclude their reading of 'Subversion of the Subject and the Dialectic of Desire' with the statement 'we must be content with what few misty glimmers have been allowed us in the course of this long, foggy night' (1994: 375).

6 Lacan describes the double condition of language as being reducible to its signifying elements (the symbolic order), and their combination in a closed order (the Symbolic order) (*É*: 169). For this reason, I distinguish between a symbolic order, which is an ordering of symbolic relations, and the Symbolic order, which is the ordering of structures of signification in relation to the phallic signifier.

7 For further discussion of Lacan's relationship to Saussure's work, see Campbell (1999).

8 See Dolar (1998) for an account of Lacan's later reformulation of the cogito as the subject of the unconscious.

9 It should be noted that Lacan derives his concept of temporality from his psychoanalytic practice, and it is a non-linear concept of time. For a further discussion of the Lacanian theory of time, see Forrester (1990: 168–218).

10 'Position of the Unconscious' was first given as a paper in 1960 before being rewritten in 1964 and published in 1966 (*Éc*: 919).

11 It should be noted that, in 'Science and Truth', Lacan slips between the knowing subject as the subject of science and the known object as the subject, reflecting a similar slippage in the distinction between the analyst and analysand as knowing subjects.

12 *Séminaire XIV, La Logique du fantasme*, unpublished. Cited in Marini (1992: 205).

13 It is ironic that this project to rationalize the unconscious is exceeded by Lacan's own clinical and textual practice, which exhibits the excesses of an unconscious which does not appear to be readily formalizable.

14 For a further discussion of the shift in Lacan's work, see Milner (1995) and Charraud (1997).

3 Knowing subjects

1 Lacan's concept of the absolute master derives from Alexandre Kojève's influential reading of Hegel. For a discussion of Lacan's appropriation of, and relation to, this concept see Borch-Jacobsen (1991).

2 This description of the sexuation of the subject is that of the 'classical' Lacan of *Écrits*. While this account of the masculine subject essentially remains unchanged in Lacan's later work, his later seminar of 1972–1973, *Encore*, reformulates his concept of the female subject. This conceptual shift is discussed below, see pp. 86–89.

3 For further discussion of the difficulties of feminine paternal identification, see below, pp. 91–92.

4 For an influential example of the feminist debate around the figure of the hysteric, see Cixous and Clément (1975).

5 For Dora's case history, see Freud (1905). For discussion of the feminist debates concerning Dora, see Bernheimer and Kahane (1985).

6 The refusal to name oneself as feminist does not mean that one does not identify with a feminist politics or project. For further discussion of this point, see below, p. 94 onwards.

7 For an example of the debates that have arisen from declarations of allegiance to a feminist politics by men, see Jardine and Smith (1987).

8 Laplanche and Pontalis note that Freud most often describes primary identification in terms of the little boy's identification with the father (1973: 336). In a footnote to his discussion of primary identification, Freud points out that since the primary identification occurs prior to the sexual differentiation of the parents in the Oedipus complex, then primary identification involves the object of the parent rather than the sexed figure of the mother or father (1923: 370). However, because of existing parenting arrangements, that parent is usually a maternal figure.

9 In the second psychical topography, secondary identification forms the basis of the psychic structure of id, ego and super-ego (Freud 1923).

10 The term 'other' is used in the psychoanalytic sense of an other to the subject, rather than in the sense of a culturally constructed Other.

4 Feminist discourses

1 An important exception is Gemma Corradi Fiumara's writing on language. For example, see 'The Metaphoric Function and the Question of Objectivity' (1994: 31–44).

2 Where the term 'Real' is capitalized, it refers to the Lacanian concept of the Real, which is discussed further below, see pp. 131–132.

3 This new signifier is not the master signifier, as it does not represent the signifier which sustains the fundamental fantasy of the analysand and which comes into existence in the course of analysis. Rather, this is a signifier of the lack of the Other.

4 For a compelling philosophical and political critique of social constructivism, see Butler (1993b: 4–12).

5 For an example of this process, see Kidder *et al.* (1995: 62).

5 Feminism's time

1 See, in particular, Lacan's doctoral thesis, *De la psychose paranoïaque* (1932), on paranoia which includes his case study of the paranoid 'Aimée'.

2 In claiming language as the foundation of human society, Lacan places himself in an important tradition of Western political thought, which runs from Aristotle's description of the speaking being to the social contract theory of Rousseau.

3 Rather, this symbolic economy is based on a refused homosexual identification. For further discussion of the repudiated homosexual relation, see the discussion of the formation of social fictions in Chapter 4.

4 However, the history of the battle for women's suffrage in the USA and Australia reminds us that in fact suffrage was often claimed not on behalf of all women, but on behalf of white women. For example, bell hooks describes how Anglo-American feminists sacrificed the vote of African-American women in their suffrage campaigns (1981: 127–128).

5 For a superb account of the relationship between democratic liberalism and feminism, see Nash (1998).

6 Butler develops her strategy from Paul Gilroy's important reading of the Enlightenment in *The Black Atlantic* (1993).

7 In her most recent work, Irigaray calls for 'a sexually-marked civil code' (1994: 9) in order 'to obtain positive rights of citizenship in the female mode' (1994: 38).
8 For an example of a compelling critique of the primacy of the Symbolic in Kristeva's work, see Butler (1993a).
9 *Séminaire XVI*, unpublished, cited in Marini (1992: 217).

Bibliography

Adams, P. (1996) *The Emptiness of the Image: Psychoanalysis and Sexual Differences*, London and New York: Routledge.

Addelson, K. Pyne (1993) 'Knower/Doers and Their Moral Problems', in L. Alcoff and E. Potter (eds) *Feminist Epistemologies*, London and New York: Routledge.

Alarcón, N. (1994) 'The Theoretical Subject(s) of *This Bridge Called My Back* and Anglo-American Feminism', in S. Seidman (ed.) *The Postmodern Turn: New Perspectives on Social Theory*, Cambridge: Cambridge University Press.

Alcoff, L. and Potter, E. (1993a) 'Introduction: When Feminism Intersects Epistemology', in L. Alcoff and E. Potter (eds) *Feminist Epistemologies*, London and New York: Routledge.

—— (eds) (1993b) *Feminist Epistemologies*, London and New York: Routledge.

Alfonso, R. and Trigilio, J. (1997) 'Surfing the Third Wave: A Dialogue Between Two Third Wave Feminists', *Hypatia: A Journal of Feminist Philosophy*, 12, 3: 7–16.

Allen, C. and Howard, J. (eds) (2000) *Provoking Feminisms*, Chicago and London: Chicago University Press.

Alston, P. and Steiner, H. (2000) *International Human Rights in Context: Law, Politics, Morals*, Oxford: Oxford University Press.

Althusser, L. (1996) *Writings on Psychoanalysis: Freud and Lacan*, trans. Jeffrey Mehlman, New York: Columbia University Press.

Antony, L. and Witt, C. (eds) (1993) *A Mind of One's Own: Feminist Essays on Reason and Objectivity*, Boulder, CO and Oxford: Westview.

Anzaldúa, G. (1987) *Borderlands/La Frontera*, San Francisco: Spinsters/Aunt Lute.

Aoki, D. (1995) 'Using and Abusing French Discourse Theory: Misreading Lacan and the Symbolic Order', *Theory, Culture and Society*, 12: 47–50.

Arneil, B. (1999) *Politics and Feminism*, Oxford: Blackwell.

Bailey, C. (1997) 'Making Waves and Drawing Lines: The Politics of Defining the Vicissitudes of Feminism', *Hypatia: A Journal of Feminist Philosophy*, 12, 3: 16–28.

Barwell, I. (1994) 'Towards A Defence of Objectivity', in K. Lennon and M. Whitford (eds) *Knowing the Difference: Feminist Perspectives in Epistemology*, London and New York: Routledge.

Baumgardner, J. and Richards, A. (2000) *Manifesta: Young Women, Feminism and the Future*, New York: Farrar, Straus and Giroux.

Benevuto, B. and Kennedy, R. (1986) *The Works of Jacques Lacan: An Introduction*, London: Free Association.

Bernheimer, C. and Kahane, C. (1985) *In Dora's Case: Freud, Hysteria, Feminism*, London: Virago.

Bhabha, H. (1994) *The Location of Culture*, London: Routledge.

Borch-Jacobsen, M. (1991) *Lacan: The Absolute Master*, trans. D. Brick, Stanford, CA: Stanford University Press.

Bordo, S. (1986) 'The Cartesian Masculinization of Thought', *Signs: Journal of Women and Society*, 11, 3: 439–456.

Bordo, S. and Jagger, A. (eds) (1989) *Gender/Body/Knowledge: Feminist Reconstructions of Being and Knowing*, New Brunswick, NJ: Rutgers University Press.

Bourdieu, P. and Wacquant, L. J. (1992) *An Invitation to Reflexive Sociology*, Cambridge: Polity.

Bowie, M. (1979) 'Jacques Lacan', in J. Sturrock (ed.) *Structuralism and Since: From Lévi-Strauss to Derrida*, Oxford: Oxford University Press.

—— (1991) *Lacan*, Cambridge, MA: Harvard University Press.

—— (1993) *Psychoanalysis and the Future of Theory*, Oxford: Blackwell.

Bowleg, L. (1995) 'Better in the Bahamas? Not If You're a Feminist', in B. Findlen (ed.) *Listen Up: Voices from the Next Feminist Generation*, Seattle: Seal.

Bracher, M. (1993) *Lacan, Discourse and Social Change: A Psychoanalytic Cultural Criticism*, Ithaca, NY and London: Cornell University Press.

—— (1994) 'On the Psychological and Social Functions of Language: Lacan's Theory of the Four Discourses', in M. Bracher, M. W. Alcorn Jr., R. J. Corthell and F. Massardier-Kenney (eds) *Lacanian Theory of Discourse: Subject, Structure and Society*, New York and London: New York University Press.

Braidotti, R. (1991) *Patterns of Dissonance: A Study of Women in Contemporary Feminism*, trans. E. Guild, Cambridge: Polity.

—— (1992) 'On the Female Feminist Subject, or: from "she-self" to "she-other"', in G. Bock and S. James (eds) *Beyond Equality and Difference: Citizenship, Feminist Politics and Female Subjectivity*, London: Routledge.

—— (1994a) 'Body-Image and the Pornography of Representation', in K. Lennon and M. Whitford (eds) *Knowing the Difference: Feminist Perspectives in Epistemology*, London and New York: Routledge.

—— (1994b) *Nomadic Subjects: Embodiment and Sexual Difference in Contemporary Feminist Theory*, New York: Columbia University Press.

Brennan, T. (1986) 'Introduction', in T. Brennan (ed.) *Between Feminism and Psychoanalysis*, London and New York: Routledge.

—— (1993) *History After Lacan*, New York and London: Routledge.

Butler, J. (1990) *Gender Trouble: Feminism and the Subversion of Identity*, London and New York: Routledge.

—— (1993a) 'The Body Politics of Julia Kristeva', in K. Oliver (ed.) *Ethics, Politics, and Difference in Julia Kristeva's Writing*, London and New York: Routledge.

—— (1993b) *Bodies That Matter: On The Discursive Limits of 'Sex'*, London and New York: Routledge.

—— (1995a) 'Contingent Foundations', in J. Butler, S. Benhabib, D. Cornell and N. Fraser, *Feminist Contentions: A Philosophical Exchange*, London and New York: Routledge.

—— (1995b) For a Careful Reading', in J. Butler, S. Benhabib, D. Cornell and N. Fraser, *Feminist Contentions: A Philosophical Exchange*, London and New York: Routledge.

—— (1997a) *Excitable Speech*, London and New York: Routledge.

—— (1997b) *The Psychic Life of Power: Theories in Subjection*, Stanford, CA: Stanford University Press.

—— (1998) 'Marxism and the Merely Cultural', *New Left Review*, 227: 33–44.

—— (2000a) *Antigone's Claim: Kinship Between Life and Death*, New York: Columbia University Press.

—— (2000b) 'Competing Universalities', in J. Butler, E. Laclau and S. Zizek, *Contingency, Hegemony, Universality: Contemporary Dialogues on the Left*, London and New York: Verso.

—— (2000c) 'Questions', in J. Butler, E. Laclau and S. Zizek, *Contingency, Hegemony, Universality: Contemporary Dialogues on the Left*, London and New York: Verso.

Caine, B., Grosz, E. and de Lepervanche, M. (eds) (1988) *Crossing Boundaries: Feminisms and the Critique of Knowledges*, Sydney: Allen and Unwin.

Campbell, K. (1999) 'The Slide in the Sign: Lacan's *Glissement* and the Registers of Meaning', *Angelaki*, 4, 3: 135–143.

—— (2001) 'The Plague of the Subject: Judith Butler's *Psychic Life of Power*', *International Journal of Sexuality and Gender*, 6, 1/2: 35–48.

Chambers, V. (1995) 'Betrayal Feminism', in B. Findlen (ed.) *Listen Up: Voices from the Next Feminist Generation*, Seattle: Seal.

Chanter, T. (1997) 'Can the Phallus Stand, or Should It Be Stood Up?', in T. Dufresne (ed.) *Returns of the French Freud: Freud, Lacan and Beyond*, London and New York: Routledge.

Charraud, N. (1997) *Lacan et les Mathématiques*, Paris: Anthropos.

Chodorow, N. (1978) *The Reproduction of Mothering: Psychoanalysis and the Sociology of Gender*, Berkeley: University of California Press.

Cixous, H. and Clément, C. (1975) *The Newly Born Woman*, trans. B. Wing, Minneapolis: University of Minnesota Press, 1986.

Cleiren, C. P. M and Tijssen, M. E. M. (1996) 'Rape and Other Forms of Sexual Assault in the Armed Conflict in the Former Yugoslavia: Legal, Procedural and Evidential Issues', in R. Clark and M. Sann (eds) *The Prosecution of International Crimes*, London and New Brunswick, NJ: Transaction.

Code, L. (1987) *Epistemic Responsibility*, Hanover, NH and London: University Press of New England.

—— (1991) *What Can She Know? Feminist Theory and the Construction of Knowledge*, Ithaca, NY and London: Cornell University Press.

—— (1993) 'Feminist Epistemology', in J. Dancy and E. Sosa (eds) *A Companion to Epistemology*, Oxford and Cambridge, MA: Blackwell.

—— (1994) 'Responsibility and Rhetoric', *Hypatia: A Journal of Feminist Philosophy*, 9, 1: 1–20.

—— (1995) *Rhetorical Spaces: Essays on Gendered Locations*, London and New York: Routledge.

Collins, P. Hill (1986) 'Learning from the Outsider Within: The Sociological Significance of Black Feminist Thought', *Social Problems*, 33, 6: 14–32.

—— (1991) *Black Feminist Thought: Knowledge, Consciousness, and the Politics of Empowerment*, New York and London: Routledge.

Copjec, J. (1994) *Read My Desire: Lacan Against the Historicists*, Cambridge, MA and London: MIT Press.

Cornell, D. (1992) 'What Takes Place in the Dark', *differences: A Journal of Feminist Cultural Studies*, 4, 2: 45–71.

Corradi Fiumara, G. (1994) 'The Metaphoric Function and the Question of Objectivity', in K. Lennon and M. Whitford (eds) *Knowing the Difference: Feminist Perspectives in Epistemology*, London and New York: Routledge.

Davis, D. (1997) 'The Harm That Has No Name: Street Harassment, Embodiment and African American Women', in A. K. Wing (ed.) *Critical Race Feminism: A Reader*, New York and London: New York University Press.

Dean, T. (2000) *Beyond Sexuality*, Chicago: University of Chicago Press.

de Beauvoir, S. (1949) *The Second Sex*, trans. H. M. Parshley, Harmondsworth: Penguin, 1974.

Decker, H. (1992) *Freud, Dora and Vienna 1900*, New York: Free Press.

de Lauretis, T. (1988) 'Feminist Studies/Critical Studies: Issues, Terms, and Contexts', in T. de Lauretis (ed.) *Feminist Studies/Critical Studies*, London: Macmillan.

—— (1994) 'The Essence of the Triangle or, Taking the Risk of Essentialism Seriously: Feminist Theory in Italy, the U.S., and Britain', in N. Schor and E. Weed (eds) *the essential difference*, Bloomington and Indianapolis: Indiana University Press.

Dent, G. (1995) 'Missionary Position', in Rebecca Walker (ed.) *To Be Real: Telling the Truth and Changing the Face of Feminism*, New York: Anchor.

Derrida, J. (1980) *The Post Card: From Socrates to Freud and Beyond*, trans. A. Bass, Chicago: University of Chicago Press, 1987.

de Saussure, F. (1916) *Cours de linguistique générale*, trans. R. Harris, La Salle, IL: Open Court, 1992.

Detloff, M. (1997) 'Mean Spirits: The Politics of Contempt Between Feminist Generations', *Hypatia: A Journal of Feminist Philosophy*, 12, 3: 76–99.

Dews, P. (1987) *The Logic of Disintegration: Post-structuralist Thought and the Claims of Critical Theory*, London and New York: Verso.

Dhanda, M. (1994) 'Openness, Identity and Acknowledgment of Persons', in K. Lennon and M. Whitford (eds) *Knowing the Difference: Feminist Perspectives in Epistemology*, London and New York: Routledge.

Dinnerstein, D. (1976) *The Mermaid and the Minotour: Sexual Arrangements and Human Malaise*, New York: Harper and Row.

Dolar, M. (1998) 'Cogito as the Subject of the Unconscious', in S. Zizek (ed.) *Cogito and the Unconscious*, Durham, NC and London: Duke University Press.

Dor, J. (1996) 'The Epistemological Status of Lacan's Mathematical Paradigms', in D. Pettigrew and F. Raffoul (eds) *Disseminating Lacan*, New York: State University of New York Press.

Doyle McCarthy, E. (1996) *Knowledge as Culture: The New Sociology of Knowledge*, New York and London: Routledge.

Drake, J. (1997) 'Review Essay: Third Wave Feminisms', *Feminist Studies*, 23, 1: 97–108.

Drake, J. and Heywood, L. (1997a) 'Introduction', in J. Drake and L. Heywood (eds) *Third Wave Agenda: Being Feminist, Doing Feminism*, Minneapolis: University of Minnesota Press.

—— (eds) (1997b) *Third Wave Agenda: Being Feminist, Doing Feminism*, Minneapolis: University of Minnesota Press.

Duchen, C. (1986) *Feminism in France: From May '68 to Mitterrand*, Boston and London: Routledge and Kegan Paul.

du Cille, A. (1990) 'Conference Call: Responses', *differences: A Journal of Feminist Cultural Studies*, 2, 3: 89–95.

Duran, J. (1991) *Towards A Feminist Epistemology*, Savage, MD: Rowman and Littlefield.

—— (1998) *Philosophies of Science/Feminist Theories*, Boulder, CO: Westview.

—— (2001) *Worlds of Knowing: Global Feminist Epistemologies*, New York and London: Routledge.

Edelstein, M. (1993) 'Toward a Feminist Postmodern Poléthique: Kristeva on Ethics and Politics', in K. Oliver (ed.) *Ethics, Politics, and Difference in Julia Kristeva's Writing*, London and New York: Routledge.

Eisenstein, H. and Jardine, A. (eds) (1980) *The Future of Difference*, New Brunswick, NJ: Rutgers University Press.

Eisenstein, Z. (1988) *The Female Body and the Law*, Berkeley: University of California Press.

Elliot, A. (1996) 'Psychoanalysis and Social Theory', in B. Turner (ed.) *The Blackwell Companion to Social Theory*, Oxford and Cambridge, MA: Blackwell.

Elliot, P. (1991) *From Mastery to Analysis: Theories of Gender in Psychoanalytic Feminism*, Ithaca, NY and London: Cornell University Press.

Evans, D. (1996) *An Introductory Dictionary of Lacanian Psychoanalysis*, New York and London: Routledge.

Feldstein, R. and Roof, J. (1989) 'Introduction', in R. Feldstein and J. Roof (eds) *Feminism and Psychoanalysis*, Ithaca, NY and London: Cornell University Press.

Findlen, B. (1995a) 'Introduction', in B. Findlen (ed.) *Listen Up: Voices from the Next Feminist Generation*, Seattle: Seal.

—— (ed.) (1995b) *Listen Up: Voices from the Next Feminist Generation*, Seattle: Seal.

Fink, B. (1995) *The Lacanian Subject: Between Language and Jouissance*, Princeton, NJ: Princeton University Press.

—— (1998) 'The Master Signifier and the Four Discourses', in D. Nobus (ed.) *Key Concepts of Lacanian Psychoanalysis*, London: Rebus.

—— (1999) *A Clinical Introduction to Lacanian Psychoanalysis: Theory and Technique*, Cambridge, MA and London: Harvard University Press.

Flax, J. (1990) *Thinking Fragments: Psychoanalysis, Feminism, and Postmodernism in the Contemporary West*, Berkeley and Los Angeles: University of California Press.

—— (1993) *Disputed Subjects: Essays on Psychoanalysis, Politics and Philosophy*, New York and London: Routledge.

Flower MacCannell, J. (1991) *The Regime of the Brother: After the Patriarchy*, New York and London: Routledge.

Forna, A. (1999) 'Sellout', in N. Walter (ed.) *On the Move: Feminism for a New Generation*, London: Virago.

Forrester, J. (1990) *The Seductions of Psychoanalysis: Freud, Lacan and Derrida*, Cambridge: Cambridge University Press.

Forrester, J. and Appignanesi, L. (1993) *Freud's Women*, London: Virago.

Fox Keller, E. (1983) 'Gender and Science', in S. Harding and M. Hintikka (eds) *Discovering Reality: Feminist Perspectives on Epistemology, Metaphysics, Methodology, and Philosophy of Science*, Dordrecht, Boston and London: Reidel.

—— (1985) *Reflections on Gender and Science*, London and New Haven, CT: Yale University Press.

Fox Keller, E. and Longino, H. (1996) 'Introduction', in E. Fox Keller and H. Longino (eds) *Feminism and Science*, Oxford and New York: Oxford University Press.

Fraser, N. (1992) 'The Uses and Abuses of French Discourse Theories for Feminist Politics', in N. Fraser and S. Lee Bartky (eds) *Revaluing French Feminism: Critical Essays on Difference, Agency and Culture*, Bloomington and Indianapolis: Indiana University Press.

—— (1995) 'Pragmatism, Feminism, and the Linguistic Turn', in S. Benhabib, J. Butler, D. Cornell and N. Fraser, *Feminist Contentions: A Philosophical Exchange*, New York and London: Routledge.

Fraser, N. and Nicholson, L. (1990) 'Social Criticism Without Philosophy: An Encounter Between Feminism and Postmodernism', in L. Nicholson (ed.) *Feminism/Postmodernism*, London and New York: Routledge.

Freud, S. (1905) 'Fragment of an Analysis of a Case of Hysteria ("Dora")', in *Case Histories I: 'Dora' and 'Little Hans'*, trans. A. and J. Strachey, ed. A. Richards, Harmondsworth: Penguin, 1977.

—— (1914) 'On Narcissism: An Introduction', in *On Metapsychology: The Theory of Psychoanalysis*, trans. J. Strachey, ed. A. Richards, Harmondsworth: Penguin, 1984.

—— (1917) 'Mourning and Melancholia', in *On Metapsychology: The Theory of Psychoanalysis*, trans. J. Strachey, ed. A. Richards, Harmondsworth: Penguin, 1984.

—— (1921) *Group Psychology and the Analysis of the Ego*, in *Civilization, Society and Religion, Group Psychology, Civilization and Its Discontents & Other Works*, trans. J. Strachey, ed. A. Dickson, Harmondsworth: Penguin, 1985.

—— (1923) 'The Ego and the Id', in *On Metapsychology: The Theory of Psychoanalysis*, trans. J. Strachey, ed. A. Richards, Harmondsworth: Penguin, 1984.

—— (1924) 'The Dissolution of the Oedipus Complex', in *On Sexuality: Three Essays on the Theory of Sexuality & Other Works*, trans. J. Strachey, ed. A. Richards, Harmondsworth: Penguin, 1977.

—— (1925a) 'Negation', in *On Metapsychology: The Theory of Psychoanalysis*, trans. J. Strachey, ed. A. Richards, Harmondsworth: Penguin, 1984.

—— (1925b) 'Some Psychical Consequences of the Anatomical Distinction Between the Sexes', in *On Sexuality: Three Essays on the Theory of Sexuality & Other Works*, trans. J. Strachey, ed. A. Richards, Harmondsworth: Penguin, 1977.

—— (1930) *Civilisation and Its Discontents*, in *Civilization, Society and Religion, Group Psychology, Civilization and Its Discontents & Other Works*, trans. J. Strachey, ed. A. Dickson, Harmondsworth: Penguin, 1985.

—— (1933) 'Femininity', in *New Introductory Lectures on Psychoanalysis*, trans. J. Strachey, ed. J. Strachey and A. Richards, Harmondsworth: Penguin, 1977.

Freud, S. and Breuer, J. (1895) *Studies on Hysteria*, trans. A. and J. Strachey, ed. A. Richards, Harmondsworth: Penguin, 1974.

Fricker, M. (1994) 'Knowledge as Construct: Theorizing the Role of Gender in Knowledge', in K. Lennon and M. Whitford (eds) *Knowing the Difference: Feminist Perspectives in Epistemology*, London and New York: Routledge.

Friedan, B. (1965) *The Feminine Mystique*, Harmondsworth: Penguin.

Friedlen, M. and Weiss, P. (eds) (1995) *Feminism and Community*, Philadelphia: Temple University Press.

Fuss, D. (1994) 'Reading Like a Feminist', in N. Schor and E. Weed (eds) *the essential difference*, Bloomington and Indianapolis: Indiana University Press.

—— (1995) *Identification Papers*, New York and London: Routledge.

Gallop, J. (1984) *The Daughter's Seduction: Feminism and Psychoanalysis*, Ithaca, NY: Cornell University Press.

—— (1987) *Reading Lacan*, London and Ithaca, NY: Cornell University Press.

—— (1988) *Thinking Through the Body*, New York: Columbia University Press.

—— (1992) *Around 1981*, London and New York: Routledge.

Gaudin, C., Green, C. J., Higgins, L., Hirsch, M., Kogan, V., Reeder, C. and Vickers, N. (eds) (1981) *Yale French Studies*, 62. Special Edition: 'Feminist Readings: French Texts/American Contexts'.

Giddens, A. (1990) *The Consequences of Modernity*, Cambridge: Polity.

Gilligan, C. (1982) *In a Different Voice: Psychological Theory and Women's Development*, Cambridge, MA: Harvard University Press.

Gilroy, P. (1993) *The Black Atlantic: Modernity and Double Consciousness*, London and New York: Verso.

Giron, T. (2000a) 'Psychoanalysis is a Science Fiction', *Umbra*, 4–7.

—— (ed.) (2000b) *Umbra*. Special Issue: 'Science and Truth'.

Greer, G. (1970) *The Female Eunuch*, London: MacGibbon and Kee.

Grigg, R. (1994) 'Lacan's Four Discourses', *Analysis*, 4: 33–39.

Grosz, E. (1990) *Jacques Lacan: A Feminist Introduction*, Sydney: Allen and Unwin.

—— (1993) 'Bodies and Knowledges: Feminism and the Crisis of Reason', in L. Alcoff and E. Potter (eds) *Feminist Epistemologies*, London and New York: Routledge.

Gunew, S. (ed.) (1990) *Feminist Knowledge: Critique and Construct*, London: Routledge.

Haack, S. (ed.) (1994) *The Monist*, 4, 77. Special Issue: 'Feminist Epistemology: For and Against'.

Habermas, J. (1972) *Knowledge and Human Interests*, trans. J. Shapiro, London: Heinemann.

Hammonds, E. (1997) 'When the Margin is the Centre: African-American Feminism(s) and "Difference"', in J. W. Scott, C. Kaplan and D. Keates (eds) *Transitions, Environments, Translations*, New York and London: Routledge.

Haraway, D. (1985) 'A Manifesto for Cyborgs: Science, Technology and Socialist Feminism in the 1980s', *Socialist Review*, 80: 65–108.

—— (1991) *Simians, Cyborgs, and Women: The Reinvention of Nature*, London: Free Association.

Harding, S. (1990) *Whose Science? Whose Knowledge? Thinking from Women's Lives*, Ithaca, NY: Cornell University Press.

—— (1991) *The Science Question in Feminism*, Milton Keynes: Open University Press.

—— (1993) 'Rethinking Standpoint Epistemology: "What is Strong Objectivity?"', in L. Alcoff and E. Potter (eds) *Feminist Epistemologies*, London and New York: Routledge.

—— (1998) *Is Science Multicultural? Postcolonialisms, Feminisms, and Epistemologies*, Bloomington and Indianapolis: Indiana University Press.

—— (2000) 'Comment on Hekman's "Truth and Method: Feminist Standpoint Theory

Revisited": Whose Standpoint Needs Regimes of Truth and Reality', in C. Allen and J. Howard (eds) *Provoking Feminisms*, Chicago and London: Chicago University Press.

Harding, S. and Hintikka, M. (1983a) 'Introduction', in S. Harding and M. Hintikka (eds) *Discovering Reality: Feminist Perspectives on Epistemology, Metaphysics, Methodology, and Philosophy of Science*, Dordrecht, Boston and London: Reidel.

—— (eds) (1983b) *Discovering Reality: Feminist Perspectives on Epistemology, Metaphysics, Methodology, and Philosophy of Science*, Dordrecht, Boston and London: Reidel.

Hartsock, N. (1983) 'The Feminist Standpoint: Developing the Ground for a Specifically Feminist Historical Materialism', in S. Harding and M. Hintikka (eds) *Discovering Reality: Feminist Perspectives on Epistemology, Metaphysics, Methodology, and Philosophy of Science*, Dordrecht, Boston and London: Reidel.

Hekman, S. (1990) *Gender and Knowledge: Elements of a Postmodern Feminism*, Boston: Northeastern University Press.

Hoffman Baruch, E. and Serrano, L. J. (1988) *Women Analyse Women: In France, England, and the United States*, New York and London: New York University Press.

—— (1996) *She Speaks/He Listens: Women on the French Analyst's Couch*, New York and London: Routledge.

hooks, b. (1981) *Ain't I a Woman: Black Women and Feminism*, Boston: South End.

—— (1989) *Talking Back: thinking feminist, thinking black*, London: Sheba.

—— (1991) *Yearning: Race, Gender, and Cultural Politics*, London: Turnaround.

—— (1994) *Outlaw Culture: Resisting Representations*, New York and London: Routledge.

Hunter, D. (1983) 'Hysteria, Psychoanalysis and Feminism: The Case of Anna O.', *Feminist Studies*, 9: 465.

Hutchings, K. (1994) 'The Personal is International: Feminist Epistemology and the Case of International Relations', in K. Lennon and M. Whitford (eds) *Knowing the Difference: Feminist Perspectives in Epistemology*, London and New York: Routledge.

Irigaray, L. (1974) *Speculum of the Other Woman*, trans. G. Gill, Ithaca, NY: Cornell University Press, 1985.

—— (1977) *This Sex Which Is Not One*, trans. C. Porter, Ithaca, NY: Cornell University Press, 1985.

—— (1984) *An Ethics of Sexual Difference*, trans. C. Burke and G. Gill, Ithaca, NY: Cornell University Press, 1993.

—— (1987) *Sexes and Genealogies*, trans. G. Gill, New York: Columbia University Press, 1993.

—— (1990) *Je, tu, nous: Toward a Culture of Difference*, trans. A. Martin, London: Routledge, 1993.

—— (1994) *Democracy Begins Between Two*, trans. K. Anderson, London: Athlone, 2000.

Jagger, A. (1983) *Feminist Politics and Human Nature*, Hemel Hempstead: Harvester.

Jardine, A. (1985) *Gynesis: Configurations of Woman and Modernity*, Ithaca, NY and London: Cornell University Press.

Jardine, A. and Smith, P. (eds) (1987) *Men in Feminism*, New York and London: Methuen.

Julien, P. (1985) *Jacques Lacan's Return to Freud: The Real, the Symbolic and the Imaginary*, trans. D. Beck Simiu, New York and London: New York University Press, 1994.

Juranville, A. (1996) *Lacan et la philosophie*, Paris: Quadrige/Presses Universitaires de France.

Kidder, L., Lafleur, R. and Wells, C. (1995) 'Recalling Harassment, Reconstructing Experience', *Journal of Social Issues*, 51, 1: 53–67.

Kristeva, J. (1987) *Black Sun: Depression and Melancholia*, trans. L. Roudiez, New York and Oxford: Columbia University Press, 1989.

—— (1993) *New Maladies of the Soul*, trans. R. Guberman, New York: Columbia University Press, 1995.

Lacan, J. (1932) *De la psychose paranoïaque dans ses rapports avec la personnnalité*, Paris: Seuil, 1995.

—— (1938a) 'The Oedipus Complex', trans. A. Kahn, in F. Peraldi (ed.) *Polysexuality*, New York: Semiotext(e), 1995.

—— (1938b) *Les complexes familiaux dans la formation de l'individu: essai d'analyse d'une fonction en psychologie*, Paris: Navarin, 1984.

—— (1945) 'Logical Time and the Assertion of Anticipated Certainty: A New Sophism', trans. R. Grigg, *Newsletter of the Freudian Field*, 2: 4–22, 1988.

—— (1950) 'A Theoretical Introduction to the Function of Psychoanalysis in Criminology', trans. M. Bracher, R. Grigg and R. Samuels, *Journal for the Psychoanalysis of Culture and Society*, 1, 2: 13–25, 1996.

—— (1951) 'Intervention on Transference', in J. Mitchell and J. Rose (eds) *Feminine Sexuality: Jacques Lacan and the école freudienne*, trans. J. Rose, London and New York: Norton, 1985.

—— (1953–1954) *The Seminar of Jacques Lacan. Book I. Freud's Papers on Technique, 1953–1954*, trans. J. Forrester, ed. J.-A. Miller, New York and London: Norton, 1991.

—— (1954) 'Introduction and reply to Jean Hyppolite's presentation of Freud's *Verneinung*', trans. J. Forrester, *The Seminar of Jacques Lacan. Book I. Freud's Papers on Technique, 1953–1954*, ed. J.-A. Miller, London and New York: Norton, 1991.

—— (1954–1955) *The Seminar of Jacques Lacan. Book II. The Ego in Freud's Theory and in the Technique of Psychoanalysis, 1954–1955*, trans. S. Tomaselli, ed. J.-A. Miller, New York and London: Norton, 1991.

—— (1955) 'Seminar on "The Stolen Letter"', in J. Muller and W. Richardson (eds) *The Purloined Poe: Lacan, Derrida, and Psychoanalytic Reading*, trans. J. Mehlman, Baltimore, MD and London: Johns Hopkins University Press, 1988.

—— (1955–1956) *The Seminar of Jacques Lacan. Book III. The Psychoses, 1955–1956*, trans. R. Grigg, ed. J.-A. Miller, London: Routledge, 1993.

—— (1956–1957) *Le Séminaire. Livre IV. La relation d'objet, 1956–1957*, ed. J.-A. Miller, Paris: Seuil, 1994.

—— (1957–1958) *Le Séminaire. Livre V. Les Formations de l'inconscient, 1957–1958*, ed. J.-A. Miller, Paris: Seuil, 1998.

—— (1958) 'Kant avec Sade', trans. J. Swenson, *October*, 51: 55–104, 1989.

—— (1959–1960) *The Seminar of Jacques Lacan. Book VII. The Ethics of Psychoanalysis, 1959–1960*, trans. D. Porter, ed. J.-A. Miller, London: Routledge, 1992.

—— (1960) 'Guiding Remarks for a Congress on Feminine Sexuality', in J. Mitchell and J. Rose (eds) *Feminine Sexuality: Jacques Lacan and the école freudienne*, trans. J. Rose, London and New York: Norton, 1985.

—— (1960–1961) *Le Séminaire. Livre VIII. Le Transfert, 1960–1961*, ed. J.-A. Miller, Paris: Seuil, 2000.

—— (1961) 'Metaphor of the Subject', trans. B. Fink, *Newsletter of the Freudian Field*, 5, 1–2: 10–15, 1991.

—— (1964a) 'On Freud's "*Trieb*" and the Psychoanalyst's Desire', in R. Feldstein, B. Fink and M. Jaanus (eds) *Reading Seminars I and II: Lacan's Return to Freud*, trans. B. Fink, Albany: State University of New York Press, 1996.

—— (1964b) 'Position of the Unconscious', in R. Feldstein, B. Fink and M. Jaanus (eds) *Reading Seminar XI: Lacan's Four Fundamental Concepts of Psychoanalysis*, trans. B. Fink, Albany: State University of New York Press, 1995.

—— (1964c) *The Four Fundamental Concepts of Psycho-Analysis*, trans. A. Sheridan, London: Peregrine, 1986.

—— (1965) 'Science and Truth', trans. B. Fink, *Newsletter of the Freudian Field*, 3: 4–29, 1989.

—— (1966a) *Écrits*, Paris: Seuil.

—— (1966b) *Écrits: A Selection*, trans. A. Sheridan, London: Routledge, 2001.

—— (1969–70) *Le Séminaire. Livre XVII. L'envers de la psychanalyse, 1969–1970*, ed. J.-A. Miller, Paris: Seuil, 1991.

—— (1969a) 'General Purport of a Conversation with Jacques Lacan in December 1969', trans. D. Macey, in A. Rifflet-Lemaire, *Jacques Lacan*, London: Routledge, 1977.

—— (1969b) 'Impromptu at Vincennes', in *Television: A Challenge to the Psychoanalytic Establishment*, various trans., ed. J. Copjec, London and New York: Norton, 1990.

—— (1970a) 'Preface', trans. D. Macey, in A. Rifflet-Lemaire, *Jacques Lacan*, London: Routledge, 1977.

—— (1970b) 'Radiophonie', trans. S. Schneiderman, in M. Blonsky (ed.) *On Signs*, Baltimore, MD: Johns Hopkins University Press, 1985.

—— (1972–73) *The Seminar of Jacques Lacan. Book XX. Encore: On Feminine Sexuality, the Limits of Love and Knowledge, 1972–1973*, trans. B. Fink, ed. J.-A. Miller, New York and London: Norton, 1998.

—— (1973) 'L'Étourdit', *Autres Écrits*, Paris: Seuil, 2001.

—— (1974) *Television*, trans. D. Hollier, R. Krauss and A. Michelson, New York: Norton, 1990.

—— (1975a) 'R.S.I: 14 janvier 1975' *Ornicar?* 3: 104–110, 1975 (S22).

—— (1975b) 'The Seminar XXII of 21 January 1975 — RSI', trans. J. Rose, in J. Mitchell and J. Rose (eds) *Feminine Sexuality*, New York and London: Norton, 1985 (S22).

—— (1975c) 'Le Séminaire du 18 novembre 1975', *Ornicar?* 6: 3–9, 1976 (S23).

—— (1975d) 'Le Séminaire du 16 decembre 1975', *Ornicar?* 7: 3–11, 1976 (S23).

—— (1975e) 'Geneva Lecture on the Symptom', trans. Russell Grigg, *Analysis*, 1: 7–26, 1989.

—— (1975f) 'Massachusetts Institute of Technology: 2 décembre 1975', *Scilicet*, 6, 7: 53–63.

—— (1976) 'Le Séminaire du 17 fevrier 1976', *Ornicar?* 8: 14–20, 1976 (S23).

Lacey, N. (1998) *Unspeakable Subjects: Feminist Essays in Social and Legal Theory*, Oxford: Hart.

Lacoue-Labarthe, P. and Nancy, J.-L. (1992) *The Title of the Letter: A Reading of Lacan*, trans. F. Raffoul and D. Pettigrew, New York: State University of New York Press.

Laplanche, J. and Pontalis, J.-B. (1973) *The Language of Psychoanalysis*, trans. D. Nicholson-Smith, New York and London: Norton.

Latour, B. (1993) *We Have Never Been Modern*, trans. C. Porter, Cambridge, MA: Harvard University Press.

Lazreg, M. (1994) 'Women's Experience and Feminist Epistemology: A Critical Neo-Rationalist Approach', in K. Lennon and M. Whitford (eds) *Knowing the Difference: Feminist Perspectives in Epistemology*, London and New York: Routledge.

Lechte, J. (1994) *Fifty Key Contemporary Thinkers*, London and New York: Routledge.

—— (1996) 'Introduction', in J. Lechte (ed.) *Writing and Psychoanalysis: A Reader*, London and New York: Arnold.

Lee, J. (1995) 'Beyond Bean Counting', in B. Findlen (ed.) *Listen Up: Voices from the Next Feminist Generation*, Seattle: Seal.

Lees, S. (1997) *Carnal Knowledge: Rape on Trial*, Harmondsworth: Penguin.

Lemaire, A. (1970) *Jacques Lacan*, trans. D. Macey, London: Routledge and Kegan Paul, 1979.

Lennon, K. (1997) 'Feminist Epistemology as a Local Epistemology II', *The Aristotelian Society Supplementary Volume*, LXXI: 37–54.

Lennon, K. and Whitford, M. (1994a) 'Introduction', in K. Lennon and M. Whitford (eds) *Knowing the Difference: Feminist Perspectives in Epistemology*, London and New York: Routledge.

—— (eds) (1994b) *Knowing the Difference: Feminist Perspectives in Epistemology*, London and New York: Routledge.

Leupin, A. (1991a) 'Introduction: Voids and Knots in Knowledge and Truth', in A. Leupin (ed.) *Lacan and the Human Sciences*, Lincoln and London: University of Nebraska Press.

—— (ed.) (1991b) *Lacan and the Human Sciences*, Lincoln and London: University of Nebraska Press.

Lévi-Strauss, C. (1958) *Structural Anthropology*, trans. C. Jacobson and B. G. Schoepf, New York: Basic Books, 1963.

—— (1967) *The Elementary Structures of Kinship*, trans. J. H. Bell and J. von Sturmer, ed. R. Needham, London: Eyre and Spottiswoode, 1969.

Lloyd, G. (1984) *The Man of Reason: 'Male' and 'Female' in Western Philosophy*, London: Methuen.

—— (1993) 'Maleness, Metaphor and the "Crisis" of Reason', in L. Antony and C. Witt (eds) *A Mind of One's Own*, Oxford: Westview.

Longino, H. (1990) *Science as Social Knowledge: Value and Objectivity in Scientific Inquiry*, Princeton, NJ: Princeton University Press.

—— (1995) 'Gender, Politics and the Theoretical Virtues', *Synthese*, 104: 383–397.

—— (1996) 'Subjects, Power, and Knowledge: Description and Prescription in Feminist Philosophies of Science', in E. Fox Keller and H. Longino (eds) *Feminism and Science*, Oxford and New York: Oxford University Press.

—— (1997) 'Feminist Epistemology as a Local Epistemology I', *The Aristotelian Society Supplementary Volume*, LXXI: 19–35.

—— (2002) *The Fate of Knowledge*, Oxford and Princeton, NJ: Princeton University Press.

Lorde, A. (1984) *Sister Outsider*, New York: Crossing.

Lovibond, S. (1994) 'The End of Morality', in K. Lennon and M. Whitford (eds) *Knowing the Difference: Feminist Perspectives in Epistemology*, London and New York: Routledge.

MacKinnon, C. (1982) 'Feminism, Marxism, and the State: An Agenda for Theory', *Signs: Journal of Women and Society*, 7: 515–544.

Mandava, B. (1995) 'Ghosts and Goddesses', in B. Findlen (ed.) *Listen Up: Voices from the Next Feminist Generation*, Seattle: Seal.

Marcus, S. (1990) 'Conference Call: Responses', *differences: A Journal of Feminist Cultural Studies*, 2, 3: 95–99.

Marcus, S., du Cille, A. and Schafer, S. (1990) 'Conference Call: Questions posed by S. Marcus, A. du Cille and S. Schafer', *differences: A Journal of Feminist Cultural Studies*, 2, 3: 54–56.

Marder, E. (1992) 'Disarticulated Voices: Feminism and Philomela', *Hypatia: A Journal of Feminist Philosophy*, 7, 2: 148–166.

Marini, M. (1992) *Jacques Lacan: The French Context*, trans. A. Tomiche, New Brunswick, NJ: Rutgers University Press.

Marks, E. and de Coutrivron, I. (eds) (1981) *New French Feminisms: An Anthology*, New York: Schocken.

Matsuda, M. (1996) *Where is Your Body: And Other Essays on Race, Gender and the Law*, Boston: Beacon Press.

Michael, L. (1999) 'Feminism and the Class Ceiling', in N. Walter (ed.) *On the Move: Feminism for a New Generation*, London: Virago.

Miles, T. (1995) 'Lessons from a Young Feminist Collective' , in B. Findlen (ed.) *Listen Up: Voices from the Next Feminist Generation*, Seattle: Seal.

Miller, J.-A. (1966) 'Classified Index of the Major Concepts', in J. Lacan, *Écrits*, trans. A. Sheridan, London: Routledge, 2001.

—— (1989) 'Elements of Epistemology', trans. L. Rodriguez, *Analysis*, 1: 27.

Miller, N. (1990) 'Conference Call: May 9, 1990', *differences: A Journal of Feminist Cultural Studies*, 2, 3: 74–81.

Millett, K. (1977) *Sexual Politics*, London: Virago.

Mills, S. (1992) 'Discourse Competence: Or How to Theorize Strong Women Speakers', *Hypatia: A Journal of Feminist Philosophy*, 7, 2: 4–17.

Milner, J.-C. (1991) 'Lacan and the Ideal of Science', in A. Leupin (ed.) *Lacan and the Human Sciences*, Lincoln and London: University of Nebraska Press.

—— (1995) *L'Œuvre claire: Lacan, la science, la philosophie*, Paris: Seuil.

Minh-ha, T. (1989) *Woman, Native, Other: Writing, Postcoloniality and Feminism*, Bloomington and Indianapolis: Indiana University Press.

Mitchell, J. (1982) 'Introduction – I', in J. Mitchell and J. Rose (eds) *Feminine Sexuality: Jacques Lacan and the école freudienne*, London and New York: Norton.

Mitchell, J. and Rose, J. (eds) (1982) *Feminine Sexuality: Jacques Lacan and the école freudienne*, London and New York: Norton.

Moi, T. (1985) 'Representation of Patriarchy: Sexuality and Epistemology in Freud's

Dora', in C. Bernheimer and C. Kahane (eds) *In Dora's Case: Freud, Hysteria, Feminism*, London: Virago.

Morel, G. (2003) 'A Young Man Without an Ego: A Study on James Joyce and the Mirror Stage', in P. Adams (ed.) *Art: Sublimation or Symptom*, New York: Other Press.

Mouffe, C. (1992) 'Feminism, Citizenship, and Radical Democratic Politics', in J. Butler and J. Scott (eds) *Feminists Theorise the Political*, London and New York: Routledge.

Muller, J. and Richardson, W. (1994) *Lacan and Language: A Reader's Guide to Écrits*, Madison, CT: International Universities Press.

Nash, K. (1998) *Universal Difference: Feminism and the Liberal Undecidability of Difference*, London: Macmillan.

Nelson, L. Hankinson (1995) 'The Very Idea of Feminist Epistemology', *Hypatia: A Journal of Feminist Philosophy*, 10, 3: 31–49.

Nicholson, L. (1990a) 'Introduction', in L. Nicholson (ed.) *Feminism/Postmodernism*, London and New York: Routledge.

—— (ed.) (1990b) *Feminism/Postmodernism*, London and New York: Routledge.

Nobus, D. (2000) *Jacques Lacan and the Freudian Practice of Psychoanalysis*, London and Philadelphia: Routledge.

Oliver, K. (1993) *Reading Kristeva: Unravelling the Double-Bind*, Bloomington and Indianapolis: Indiana University Press.

Orr, C. (1997) 'Charting the Currents of the Third Wave', *Hypatia: A Journal of Feminist Philosophy*, 12, 3: 29–45.

Patel, P. (1998) 'Third Wave Feminism and Black Women's Activism', in *Black British Feminism: A Reader*, London and New York: Routledge.

Pateman, C. (1988) *The Sexual Contract*, Stanford, CA: Stanford University Press.

Payne, M. (1993) *Reading Theory: An Introduction to Lacan, Derrida and Kristeva*, Oxford: Blackwell.

Ragland-Sullivan, E. (1987) *Jacques Lacan and the Philosophy of Psychoanalysis*, Urbana and Chicago: University of Illinois Press.

—— (1989) 'Seeking the Third Term: Desire, the Phallus, and the Materiality of Language', in R. Feldstein and J. Roof (eds) *Feminism and Psychoanalysis*, Ithaca, NY: Cornell University Press.

—— (1991) 'The Sexual Masquerade: A Lacanian Theory of Sexual Difference', in E. Ragland-Sullivan and M. Bracher (eds) *Lacan and the Subject of Language*, London and New York: Routledge.

Ramas, M. (1985) 'Freud's Dora, Dora's Hysteria', in C. Bernheimer and C. Kahane (eds) *Dora's Case: Freud, Hysteria, Feminism*, London: Virago.

Ringer, F. (1990) 'The Intellectual Field, Intellectual History, and the Sociology of Knowledge', *Theory and Society*, 19: 269–294.

—— (1992) *Fields of Knowledge: French Academic Culture in Comparative Perspective 1890–1920*, Cambridge: Cambridge University Press.

Rose, H. (1983) 'Hand, Brain, Heart: A Feminist Epistemology for the Natural Sciences', *Signs*, 9, 1: 73–90.

Rose, J. (1982a) 'Introduction – II', in J. Mitchell and J. Rose (eds) *Feminine Sexuality: Jacques Lacan and the école freudienne*, London and New York: Norton.

—— (1982b) 'Chapter Six', in J. Mitchell and J. Rose (eds) *Feminine Sexuality: Jacques Lacan and the école freudienne*, London and New York: Norton.

—— (1986) *Sexuality in the Field of Vision*, London: Verso.

Roudinesco, É. (1990) *Jacques Lacan and Co.: History of Psychoanalysis in France, 1925–1985*, trans. J. Mehlman, London: Free Association.

—— (1997) *Jacques Lacan*, trans. B. Bray, Cambridge: Polity.

Roustang, F. (1990) *The Lacanian Delusion*, trans. G. Sims, New York and Oxford: Oxford University Press.

Ruddick, S. (1993) 'New Feminist Work on Knowledge, Reason and Objectivity', *Hypatia: A Journal of Feminist Philosophy*, 8, 4: 140–149.

Sartori, D. (1994) 'Women's Authority in Science', in K. Lennon and M. Whitford (eds) *Knowing the Difference: Feminist Perspectives in Epistemology*, London and New York: Routledge.

Scheman, N. (1987) 'Othello's Doubt/Desdemona's Death: The Engendering of Scepticism', in J. Genova (ed.) *Power, Gender, Values*, Edmonton: Academic Printing and Publishing.

—— (1993a) *Engenderings: Constructions of Knowledge, Authority and Privilege*, New York: Routledge.

—— (1993b) 'Though This Be Method, Yet There Is Madness in It: Paranoia and Liberal Epistemology', in L. M. Antony and C. Witt (eds) *A Mind of One's Own: Feminist Essays on Reason and Objectivity*, Boulder, CO and Oxford: Westview.

Schor, N. and Weed, E. (eds) (1994) *the essential difference*, Bloomington and Indianapolis: Indiana University Press.

Scott, J. (1988) 'Deconstructing-Equality-Versus Difference: Or, the Uses of Post-structuralist Theory for Feminism', *Feminist Studies*, 14, 1: 33–51.

Seller, A. (1994) 'Should the Feminist Philosopher Stay At Home?', in K. Lennon and M. Whitford (eds) *Knowing the Difference: Feminist Perspectives in Epistemology*, London and New York: Routledge.

Seshadri-Crooks, K. (2000) *Desiring Whiteness: A Lacanian Analysis of Race*, London: Routledge.

Shepherdson, C. (1993) 'On Fate: Psychoanalysis and the Desire to Know', in T. Flynn and D. Judovitz (eds) *Dialectic and Narrative*, Albany, NY: State University of New York Press.

Sheridan, A. (1977) 'Translator's Note', in J. Lacan, *Écrits*, trans. A. Sheridan, London: Routledge, 2001.

Showalter, E. (1987) *The Female Malady: Women, Madness and English Culture 1830–1980*, London: Virago.

Siegel, D. (1997) 'The Legacy of the Personal: Generating Theory in Feminism's Third Wave', *Hypatia: A Journal of Feminist Philosophy*, 12, 3: 46–75.

Silverman, K. (1983) *The Subject of Semiotics*, Oxford and New York: Oxford University Press.

—— (1988) *The Acoustic Mirror: The Female Voice in Psychoanalysis and Cinema*, Bloomington and Indianapolis: Indiana University Press.

—— (1992a) 'The Lacanian Phallus', *differences: A Journal of Feminist Cultural Studies*, 4, 1: 84–115.

—— (1992b) *Male Subjectivity at the Margins*, London and New York: Routledge.

Smith, D. (1987) *The Everyday World as Problematic: A Feminist Sociology*, Boston: Northeastern University Press.

Spivak, G. (1984–1985) 'Criticism, Feminism and the Institution: An Interview with Gayatri Chakravorty Spivak', interview by E. Gross, *Thesis Eleven*, 10/11: 175–187.

—— (1987) *In Other Worlds: Essays in Cultural Politics*, London: Methuen.

—— (1989) 'Feminism and Deconstruction, Again: Negotiating with an Unacknow-ledged Masculinism', in T. Brennan (ed.) *Between Feminism and Psychoanalysis*, London and New York: Routledge.

Stanley, L. (ed.) (1990) *Feminist Praxis: Research, Theory and Epistemology in Feminist Sociology*, London and New York: Routledge.

—— (1994) 'The Knowing Because Experiencing Subject: Narratives, Lives and Autobiography', in K. Lennon and M. Whitford (eds) *Knowing the Difference: Feminist Perspectives in Epistemology*, London and New York: Routledge.

Strickland, S. (1994) 'Feminism, Postmodernism and Difference', in K. Lennon and M. Whitford (eds) *Knowing the Difference: Feminist Perspectives in Epistemology*, London and New York: Routledge.

Tanesini, A. (1994) 'Whose Language?', in K. Lennon and M. Whitford (eds) *Knowing the Difference: Feminist Perspectives in Epistemology*, London and New York: Routledge.

—— (1999) *An Introduction to Feminist Epistemologies*, Oxford: Blackwell.

Thompson, J. (1994) 'Moral Difference and Moral Epistemology', in K. Lennon and M. Whitford (eds) *Knowing the Difference: Feminist Perspectives in Epistemology*, London and New York: Routledge.

Tuana, N. (ed.) (1989) *Feminism and Science*, Bloomington and Indianapolis: Indiana University Press.

Turner, B. (1996) 'Introduction', in B. Turner (ed.) *The Blackwell Companion to Social Theory*, Oxford and Cambridge, MA: Blackwell.

Verhaeghe, P. (1997) *Does the Woman Exist? From Freud's Hysteric to Lacan's Feminine*, trans. M. du Ry, London: Rebus.

Walker, R. (1995a) 'Being Real: An Introduction', in R. Walker (ed.) *To Be Real: Telling the Truth and Changing the Face of Feminism*, New York: Anchor.

—— (ed.) (1995b) *To Be Real: Telling the Truth and Changing the Face of Feminism*, New York: Anchor.

Weedon, C. (1987) *Feminist Practice and Poststructuralist Theory*, Oxford: Blackwell.

Whitford, M. (1991) *Luce Irigaray: Philosophy in the Feminine*, London and New York: Routledge.

Williams, C. (1994) 'Feminism, Subjectivity and Psychoanalysis: Towards a (Corpo)real Knowledge', in K. Lennon and M. Whitford (eds) *Knowing the Difference: Feminist Perspectives in Epistemology*, London and New York: Routledge.

Williams, P. (1993) *The Alchemy of Race and Rights*, London: Virago.

Zita, J. (1997a) 'Introduction', *Hypatia: A Journal of Feminist Philosophy*, 12, 3: 1–6.

—— (ed.) (1997b) *Hypatia: A Journal of Feminist Philosophy*, 12, 3. Special Issue: Third Wave Feminisms.

Zizek, S. (1989) *The Sublime Object of Ideology*, London and New York: Verso.

—— (1991) *For They Know Not What They Do: Enjoyment as a Political Factor*, London and New York: Verso.

—— (1992) *Looking Awry: An Introduction to Jacques Lacan through Popular Culture*, Cambridge, MA and London: MIT Press.

—— (1998a) 'Four Discourses, Four Subjects', in S. Zizek (ed.) *Cogito and the Unconscious*, Durham, NC and London: University of Duke Press.

—— (1998b) 'The Seven Veils of Fantasy', in D. Nobus (ed.) *Key Concepts of Lacanian Psychoanalysis*, London: Rebus.

—— (2000) '*Da Capo senza Fine*', in J. Butler, E. Laclau and S. Zizek, *Contingency, Hegemony, Universality: Contemporary Dialogues on the Left*, London and New York: Verso.

Index